Sexy Serenity

A Memoir

Miranda K. Simon

Adamo Press
Aliso Viejo, California

SEXY SERENITY: A MEMOIR
FIRST EDITION, Copyright © 2014 by Miranda K. Simon.
Published by Adamo Press.

Library of Congress Control Number: 2014944894

Cover photograph by Gabriel S. Delgado C. Used with written permission.

ISBN 978-0-9897037-4-1

Dedicated to the single parents working their way through college

PART ONE
DANCE HOSTESS

Chapter One
The Beginning

No matter what anyone says, I'm not a whore.

Let me clarify. I didn't join the adult entertainment business as a social experiment or a research project or out of boredom to get my kicks. No, it found me.

It was a cure for my financial desperation. I spent five years in the "sex industry" as a hostess dancer and exotic dancer—bikini, topless, and all-nude.

I know what you may be thinking, and no, not all women in the sex industry are drug addicts, sluts, and prostitutes. I didn't know that then. Now I do.

Raised with a healthy dose of Christian guilt, I used to think no upstanding woman in good conscience could take off her clothes for money and maintain a decent reputation. A stripper wouldn't fit into my circle of friends.

What a hypocrite I turned out to be. Life's funny like that.

* * *

Spring 1996

I hated onions, garlic, and mushrooms–always had–until the cravings for them started after I turned eighteen. *How odd,* I thought.

Sitting atop the crinkly white paper on the examination table in the doctor's office, I glanced at the white plastic wand on the counter which held my future in its window. When I slept with Ricky for the first time, the condom had broken. I had rushed to the bathroom and washed my insides out with soap, hoping, hoping.

Faded pink lines came into focus.

The nurse picked up the stick. "You're pregnant."

"No, I can't be." I had four more months of high school before I moved into a college dorm. "The lines are too faint."

She waved the wand at me. "Honey, the plus sign means the test is positive."

"But it's more negative. The other line is hardly noticeable. It can't be a plus." Ricky's green eyes, dark skin, and broad shoulders—my final fling before college—flashed through my mind. We had only met a few weeks ago, introduced by a common friend.

The nurse placed a hand on my shoulder. "Make a prenatal appointment on your way out."

I sat there, shaking my head. So much for all my Advanced Placement scores, honors classes, and late-night study sessions. What a waste. How to break the news to my divorced parents who always expected the best from me and my siblings? I shuddered.

At home, I flipped through some on-campus university housing pamphlets and imagined myself strolling across grassy lawns like the college students in the pictures, backpack slung jauntily over one shoulder. The perfect sunny Southern California location. I loathed the cold and snow, so I hadn't applied to an Ivy League school back East. I wanted to be near the beach.

None of that mattered now. Amid my tears, I tore up my university acceptance letter. Can't bring a baby into the dorms.

Months before the baby was due, Ricky turned violent and abusive. Yet I had nowhere else to live because of my dad's recent cancer diagnosis and my mom's foreclosure, so I stayed with Ricky with the intention of getting out as soon as I could.

I enrolled in the local junior college and signed up for summer classes. Philosophy? Couldn't think of a better subject. Getting a grade for answering "why me?" Why not?

Jacob was born a day early. Labor was sporadic and if I had listened to the advice nurse who advised me to stay home until my contractions came at regular intervals, it would've been a home birth, not the ideal "place of birth" for my baby's birth certificate.

"What's 'colic'?" I asked the pediatrician. "Is that why he can't hold down formula, has projectile vomiting and can't sleep for more than a few hours at a time?"

The doctor nodded. "Quite possibly."

"What can I do?" I looked down at Jacob's harmless smile.

"Not much. Hopefully, he'll grow out of it."

Hopefully.

Ricky's physical and psychological abuse continued while I attended spring semester as a full-time college student.

The following summer Ricky—the "sperm donor" as I refer to him—threatened to kill me. He held me hostage with a butcher knife while nine-month-old Jacob slept in his crib nearby. Hours later, by sheer luck or God's grace, I was able to sneak on the phone to dial 911. The police came with sirens wailing and guns drawn. They arrested Ricky and escorted him to jail. That is another story. All that mattered was that I had survived.

My mom, my brother Kirk, my son and I—restraining orders in hand—made immediate plans to move.

I phoned Yessenia. She and I had been close friends for five years, ever since our first day of high school. Yessenia looked like a cross between Cindy Crawford and Julia Roberts. She lived at home with her parents who were against her modeling even though she'd been approached multiple times. She had no interest in college and instead worked part-time at a grocery store.

"I'm excited about moving and starting a new life. I might major in accounting." I paused, eager for her to share my joy. "Why are you being so quiet?"

"You have no idea what I'm going through," Yessenia whispered into the phone, her voice muffled and shaky.

"What happened?"

"I almost drove my car off a cliff." She sounded as if she had been crying.

"You got into an accident?"

"No." She was silent for a moment. "But I wish I had. I can't take him anymore."

"Who?"

"My dad," Yessenia said. "All he does is put me down. I'm a whore, a slut, a stupid, no-good piece of trash. Always have been." She took a breath. "I'm going to finish off what I should have done earlier."

Was Yessenia—who had stuck with me through many of the worst moments of my life—about to commit suicide? I panicked. "We're moving this weekend," I said. "Do you want to come with us?"

There was a long pause. "Are you serious?"

"Totally."

"Your mom won't mind?"

"Of course not. You know she adores you."

She sniffled. "You don't know how much this means to me."

No longer would beautiful Yessenia be subjected to a middle-Eastern father who emotionally abused her and a weak mom who didn't protect her.

I found a job as a cashier at a big box retailer and Yessenia found an office job at a call center. The downside was that I had to wear a uniform of collared shirts and pleated khakis, unflattering for a girl who had what my first boyfriend's mom referred to as "good birthing hips." The upside was getting a paycheck.

That paycheck wasn't enough to support my son so I had no other option but to apply for public assistance.

I was lucky enough to get Jacob into the childcare center at my college. I kept working hard. My grades were stellar. Life was improving until eight months later when Social Services cut off my son's financial aid and food stamps. "New guidelines" handed down by the government meant he and I only qualified for help during my first two years of college, after which I was expected to get a full-time job. But when I chose to keep my baby rather than give him up for adoption—something I had seriously considered—I'd promised myself I would earn a Bachelor's Degree to be able to support him and give him the good life he deserved. A local university had already accepted my transfer application.

I needed cash. My college financial aid package wouldn't cover living expenses. Either I would have to drop out of school or find another way.

* * *

MARCH 1998

"You quit?" I set my textbook aside and stared at Yessenia. "Why?"

"My boss reminded me too much of my dad."

"What are you going to do? How are you going to pay the rent?"

"Don't know." She flipped through a *Vogue* magazine. "Don't care."

"Well, tell me when you figure it out because I'm in trouble, too."

The next day Yessenia handed me the newspaper's classified section with a few waitressing ads circled.

"But I'm so clumsy," I said. "You and Kirk make fun of me for bumping into walls." My little brother relished any opportunity to laugh at me. "I can't serve food or drinks. I'll spill on customers and get fired."

"That's your choice. I'm doing it."

Yessenia and I drove the thirty-five miles to Los Angeles, map and job ads in hand.

She had clipped out three vague listings offering full or part-time employment for women eighteen years and older as a "hostess/dancer/waitress" in Los Angeles. Yessenia and I were both twenty years old and L.A. was only forty-five minutes away. Previous job experience? None needed. Company contact info? Only an address and phone number. But—showing the same meticulousness with which I chose Mr. Dreamy Green Eyes—I was too desperate to care.

While Yessenia drove, I stared at her manicured nails, tanning-salon bronze skin, blonde highlights and mesmerizing blue contact lenses. She looked glamorous and people would probably tip her well.

I flipped open the visor mirror. Although my blue-green eyes were genuine, my skin was pale, my bangs simple, and my long hair dark brown. Optimistically, I decided I'd smile a lot and go for the girl-next-door look.

Under the late-afternoon sun, Yessenia pulled up to our first stop, Club Moonlight*. What an odd name for a restaurant. The neighborhood was pretty odd, too. Work trucks and vans were parked up and down the barren streets. We had expected to find a high end dining establishment, not a nondescript stucco building protected by a chain-link fence.

Inside we saw nothing but high-backed leather booths, a tiny stage, mirrors everywhere, and ghastly neon lighting. It wasn't like any of the restaurants or nightclubs I had been to.

A short Asian woman calling herself *"Mama-san"* swooped down on us. Deep lines alongside her mouth drooped into a set frown. Her eyebrows scrunched together, her forehead wrinkled, and crow's feet around her eyes pulled her face into a scowl.

"You girls work tonight?" *Mama-san* asked in a choppy Asian accent.

"What would we do here?" I said. "Serve food?"

"No, no food. Drinks only."

"So we'd serve drinks like a cocktail waitress?"

Mama-san shook her head. "No, not waitress. You hostess."

"So we seat the customers?"

"No, I arrange customers with hostesses."

At the time, I thought the term "hostess" only applied to the people who stood at the podium near the front entrance of restaurants and seated guests, so the more *Mama-san* said, the more confused I became. I now know *Mama-san* is the traditional name for matrons who run prostitution houses or Geisha clubs in Japan. Back then I wasn't so worldly.

"Where is everyone?" I asked.

"Club not open day, night only. Come, I give you private tour." *Mama-san* motioned for us to follow. "Only business men, high-class men come here." She smiled and raised her eyebrows. "Pretty hostess do good."

"Only men?" I asked. "No women?"

She laughed. "No, no. Male clients. You entertain them."

My eyes widened. "Entertain them? How?"

"You talk to men. Entertain. Serve drinks, flirt, karaoke, dance if you like. Only good men with money here." Her voice became more stern. "I match you two with very rich Asian men. But you talk, smile. If they have good time, they come back and ask for you. The men come here to relax, have good time. You give them good time."

I stared at Yessenia who stared back. We needed more time to think.

"I hire you," *Mama-san* said. "Tonight? Tonight?"

"Thank you for the kind offer," I said. "We'll let you know. We have a few places to check out."

"Where?"

"Club Flamingo and Valley View*," Yessenia said.

She shook her head. "No, no, those places dirty. This club is classy." She wagged her finger at us. "You nice, pretty girls. Make more money here. You see."

Yessenia and I left in search of the second club hoping it would be less sleazy.

Club Flamingo was in an even seedier part of Downtown L.A., not a place where you'd want to be late at night. In the gathering darkness, we could still see the neighborhood was full of bums, druggies, and panhandlers. After debating whether or not to check it out, we ascended a narrow staircase tucked tightly between two dark walls.

At the top, the club entrance consisted of an ordinary black door. We pushed inside and I let my eyes adjust to the dim lighting.

Young women, mostly Hispanic, sat on red couches to our right. On a lonely dance floor beyond them, couples swayed. A DJ spun slow songs from the '70s and '80s, not the fast-paced techno-electronica music we were accustomed to. The men were my grandfathers' age.

The bored-looking security guard at the entrance steered us toward the owner, a stern middle-aged Japanese man dressed in a white collared shirt and black slacks who led us back to his office. As he described his club—a hostess club—in proud, reverential terms, I noticed his crooked teeth weren't as presentable as his attire. Then it occurred to me that his full head of jet-black hair looked dyed and the wrinkles around his almond eyes cut much deeper than they'd seemed at first glance.

Again someone was telling me I would be paid to dance with and "entertain" random men and again I wondered how far the entertaining would be expected to go.

He flattered us and assured us that attractive, intelligent young white women who could hold a conversation were in high demand. Seemingly detecting our hesitation, he offered to let us speak with one of the girls.

A pretty Caucasian girl approached us. Nicole stood out like a gem among the coarse rocks. Instead of the skimpy attire of the gaunt cheek-boned or pudgy-faced girls, Nicole wore a gray pencil skirt and a white blouse. Her straight-cut blonde hair was held back with a tasteful headband and hung neatly down her shoulders, exposing the fair complexion of her high forehead. She could have passed for a court reporter rather than a "hostess."

"You don't like this place?" she asked. "Why not?"

"It's a little dark," I said carefully.

Yessenia added, "Club Moonlight was classier."

"I wouldn't work there," scoffed Nicole.

"Why not?" Yessenia asked.

"I used to work there. Yeah, it looks nicer and the owners seem nice and at first you'll probably make good money." Nicole nodded. "But after a while they'll push you to date the clients—if you know what I mean—and if you refuse they'll throw you out."

I practically shoved Yessenia out the door. Outside, I asked, "Does 'date' mean what I think it means?"

She started the engine and jerked the car away from the crumbling curb. "Does 'starve' mean what you think it means?"

I shuddered.

On our way to our third and final destination, the Valley View*, I stared out at the buildings blurring by. "I won't sleep with men for money, so apparently I don't have anywhere to work."

Yessenia was silent.

I looked at her. "Would you sleep with men for money?"

"You don't know if Nicole was even telling the truth," she said.

We parked across the street from what looked like a neon-encrusted bomb shelter. The sidewalks shook under the assault of endless pounding club music. A dozen men, some in unlaced boots, jeans riddled with holes, and wife-beater t-shirts, smoked, drank, and shouted at each other in Spanish.

"I don't want to walk by those guys."

Yessenia took my arm and marched me past a barrage of cat calls and whistles until we were safely inside the club.

Minutes later, a fat Hispanic man was looking us up and down. "Yeah, I'm the manager," he wheezed. "Ay, go ahead and look around. Come back and see me if you want to work."

A quick glance around confirmed that Yessenia and I stood out like two poodles in a pack of wolves. The trouble was not only did we look clean-cut and innocent; we *were* clean-cut and innocent…at least at the time.

Yessenia and I squeezed by couples—now we knew they were hostesses and clients—who were in various stages of conversation or dancing.

We passed through an area with couches and a room with a large dance floor before we found enough breathing space to take in the surroundings.

An older man clutched his arms around the waist of a Hispanic girl young enough to be his granddaughter and rubbed himself against her ass—and she let him. Another young girl had her hands in a guy's gray hair and was grinding her thighs into his crotch. We were watching a roomful of dry-humping.

Yessenia pointed to the room's darker areas. "There's more than dancing over there." Young girls and old men were groping each other.

The men were staring at us. Some smiled, their eyes travelling up and down our bodies. A few licked their lips. One winked and blew a kiss. I felt suffocated.

There were no security guards to be found, so I searched for an exit. The room was shrinking and getting hotter and stuffier. I needed air. I reached for Yessenia's hand and we pushed our way back to front door. The cool outside air hit my skin and opened my lungs.

By the time we were back inside her car with the doors locked I wanted to cry. I was frustrated and disgusted.

"I'm so sorry," Yessenia gasped. "The ads didn't say anything about this."

"What are we going to do?" I said. "Rent's due."

"I don't trust *Mama-san*," said Yessenia, "but I'll give Club Flamingo a try if you will."

So we drove back to Figueroa Street, parked in the pothole-ridden lot, and crawled back inside Club Flamingo with our tails between our legs.

I plunged into my first shift with a smile plastered on my face and every ounce of optimism I could muster. Unfortunately the evening had a few ugly surprises in store for me.

"What name do you want?" the owner asked.

"Name?" I tilted my head.

"I'm making your time card," he said impatiently. "Pick a name."

"Uh…Cassie?"

"Fine." He pointed to a paper. "Write it there."

I obeyed.

"Okay, you've signed everything. Now pay attention because I only want to go through this once." He seemed short-tempered, not kind like when we met hours earlier.

He gave me a two-minute training session on how to "clock in" when a customer wanted to buy a dance with me. I had to take a blank card and punch it in a time clock, which stamped the current time on the card. Then I had to put the card in front of my name so the management would know I was working. When a customer was through with me, I had to take the card and clock out, then bring it to the register so the cashier would know how much time to charge the customer.

At the end of the training session, I was still thoroughly confused as to how I was actually going to make money at this but I didn't want to endure his breath or his irritation any longer so I simply nodded when he asked if I understood the procedures.

"Okay, go sit over there where your friend is." He pointed to a couple of red vinyl couches. Unlike the rest of the club's dim lighting, the couches were illuminated with blinding spotlights, so the faces of the girls sitting on them stood out like paintings in a gallery.

I sat down on a red couch, feeling the heat of the spotlights and of the other girls' stares. Yessenia was nowhere to be seen.

Someone tapped my shoulder. I turned and could barely make out a man beckoning me over as one would do to a dog. I stood up and approached him—what else was I supposed to do?

He nodded toward the time clock. "Don't you need to clock in?"

"Oh, yeah." I stuck a blank card into the time clock two or three times with no luck. Finally the customer showed me how to do it. It clicked and I stuck it behind my strange new name, "Cassie."

He took my hand and pulled me toward the dance floor. He didn't ask me my name or where I was from. He dragged me to a crowded dark corner, held me close, and grabbed my ass with both hands. I jumped back. "What are you doing?" I yelled.

Instead of answering, he grasped my wrists and pressed his body up against mine. I felt a hard lump on my lower abdomen. I screamed, but no one could hear me over the loud music.

My customer shook his head and scowled. Then he dragged me back to the time clock.

The owner gave me a dirty look as he rang up the bill and tossed me a red ticket. My customer handed a five-dollar bill to the owner and one to me and marched away. I stood there, speechless.

"What are you waiting for? Go back to the couch," the owner said. "Next time, stay clocked in for longer."

I spun around but before I could reach the couches, another guy tapped me on the shoulder. This one was either deaf or didn't speak English, since he didn't say a word but only motioned with his hands. He led me back to the dance floor. This time, the customer slow danced with me in the middle of the room away from any dark corners. At first I was relieved but then I stiffened as he gradually pressed our bodies closer together. But he seemed more interested in simply being close to me than in grinding against me.

In fact, it might have been almost bearable if it weren't for the stench of his clothing soaked in body odor and freshly-cut grass. Before I could object his rough calloused fingers were intertwining with mine, his hot greasy sweat spreading onto my palms. It was like trying to choke down a horse pill without gagging.

When the next song started, my greasy customer began steering me towards the dark corner and soon I was trapped in the same situation as before.

I removed his hands from my ass and pulled away. He sighed and returned me to the register.

"Where's your card?" the owner asked.

My eyes widened. "Oh, no…I forgot."

"Go clock out and bring it."

"I forgot to clock in."

His cheeks flushed. "You have to clock in!" he yelled. "You're going to make me lose money! This is a warning, do you understand?"

Heat rose to my face and I nodded.

My customer didn't tip me and at the time I didn't argue. Nowadays I would never accept it. Nowadays I would demand a tip just for wasting my time. But back then I was so green that I allowed men to take advantage of my debilitating shock.

Again I was chosen by a customer immediately. It was flattering. I couldn't help but notice I was getting more attention than most of the other girls and at first I thought my open smile, bright green eyes, or even my soft curves made me the belle of the ball.

However, after I slapped the tenth set of hands off my butt or squirmed out of the dark corner for the tenth time, I started to wonder what I was doing wrong. None of the other girls looked alarmed by their groping suitors. If anything they looked bored. Was I being too sensitive?

Then—on the dance floor—I spotted one other girl whose misery seemed to mirror mine: Yessenia. She moved like a zombie in the arms of a slimy creep that a week earlier she would never have given the time of day to.

By the end of the night, after getting warned over and over for not turning in my red tickets, my feet pulsed in pain from the high heels, my head throbbed from the pounding music, and my will to squirm had nearly dissolved. Yessenia and I each pocketed close to $100 cash in tips.

When we finally escaped from Club Flamingo my body was shaking from the cold. Nausea bubbled up my throat.

Yessenia linked her arm in mine and together we trudged to her car in silence.

What did we do with the money? On the way home, we stopped at an all-night drive-through and ordered too much food. We sat in her car and I shoved a chicken pita, fries smothered in cheese and onion rings dripping in oil into my mouth.

I hadn't eaten that much in one sitting, ever.

"I never buy anything over a dollar," I said, "and now I can afford all this. I spent seven dollars just on me."

Yessenia nodded. "Yeah, no more digging through the couch cushions or my car to find enough change to share the two-for-ninety-nine-cents tacos."

I gave her a hug. "We can pay our rent."

She pulled back, quiet. "I don't know if I can do this."

"Do you see any other choice?" Then it hit me. The whole night replayed in my head.

I burst into tears. So did she.

CHAPTER TWO
THE RED COUCH

APRIL 1998

YESSENIA SET DOWN HER curling iron, wiggled out of one black mini skirt and into another one, and applied mascara to the lashes above her large brown eyes.

"You look gorgeous," I said.

Yessenia frowned into the mirror, took off her white tank and slipped into a red halter top. Then she brushed on more powder and used baby hair clips to secure two locks of her long blonde and brown tresses to the sides of her head, allowing other curls to hang down and frame her oval face.

I paced across our messy bathroom. "Can we go?"

"What's the big hurry?"

"Jacob's asleep, my mom's home from work to watch him, and I don't want to be late."

"You just don't like the questions your mom's been asking," she said. "I don't give a damn what my parents think."

"Well I do. Can we go now? I need to make money."

She ignored me and put on more makeup. I went into my bedroom to check on Jacob. He'd gotten pretty adept at climbing out of his crib so I had to move him into a toddler bed. Maneuvering around the two room dividers I used to section off a corner to create a "bedroom" for him, I peered into the darkness. The dividers had been my mom's idea. They gave me some privacy and reduced Jacob's bedtime distractions. They weren't as good as a separate room, which was a luxury I couldn't yet afford.

My eighteen-month-old had his teddy bear under one arm but

15

had kicked off his covers. Inching closer, I pulled the comforter up, tucked it under his chin, and softly kissed his cheek. He stirred.

I froze. If he were to wake up, it would take me another half hour to get him back to sleep. A half hour less to make money.

Jacob's deep breathing resumed. With his green eyes closed, his brown hair soft from his earlier bath, and his creamy white skin, he looked like a sleeping angel. I fought my urge to grasp his tiny hand and instead tiptoed back to the bathroom.

Yessenia still wasn't ready to leave. Lost-dollar signs flashed before my eyes. I wrapped myself in the knee-length sweater jacket I used to hide my "work uniform" and headed to the living room where I found my mother.

She had her ankles up on the coffee table and her nose in a book: a Christian romance novel. I could never get into that smut. I sat next to her on the couch.

She took off her glasses and rubbed her eyes. "I thought you'd left already." She lowered her chin and gave me a motherly stare. "Aren't you going to be late?"

"Yessenia has her own personal schedule."

Mom frowned. "When you worked at the department store you had normal hours, not this all-night business."

"I also had more money problems because they only paid me minimum wage. I couldn't pay for college and take care of Jacob on minimum wage."

"But what about all the financial aid, daycare help, food stamps, and welfare?" Her thin pink lips pursed shut. "Doesn't the government take care of you?"

I hated my mother reminding me that I received public assistance. When my younger brother Kirk and I were growing up, my mom occasionally accepted food boxes from our church, but she resorted to working as many as three jobs at a time rather than ask for government aid.

"Not anymore. 'Welfare reform' means the government financially cuts us off. That's why I had to get the job at the department store to keep going to college."

"I wanted to finish school. But things didn't work out for me."

"Well, I may have to quit school," I snapped.

"Don't be stupid. Do you know how hard it was for me to take care of you and your brother as a single mother without a degree?"

"I didn't say I *wanted* to quit school. But Social Services says when

I finish my two-year degree in May I can't get food stamps or money anymore. They would rather I stop going to school and work full-time."

"I thought you were going to transfer to the university."

"I can't afford it."

"What about child support?"

"That jerk has never given me a dime."

She shook her head. "If your father or I had known that man had put his hand to you…he'd be dead. You just make sure you keep Jacob away from him."

"Yes. That's why I'm going to college and that's why I work the evening shift, so I can get a better job and I'll never have to ask anyone for money ever."

She softened her tone. "If I had money, I'd give it to you."

I smiled. "I know, but I want to do it on my own."

"I don't see how a waitress can earn enough for herself, let alone a baby."

I bit my lip. "I'm a really good waitress."

Yessenia finally emerged from the bathroom. "Shall we?" she said brightly.

Mom stared at Yessenia's provocative outfit. "You'll definitely make good tips dressed like that."

My stomach churned.

*   *   *

I sat in the spotlight on the red couch and crossed my legs demurely.

"Cassie," Yessenia said, "money heading your way."

I squinted into the darkness. A man was pointing at me and motioning me over. Oh, thank God he's a suit, I thought. I peeled my sweaty skin off the vinyl couch and stood up. I tugged down the hem of my beige suede mini. I had bought the skirt a couple of years ago during my junior year in high school—the only short skirt, after much begging, that my dad had ever allowed me to buy—and was proud it still fit. Memories of my conservative, well-educated daddy were totally unwelcome at that moment, especially when my new customer could easily turn out to be my daddy's age. I shifted my bra to better showcase my ample natural cleavage.

After a final shove to get Daddy out of my brain, I smiled and strutted to the column in the center of the room. I slid a blank card into the time clock. It clicked. Cassie was clocking in.

When Cassie clocked in, Miranda clocked out. No longer was I a college student or a single mother. I became a paid companion, a fantasy.

My own fantasies were nothing like this, of course. Ever since I could remember I'd fantasized attending a prestigious university, advancing in a high-paid career, getting married, then having children.

I recognized the Asian man wearing a dress shirt and gray slacks as one of my regulars. I smiled in delight as he handed me a coupon for "Ten Free Minutes." Goody: ten minutes of lost money. I let him guide me toward the dance area, since he was old enough to be my father.

We passed through pockets of dank and dusty air surrounded by black walls. I tried not to trip over the creases in the stained red carpet, or what was left of it, and avoided eye contact with the other women who I'd learned were only too ready to view any glance as gloating, ridiculing, or a challenge. To my right and left, they sat on red couches eyeing me from behind the cast-iron railings.

My heels clicked on the worn wooden floor. Head held high, my customer escorted me in a princely fashion past the DJ who was spinning another slow song. The gentleman's arm was wrapped around my waist. His obvious pride was flattering in a way.

My client was passionate about dancing. I twirled around the room at his direction. He paused to wipe sweat from his forehead with his handkerchief. I'd once dreamed of being courted by a gentleman who waltzed me across the dance floor. Maybe this was my dream coming true.

Smile. Flirt. Maintain the illusion. Keep him entertained, so he'll keep me on the clock.

He peered into my eyes but wouldn't say a word. He didn't stare hungrily at my lips or down at my breasts. He didn't slip his hand down to squeeze my butt. Club Flamingo's version of a real gentleman.

The "Ten Free Minutes" offer ended; men and their hostesses lined up at the cash register in the lobby. Not me. Lucky me: my client danced with me for twenty more minutes.

A fast song spoiled his mood and he led me back to the cashier who calculated the total due. For spending thirty minutes with me, my customer paid the club ten dollars and handed me a twenty. He was a true gentleman: he gave me what the bill would have been without the cheesy coupon plus eight dollars extra. And—best of all—he didn't ask for a date even though the owners had helpfully provided a stack of paper on the counter for writing down the girls' names and phone numbers.

I gave him a polite hug before we parted. He headed out the door and back to his other life; I returned to the red couch to signify my availability. The stack of paper on the counter served as a reminder that while the owners' official position was that the girls were to see clients exclusively inside the club so the club could get their cut—the implication was we girls should do whatever we had to do to ensure the customers kept coming back. I played dumb, pretending not to understand what the stack of paper was for.

For every hour I was on the clock, the club raked in twenty-four dollars and so did I, more or less. In a good four-hour shift, I could make about $100—enough to cover daycare, food, and gas.

A muffled sound came over the loudspeaker.

"Hey, Kim." I poked the bony girl with stringy blonde hair sitting next to me. "What did they say?"

She rolled her eyes. The spotlights cast shadows on her face, making her cheeks look sunken. "Another ten-free-minutes special. Damn, business is slow. I gotta make my rent."

I was thinking the same thing.

Kim's brown eyes widened. "Oh, shit. Here comes Hector-the-molester."

An old man with sweaty gray locks that encircled a widening bald spot waddled towards us. His striped shirt's top two buttons were open, partially exposing his curly gray chest hair. His belt kept his shirt tucked into his slacks, thankfully, but his belly hung over the belt. He upturned the corners of his lips in a smile revealing his crooked, stained teeth.

I choked back a gag. "Eww." I stood up. "I'm going to go hide in the locker room."

"My ex ain't paying his child support. My three kids gotta eat. I need cash and minutes. I've been warned twice." She grimaced. "So I'll be staying out here."

When a dance hostess consistently fell short on minutes, the owners either put her on probation or fired her. They expected 120 minutes a night per girl, which wasn't easy.

Most girls quit hostess dancing after a couple weeks anyway. This was not a career choice for young women, more like an act of desperation, so I didn't get to know any of them.

A young man covered in engine grease with slicked back hair pointed at me. Ick. I pretended not to notice him, and continued my exodus toward the hostess locker room.

I bumped into Yessenia looking, as usual, as if she should have been strutting across a catwalk or gracing the cover of a magazine rather than dancing here at Club Nasty. Holding an unlit cigarette between her long, manicured fingers, Yessenia leaned close to a mirror and adjusted her long fake eyelashes. Even false eyelashes looked good on her. On me they looked like dead caterpillars.

"Hiding from the ten-free-minutes special hmm?" I grinned.

"Hell yeah. I'm not a charity." She looked at me. "I'm going for a smoke."

I followed her through a maze of dark corridors. The club operated from half of the gutted-out second-floor of a crumbling brick building; the other half was off limits, containing locked and abandoned offices or rooms, most of which were unfit for human use except for the hostesses' "Smoking Lounge."

The small square room featured peeling paint and a "balcony" (fire escape) the braver girls used. I didn't smoke, but I appreciated the "fresh air." I preferred stale cigarette smoke to humid body odor, reeking sweat, and musky cheap cologne. Plus, I could commiserate with Yessenia.

Tired from squatting, I used my purse as a cushion from the splintered floorboards. I sat and stared out the open window, beyond the fire escape. City lights sparkled. High-rise buildings competed for the sky. Maybe one day I'd work in one with a sweeping view of the city.

A new hostess, a barely legal Hispanic girl, joined us. "Can I bum a smoke?" She yanked at black spandex not long enough to be called a skirt.

"Sure." Yessenia held her cigarette in between her lips while she took out another one.

"Watch out." I pointed down at some rotted beams in the floor. "Careful of the hole in the corner."

She gave a half-assed shrug. "I'm going to fall through the cracks sooner or later."

"I can't believe this place hasn't been condemned," I said. "I'm sure it's violating a dozen health codes. I wonder if OSHA would give us a reward for turning the owners in."

Yessenia took a long drag. "It's probably some fucking historical building."

Yeah a historical building that housed a hostess club. Sometimes I imagined the girls in this line of work decades or centuries before me. There were other names for it. Rather than a hostess dancer, I could have been a taxi dancer or a Geisha girl descended from a long tradition of men paying to be entertained by society's most refined, attractive women. It was true my best money came from flirtatious, intelligent conversations with classy businessmen. But—unlike Geisha girls with white painted faces and bulky kimonos who performed traditional dances *for* their clients—we adorned our faces with natural-looking makeup, wore outfits to showcase and flatter our figures, and danced face-to-face *with* our clients.

Years later I realized hostess clubs and the red couches where we girls sat on display were unlike anything else in the world: strip clubs, disco clubs, brothels, bars, lounges, coffee houses. Hostess clubs, rare in America, descended from the Japanese Geisha tradition of Geisha girls charming men. That sounded like more fun.

But I would snap back to the reality of Los Angeles, California circa 1998 and the degrading reality that I couldn't pick my dance partners at all.

The newbie finished her cig and rushed back to earn more minutes and cash.

I stood up and my heel sank into the floor. I steadied myself. "This place is a piece of shit."

Yessenia took a long drag. "No worse than this shitty job." She blew smoke into the air, which without a breeze stayed suspended in place.

"Are you ready to go back out there?"

She flicked her hand. Ash trailed to the floor. "Just ready to go home."

After our shift ended, Yessenia and I linked arms to descend the dark creaking staircase. We staggered toward the parking lot, stepping around hypodermic needles and used condoms. The initial shock had worn off.

During the drive home, we discussed our night.

"Some guy tried to touch me in the TV room," I said. The TV room was the same size as the dance area with private leather loveseats several rows deep.

"And? At least you didn't have to sit next to some girl who let a guy finger-bang her under his jacket."

"Seriously? Guys better not expect that from me."

"We sit on couches waiting for sick fuckers to clock us in. What do you expect?"

"A little respect."

"You want respect? Quit and go get your office job."

"You know it doesn't pay enough. At least we get tips here."

"Yeah, I love getting my leg humped by someone old enough to be my grandpa. I should be paid more for this. There's gotta be a better way to make money."

I shook my head. I didn't know what else we could do.

Chapter Three
Balancing Act

MAY 1998

JACOB SCREAMED, WAKING ME up. I bent over the side of my bed to find him sitting wide-eyed on the carpet. I reached over, scooped him up off the floor and placed him on the pillow next me.

He jumped on the bed and tried to slide down my bent knees onto my stomach, which felt like a punch. He was more effective than any alarm. I stretched and realized I was still in my mini skirt and halter top from work—one of the downsides of getting home at 3 AM and being too exhausted to change.

I reached for my clock. It was after 8 AM and my first class started in an hour. I wiped the smeared mascara off my face.

After wrestling my book bag and Jacob's diaper bag into the trunk, I fought Jacob to buckle his squirming body into his car seat. Then I floored the gas pedal all the way to the daycare center at my college.

I delivered Jacob and his diaper bag to his classroom with only five minutes left to drive to my own class. I spun in place and prepared to sprint back to the car when I felt his little arms wrap around my legs.

"I love you, mommy." He smiled. I squatted down and he gave me the biggest little bear hug ever. "Love you, love you, love you."

"I love you, too." I kissed his forehead and rubbed his back praying he wouldn't make a scene. "I have to go now, but we can go to the park later if you want to."

"No, Mommy, don't go." He nuzzled his head into my neck. "Come play." He grabbed my hand and yanked me in the direction of the toy shelves.

I pulled back. "We can play later. I need to go."

He sniffled. "No, don't go, Mommy." Tears welled in his big green eyes.

The look of pain and abandonment on his face made my stomach drop.

"Mommy! I want you!" He wailed louder and louder. I squatted back down. He grabbed my neck and squeezed. "Don't go. Pease Mommy."

"Honey, I love you so much, but Mommy has to get to class."

"No, I want you."

"Please, Jacob. I'll pick you up as soon as I can." I wiped his face with my sleeve. "I'm going to be late."

The preschool teacher who had been busy with other toddlers finally came to the rescue. "Jacob, do you want to come over and color with me?"

He shook his head and maintained the death grip around my neck.

I pried his arms away, gave him another kiss and handed him to the teacher. He pouted and stretched out his arms toward me.

I blinked back tears as I rushed to my car. I hoped Jacob didn't see me crying. I didn't know how much longer I could keep passing him between babysitters, preschool teachers and my mom so I could work and go to school. I was doing all this for him but I was too exhausted to pay much attention to him when I was actually with him.

After finding a parking spot, I jogged into my class, ten minutes late as usual. And—also as usual—my teacher's monotonous lecture on mathematical calculations quickly lulled me to sleep.

My head smacked onto the table and I jolted upright, hoping my professor didn't notice. Luckily, the back of his gray head was to me as he scrawled a balance sheet equation on the board. I rubbed my eyes, straightened up, and robotically copied the numbers into my notebook.

The next time I fell asleep, a classmate jabbed me helpfully in my side. My head slipped off my hand. I yawned, wiped drool from the corners of my mouth, and opened my eyes.

"All right, be back here in about ten," my professor announced. He took off his glasses and wiped the sweat from his nose. "Oh, and I posted the grades, which include the last test, outside the door."

Stacey, my helpful classmate, hissed in my ear. "He was looking at you." She shook her head, picked up her purse and joined the rush of students who gathered around the grade sheets outside.

My professor sat down at his desk and shuffled through his lecture notes.

I approached him. "Excuse me, Mr. James."

He glanced over his glasses at me. "Yes?"

"I want to apologize for falling asleep. I have a new baby at home."

"Well, please do try to stay awake."

Outside, I examined the grade sheet. All A's, like most of my grades had been since first grade. I turned to find Stacey behind me.

"I don't understand how you do that," she said.

"What?" I asked.

"You're always late to class and falling asleep. I study every day, get here on time, stay awake, yet I'm the one with a C."

"I study a lot at home." A lie. Numbers and school came easy to me.

I tried to keep my hostessing job from affecting me, my son, or my life. When people through polite conversation would ask me about my job, I would mumble something about studying in college and change the subject. When people at the hostess club asked me about my life, I wouldn't mention Jacob, but would say I needed money for college then drive the conversation back toward them.

* * *

The dancers had nicknames for our most notorious customers like "Hector-the-Molester." One night he clocked me in and led me to the dark "grinder's corner." Hidden from the rest of the dance floor by a support pillar, this was where the customers who wanted to grind themselves on the hostesses took them. Having to remain pleasant while older, unattractive, uneducated men with whom I wouldn't even flirt in the outside world were rubbing themselves against me, felt repugnant. Some hostesses, seemingly to compensate for not being as smart or pretty, spent their entire shift over there, one man after another pressed against them.

Yessenia and I learned to avoid the spot. It was like a disease because if one client saw you allowing customers to grind over there, every other man who clocked you in would expect the same service. And sooner or later your will or self-esteem would be completely worn down and you wouldn't bother to protest.

Yessenia and I donned a don't-even-try-it look, so we weren't often subjected to grinding sessions. Whenever a customer tried to maneuver me over there, I pushed us back out into the open. Eventually most of those men tired of the game and clocked me back in, occasionally without a tip.

Once in a while, if I was having a particularly rotten night tip-wise, I might put up with some light contact dancing. The contact may have been light but I paid heavily for it by feeling like shit about myself later. There was nothing worse than allowing a strange man to squeeze his body together with yours and pant against your neck while you had to smile and pretend to enjoy it. I would imagine my son treating a woman that way someday—or worse my future grand-daughter being used that way—and I wanted to scream and punch the guy.

One evening, Hector-the-Molester clocked me in before I had a chance to consider the warnings I'd heard about him from the other girls. I thought I recognized the gray strands of hair circling the bald spot, the beer belly protruding far enough to have un-popped a button, and the yellowed, crooked teeth. He was old enough to be my grandfather. He steered me toward the grinders' corner, tightly gripping my waist and hands.

At first, many men seemed shy about letting me know what was on their sweaty little minds—as if I couldn't figure it out—but Hector's forcefulness and strength made me feel violated. He panted in my face, dripped sweat all over me, and stared at me with a sick concentrated look that made me want to vomit. I was his humping post. No money was worth this.

I didn't know what to do. The men were supposed to decide when the "dancing" started and stopped and it was frowned upon to deviate from this custom. Usually when I became uncomfortable with a customer's behavior, all it took was for me to refuse to meet his demands. That didn't work with Hector.

I tried my best to squirm away from him, but he pulled me closer and rubbed against me more vigorously.

Over and over I would writhe out of reach and he would yank me close. Finally he tired of these power struggles and checked me back in.

I ran to the locker room to detox, blinking back tears, stomach churning. I sat in a daze and stared at my reflection in the mirror. I couldn't even recognize the lonely grayish-green eyes gaping back. They belonged to a stranger, as did the long, tangled hair, chapped lips, and freckles splattered across the pallid nose. It wasn't me. I couldn't find myself in that sad girl's face.

The eyes alarmed me the most—they looked hollow and empty, as if they'd never seen joy or love. I saw no trace of my happy childhood, my joy from serving in my community, my serenity from serving in my church, and the pleasure I'd taken in my studies. Where was the girl who found adventure in climbing trees, hopping on stones, and scrambling through ditches?

As much as I despised the work I was doing and the nightmarish creatures it brought into my waking life, I knew it wasn't the only thing making me sad. And I couldn't blame my misery on my son's father—the "sperm donor"—whom I'd never loved. No, it was my first boyfriend back in high school, Henry, who gave me my first nudge toward this dungeon.

Henry took everything from me.

I was a trusting fifteen-year-old. Henry wooed me, my friends, and my family, and ended up isolating me from everyone.

Henry wrote me love letters folded into paper hearts every day. He sang "You Are So Beautiful." He brought me red roses and gave me my awkward first kiss.

Henry also grabbed me by the hair and held my head down to perform fellatio on him. I was definitely unwilling. As my tears poured down onto his dark bare skin, I begged him to let me go. He ignored my pleas.

Henry smiled like a gentleman with my family, befriended my little brother, and helped my mom around the house. He also destroyed several of my friendships over what I mistakenly assumed were false accusations of his sexual advances.

Henry proudly took me to our high school dances and patiently taught me to drive. He also coerced me to do more sexual acts before I turned seventeen than many women do in their entire lives, some of which he secretly videotaped.

Henry would then alternate between being with me and shunning me while making advances on other girls. He begged me for help with his math homework then kissed another girl behind my back on the school bus. The mixed emotions broke me down. I clawed at my wrists until they were bloody, both out of wanting to feel again and wanting to never feel again.

With battered pride, I hid this from everyone except him, and he didn't care.

He seemed to take pride in ignoring the word "no"—at least when I would say it. "No" became meaningless and only spurred him on. When I tried to break up, he raped me while I lay helplessly frozen in shock. He acknowledged what he had done but showed no remorse.

Yet I still ended up back by Henry's side.

Henry broke my heart, betrayed my trust, and laid the foundation for the wall I would build.

After we broke up once more, Henry came over to my house while I was home alone and tried to rape me a second time. I froze. In my head I said no, but lay there; my mind separated from my body.

To this day, I can't remember if his second attempt was successful or not.

I checked myself into counseling. It took months of intense practice with my psychologist before I could literally mouth the word "no." She taught me to recognize the cycle of abuse and helped me to rebuild my self-esteem. I finally gathered the strength to tell Henry to fuck off.

From the backseat of my mom's pick-up truck during a lull in our conversation, I whispered to her, "Henry...raped me." Words barely audible, but loud enough to be heard.

Mom paused then moved on to another topic. As she had with her own traumatic childhood, she blocked out my confession, unable to hear it.

Once again I was alone and victimized.

Hector-the-Molester had somehow unlocked a flood of awful memories of Henry. I felt powerless again. "No" was again meaningless. I couldn't even cry. I felt numb. I was twenty years old.

While I stared at my reflection, Yessenia rushed in, mascara streaming down her cheeks.

"Oh...my...God," she gasped. "I can't believe he jizzed on me."

Before I could ask what she was talking about, I saw it. Below Yessenia's halter top, the front of her skirt displayed a circular wet spot.

My jaw dropped. I was shocked. The possibility had never occurred to me. Duh.

Another girl jumped up to help Yessenia, who was already in the bathroom furiously scrubbing her skirt with a paper towel and soapy water. The spot had grown huge.

"Stupid ass," the girl said, "They're supposed to wear condoms."

Condoms? They're not supposed to whip out their dicks. I doubted the Geisha girls had had these problems. We and Geishas both entertained men, but there seemed to be a separation of class and we were apparently stuck at the lower end.

Yessenia sobbed. "I can't go back out there like this!"

I wanted to help her. I wanted to hug her, to tell her it would be all right. I wanted her to believe life would get better, but my mouth was glued shut because I wasn't actually sure. I felt like she and I had made a deal with the devil to pay our rent and the devil could collect any day if he wasn't already doing so.

At least Yessenia and I still had our moral limits since we weren't stripping off our clothes or giving hand jobs in an alley.

"Don't worry, honey." The girl guided Yessenia back toward the lockers. "I have another skirt you can borrow. It'll be okay."

No, I didn't think so. Nothing was going to be okay.

Neither Yessenia, nor I, made much money that shift. To top it off, we were hassled by the owner when it was time to turn in our tickets to account for our time. He paced across the room and ran his hands through his charcoal hair.

"Why so little tickets?" he yelled.

"We had a bad night," I said. "You know, we usually do well."

"Fire me if you want." Yessenia tossed her tickets onto his desk.

"Come on," I said. "We get a lot of minutes most of the time."

He narrowed his almond eyes at us for a moment then broke into a half-hearted smile. "Fine, fine, it's okay. But you do better next time."

While he spoke, I watched the "grinder" girls struggling to add up all the minutes they had accumulated. I wondered if they felt the money was worth the misery, but who was I to judge? There had to be girls willing to satisfy those types of clients. I couldn't survive working as a hostess much longer if I had to endure too many more Hectors. Then again, I didn't know how else I could support Jacob until I could finish my bachelor's degree, which was at least two more years away.

* * *

Daytime was my life; nighttime my job.

During a late shift at the hostess club, a lanky customer in jeans and a trench coat approached me. His long gray hair was partially dyed brown and held back in a ponytail. He clocked me in and took me to "grinder's corner." I didn't hear him unzip his pants, but through the darkness, I saw his one-eyed snake start to rear its ugly head.

Horrified, I jumped back several feet. "Put that thing away. Now."

"C'mon, I tip you good," he said and reached for my hips.

I threw his hands down. "Do you want to get me fired? If you want me to dance with you, you better zip it back up now."

He must have felt my icy stare. Quickly, he complied.

That was a first. It did make me wonder though, if I hadn't been paying enough attention during my dances with other men. What if...? I shook off the chilling thought and focused on mentally counting how much money was in my purse and how many minutes I had accrued. Had I earned enough to buy groceries and gas?

Denial and compartmentalization were safety mechanisms I employed effectively. Reality was too painful.

CHAPTER FOUR
FAMILY AND SCHOOL

MAY 1998

EVEN THOUGH THE CLASS wasn't required, I was nervous during my first graded performance on the piano.

"Miranda, you're up next," said my professor, a middle-aged man with a large nose that gave his long face a friendly but comical appearance.

I bit my lip, hung my head, and descended the steps to the center of the stadium style classroom. The spotlights from the ceiling reflected off the glossy black wood of the grand piano—I could only wish that one day I could afford such a beautiful instrument. I opened my piano book and sat down on the bench. Straightening my posture, I dangled my hands above the keys and held my foot over the pedals. I hoped my teacher couldn't see my shaking.

He cleared his throat. "Start with 'When the Saints Go Marching In,' and follow up with whichever pieces you've chosen."

I nodded, closed my eyes for a moment and let my hands loose. I hit the keys with powerful strokes and started making music. My shoulders danced to the tune. Next I played Simon and Garfunkel's "Scarborough Fair" and Eric Clapton's "Tears in Heaven." Every note reverberated through my heart. When I returned to my seat, my professor handed me my grade. The paper read: *Good job! You earned an "A" but the clicking of your nails on the keys is distracting. Please cut them.*

My manicured nails. I remembered when he mentioned short nails were best for playing piano, which I loved to play. Unfortunately, manicured nails were best for hostessing, and hostessing was paying my bills.

*   *   *

As the weeks went by, I noticed several things about the hostess club, one being that many men came into the club merely to stand across from the red couches. They'd gawk at us girls like awkward adolescents at a junior high dance. Although they paid the entrance fee, they didn't check-out any hostesses. Occasionally, they'd do a "ten-free-minutes" deal, tip the girl five dollars, return her after ten minutes, and await the next special or leave. I figured these guys were incredibly hard-up for attention or cash, and I avoided them.

After the owners announced another promotion, a man in a soiled white t-shirt and grease-stained jeans pointed at me, signaling his desire to dance. I turned my head and made small talk with the girl beside me. I figured if he didn't have the balls to come over and ask for permission in English to dance with me, then I didn't want to be clocked in by him.

On the other hand, I couldn't be too smug, especially when the owners were watching. Fortunately, the man picked another hostess.

One night, a customer who couldn't manage to get me to give his crotch the kind of attention he wanted pulled me by the hand and stomped back to the register. I knew other customers watched to learn what each girl would and wouldn't do. This could be bad for my earnings. So, I made friendly eye contact with other men on my way back, smiled, and gave a shrug as if to say I have no idea what this idiot's problem is.

I learned that much like me and Yessenia, some customers held themselves in higher regard than others. The "suits"—men who dressed in white-collar business attire (not always, but typically) had more dignity. They probably had the same carnal intentions as the rest but pursued those more discreetly. Many wanted companionship more than a quick sexual fix.

Most suits tipped me higher and treated me better. Some returned to see me multiple times. Each subsequent visit, they tried to get to know me through conversation and by scooting a little closer to me in the booths. I knew it was a game. But what they didn't know was I had been performing drama on stage in school since age five and playing chess since age seven. I considered myself a wily and formidable opponent.

Yessenia and I discovered some girls had been receiving gifts in addition to monetary tips. I didn't understand how and wanted to know more. When it finally started to happen for me, work became a bit more fun.

An Italian jewelry store owner was one of my first "regulars." He pushed my hair back from my shoulder, saying, "You never seem to wear any jewelry. I could bring you a necklace."

"Oh? What kind of necklace?" I figured he was bullshitting me to get better service.

"A beautiful one, made in Italy."

"I would love that. Would you bring it for me next time you come?"

"I'll bring it next week."

He didn't show up the next week. The following week, he "forgot" it. I played along and pretended to be disappointed, never expecting to see anything.

I grew tired of him. He didn't tip particularly well, so I was wasting my time clocking in with him when I could have been making more money from another "suit."

When we danced again, he pulled a plastic bag from his coat pocket and out came a lovely silver bracelet, with intricate detail and alternating braided patterns on each side.

I smiled. Too bad it wasn't gold. Then I could pawn it for money. Still, I was appreciative and kept it. Yessenia didn't accept gifts because she didn't want to take home with her any reminders of the job. I didn't attach meaning to the bracelet; it was only a material object, a little trophy.

*   *   *

The doorbell rang and I opened the front door to find Joe, Yessenia's boyfriend of the past two years, illuminated by our porch light. His smiling blue eyes and baby-face covered up a harsh childhood— watching his dad walk out on his mom when Joe was only a toddler. This was why he had a soft spot for my Jacob.

I appreciated the attention and gifts Joe lavished on my son; it helped relieve some of the intense guilt I carried because Jacob had no real male role model. I took full responsibility for my poor decision to have sex with a stranger. And even though it hadn't been my fault the condom broke or that the sperm source had been better suited for prison than fatherhood, I still felt that every misery Jacob endured was my fault and that I'd disappointed everyone: my parents, my teachers, and my priest.

"Hey, Joe." I turned my head and yelled. "Yessenia! Joe's here."

He threw his chin up in a nod, which reminded me of the greeting I'd seen gangsters in Los Angeles use to say hello. "How's my little man? He asleep?"

"No, he should be, but he's not."

Joe grinned and pulled a bag out from behind his back. "Aw, go get him. I got stuff for him."

Yessenia appeared, dressed for a hot date with her man, curls cascading down her shoulders. She wrapped her arms around Joe and gave him a sexy kiss.

I went back to our room to get Jacob. He had smashed some yellow Play-Doh into the carpet. Ignoring his mess for the moment, I convinced him to go say hi to Joe.

By the time I led Jacob out by the hand, Yessenia and Joe were yelling at each other. They shut up when they saw us. Yessenia backed away while Joe squatted down and outstretched his arms. "Hey, Jacob. How you doing? Getting so big!" Joe tossed him up in the air. "I got something for you."

"What?" Jacob clutched his shoulder.

Joe set my son down and opened the bag. "He probably don't want this stuff, but here." He tossed me a couple of jumpsuits from the clothing manufacturing company where he worked. "But, hey, guess what I got?" He pulled out a teddy bear.

"Yay!" Jacob grabbed it.

"Say 'thank you,'" I said.

"Thank you," Jacob said and gave Joe a hug.

"Now you be good for your mommy, k?" Then Joe looked at me and glanced over at Yessenia. "I'm taking off."

I was confused. "Didn't you two have a date?"

Yessenia snickered and left the room.

"Love you, too, babe!" he yelled and sauntered out.

After locking the door behind him, I approached Yessenia. "What was that about?"

She shrugged in her usual way, keeping her emotions tucked inside.

I was annoyed. "We didn't go to work tonight because you wanted to see him."

"I hate our job."

"Me, too, but I need the money. Why don't you tell him the truth, that we're not waitressing?"

"Why don't you tell your mom or your college friends or the guys *you* date? You lie to everyone, too."

"But he's your boyfriend. Besides, nobody's ever heard of hostess clubs. We didn't even know what they were."

"Exactly. He'd die if he knew about it. It's gross. Who wants their girlfriend doing that shit?" She picked up her curling iron and wrapped a strand of hair around it.

"So why's he mad?"

"Because he doesn't understand why I won't let him visit me at work. He thinks I'm embarrassed about him or something."

"That sucks."

"Whatever." She shrugged. "It is what it is."

*   *   *

Back in high school while we were walking between classes, Yessenia had expressed a desire to make a living as a cocktail waitress.

My jaw dropped. "Are you crazy? Don't be a bimbo. You actually have brains."

"Just because I take honors classes with you doesn't mean I'm a goody-two-shoes."

"Oh, so that's what you think of me? Because I'm smart enough to actually do something with my life?"

"Whatever." Yessenia had always relied on that tired expression.

"Why don't you go to college to get a real career like I'm going to get and don't parade around in short skirts for money? How degrading. I'd never stoop to that level."

My, my, my. Circumstances sure had changed.

Not long after that conversation, I discovered Yessenia's dark family life. During the school year, she used to spend many nights at my house, but never once invited me to spend the night at hers. Soon I learned why.

Her dad had dropped her off at my home for the evening. She didn't say a word while she took her bag and pillow to my room. Her eyes were red and puffy.

"What happened?" I asked.

"Nothing."

"That's not true. You've been crying."

"My dad's an ass."

"Yeah, I get mad at my mom." I sat down on the bed next to her. "What did he do?"

"I'm tired of his shit."

"Of what?"

"Nothing."

I let the issue drop and instead told her about the colleges I wanted to apply to and which majors I was considering. "Guess what I found out from our school counselor? I'm like 11th in our class of over 300! With my AP scores, and SATs, plus being the president of a club and all the other extra-curricular activities, I think I have a good chance at getting into one of the good universities. Look—an Ivy League school sent me a brochure."

Yessenia started crying.

"What's wrong?" I asked.

"You know, when I was in kindergarten, I wanted to be a veterinarian."

"So? Do it. I don't get it. You have good grades. You've taken anatomy and physiology, which there's no way I could do. I can't stand the sight of blood. What's the problem?"

"My dad said working with animals is dirty and it'd bring shame to our family name."

"Shame? What the fuck? Is that a Muslim thing? I thought your dad wasn't practicing."

"He said I should be a doctor or lawyer or dentist. He said if I was a veterinarian, then he wouldn't be able to tell his relatives in Malaysia and Pakistan because it would bring shame to the family."

"Who cares what your dad thinks or some relatives you've never met?"

"You don't get it. Anything I do isn't good enough. You're lucky. You got to do cheerleading in junior high. He wouldn't let me because of the short skirts. He said I'd be using my body like a prostitute."

"That's crazy."

Tears streamed down her cheeks. "Since before middle school, he's told me I'm a good-for-nothing whore or a fucking slut."

"He talks to you like that?"

"And that's not as bad as what he's done to my brothers. Did I tell you about the time he choked my brother? He had his hands around Yosef's neck. Yosef's feet were dangling in the air. I swear to God he would've killed him if my mom hadn't thrown a shoe at him and screamed at him to stop."

"Are you freaking kidding me?" My father—gentle, caring, and kind—had never put a hand to my brother, my sister, or me. I had nothing but respect for my dad, who bragged about us kids and spoke to me as an equal. "What did Yosef do to piss him off?"

"He got a bad grade and lied about it."

"Was your dad drunk?" My dad never drank and my mom rarely touched alcohol but I'd heard about alcoholic parents.

She shrugged. "He's fucking insane."

I handed her some tissues. "Has he ever hit you or hurt you?"

"No, but I'm the only girl. I heard my aunt was abused by her husband, so he doesn't want me to be dependent on a man like his sister was. That's why he wants me to be a doctor, lawyer, or dentist."

Was she defending her dad? "But what he did was evil. Do you think he would've killed your brother?"

"I don't put anything past him. Remember I told you about when I was five and my best friend's dad tried to molest me and get me to touch his dick?"

"Oh my God, yeah." Up until that point in time, I had never witnessed nor experienced any physical or sexual abuse. "Didn't you tell your parents? Didn't the creep get arrested?"

"I ran home crying and told my mom, but she said I better not say anything about it to my dad or he'd go over and kill the guy and end up in jail."

"Did your mom at least call the cops?"

"Nope. She enables him. But, yeah, my dad would have killed that pervert. He loses his temper all the time. I think he saw some crazy shit while he was growing up in Pakistan."

"Well, this is America and he needs to leave you and your brothers alone. Haven't you told anyone? Aren't there 'social services' for this kind of stuff?"

"A teacher in junior high wanted to call my parents when I got in trouble but I begged her not to because my dad would have beaten me up." She sighed. "I don't want to talk about it anymore. What's done is done."

I couldn't understand how she lived in such a dangerously, dysfunctional family.

But that was her reality.

CHAPTER FIVE
REGULARS

MAY 1998

MY MOM, DRESSED IN her usual floor-length flower-printed cotton nightgown, stared down at us from the top of the staircase. "Where are you two going?"

"To work." I slipped on my strappy heels.

"Dressed like that? Where do you work?" She ran her fingers through her brown bobbed hair.

I put my arms into my sweater, wrapped it closed, and grabbed my velveteen evening purse. I no longer put much effort into concealing my work attire from my mom.

"I told you," I said. "We're waitressing."

"What type of waitresses dress like that?"

"We're going to be late. Let's go, Yessenia. Thanks for watching Jacob; he's asleep already. Bye, I love you."

Yessenia and I darted outside before my mom had a chance to ask me any more questions. It felt uncomfortable to have my mother go from bragging about my straight A's in school to questioning my integrity and source of income, and rightfully so.

* * *

I didn't have life as under control as I thought. Hostessing wore on me. Balancing a night job which didn't allow me to get into bed before 3 AM with daytime college classes packed with homework and studying and taking care of my one-and-a-half-year-old Jacob who I, along with the daycare center, believed was showing signs of ADHD and mild Autism, stressed me.

To relieve the stress, I went out dancing and partying at nightclubs with Yessenia or other friends after Jacob had gone to bed. To combat my loneliness, I went out on dates with different men whom I met off the Internet. With a schedule like mine, I didn't have time to meet men the old-fashioned way—in person.

After several first dates with a number of men, I started communicating online with Jason, a massage therapist. I knew I would go out with him if he asked.

At home, I turned on the computer and dialed into the Internet on our second phone line. After a busy signal, two dropped connections, and a bunch of loud annoying beeps and static noises, I was online. I hopped into a chat room. Men started to contact me. A rapid succession of text boxes jumped out at me. While I layered the ten chat boxes on the monitor, I kept track of the different men I was flirting with. I kept a notepad at hand where I jotted down their computer screen names, real names, ages, locations, and other factoids.

"*A/s/l?*" A box popped on screen. *A* stood for age, *L* for location, and *S* for sex, meaning male or female—one never could tell on the Internet.

"20/no thanks/southern CA." I smirked as I hit *Send*.

"Got pic?" the mystery man typed.

"No," I lied.

"*W/h?* Describe what you look like?" He requested my weight and height.

"200lbs, 5'2", but I have a great personality," I typed, laughing to myself. This exaggeration of 80 pounds and two inches too short was my way of trying to get the men to like me for me rather than for how I looked. It was one of my ways of weeding through the onslaught of communication.

He disappeared from the conversation so I closed his chat box.

Another box popped up—Jason.

"Hey, hon'!" he greeted. "How's ur nite going?"

As I chatted with Jason, I realized that after a couple of weeks I still hadn't sent him a picture (and he hadn't asked for one) yet we still enjoyed talking. I knew he was different.

Our relationship moved from the Internet to the telephone. I soon found myself spending several hours a night on the phone with him, discussing everything from my past and present to the meaning of life and the universe.

An only child, Jason was a free spirit who worked only as much as he needed to to pay his rent. He professed the teachings of the Dalai Lama and made a point of not judging others. He listened to everything before sharing his often profound insight.

"Everything has a purpose," he said. "Things happen for a reason. What have you learned?" He was *so* deep.

I swiveled in the desk chair with the phone pressed against my cheek. "I don't know why some things have happened, like getting pregnant."

"You don't know how that happened?" He chuckled.

"No, you know what I mean." I slouched down into the seat and rested my feet on the desk. "I get so depressed about everything sometimes. Life's hard, especially since I have to do everything on my own. Sometimes I feel like I need to prove myself to people. But I've let everyone down."

"Does it matter what other people think?"

"I know I shouldn't care, but I can't help it." At times when I talked with Jason, I felt like I was conversing with Emerson or Thoreau. I should have been transcribing every word of his.

"Do you think you have difficulty trusting yourself or others?" he asked.

"People will let you down. I need to rely on myself."

"But Miranda, if you open yourself up to new experiences, opportunities will come to you. You should try to put positive energy out there. Negativity breeds negativity."

"You're right, but it's not easy."

Jason was the most spiritually deep man I'd ever met up to that point. If only I had realized how rare our connection was, I might have treated our growing relationship differently. But even though my twenty-year-old eyes had already seen more than their share of troubles, I hadn't experienced enough of life to know what I wanted from a man, how to convey my desires and needs, and how to appreciate a good bond once I'd found one.

We finally exchanged pictures and I at least was not disappointed. I'm guessing Jason wasn't, either, because we decided to meet in person.

When I first saw him, he smiled and his green eyes lit up. The wrinkles which had begun to form on his twenty-eight-year-old face only accentuated his smile. His long light brown hair was pulled back in a ponytail and his posture was impressively straight. His shirt outlined his muscular arms and broad chest as he walked towards me.

"Hey, Miranda." Jason beamed. "You're so much prettier than your picture." The delivery of that line felt different than the pick-up lines I had grown accustomed to hearing.

"I don't know about that." I don't know why I couldn't accept his compliments, other than that they felt real and a simple response like "thanks" felt fake.

We ended our first date not with a kiss but with an extended embrace. When he pulled me close against his body, I melted into his arms and didn't want him to let go. I felt like our spirits connected through our hug.

"When will we see each other again?" I asked.

"Whenever you want." His soft fingers—soft in the way only a masseuse who worked with lotion every day could maintain— smoothed my hair from my face. A deep sense of peace came over me and stayed with me long after we'd parted.

*   *   *

During a shift at the club, one of any hostess' worst nightmares came true: some guy stiffed Yessenia out of a tip. He was a younger, mildly attractive man who was like a fish out of water in this type of establishment. After spending almost two hours with her, he checked her back in and his bill came to $48. With an innocent smile, he proudly handed her $10.

An argument ensued. He thought he was being fair in tipping her more than 20%. She was in tears. He accused her of trying to swindle him.

I led him over by the pool tables for a quick bit of education while Yessenia continued to fume. "This isn't a restaurant," I said to him. "Everyone knows you're supposed to tip the girls at least the same amount as the bill."

Somehow hearing this from another person made it truer.

"But I didn't know," he said. "I don't have any more money."

I felt horrible for Yessenia, but if he didn't have the cash, he didn't have it.

That's when we swore to follow the other girls' advice to not spend too much time with any new customer, until we knew whether he was good for some real money.

*   *   *

Life became a little better when we focused our energy on establishing "regulars" for ourselves.

Hiroki, a middle-aged, pudgy, balding Japanese man with glasses, seemed like any other "suit" with his three-piece neatly pressed. Rather than merely matching the $12 bill, or even generously giving me $20, Hiroki caught my attention by tipping me $50 for less than thirty minutes of my time. When he, like many other customers, handed me a piece of paper with his number, something compelled me to put it into my wallet as opposed to ripping it up and discarding it. But I couldn't work up the nerve to call him.

A few days after meeting Hiroki, I was clocked in by Mark, an older Filipino man. Unlike Hiroki, who had a slightly expanded waistline, Mark was shorter and fitter, with a full head of thick black hair and a slight accent. Rectangular gold glasses framed his round chestnut face, but it was his gold nugget ring which caught my attention. Seeing wedding rings made my stomach churn at the broken promises on display. It made me question the sanctity of marriage and whether or not it was a life choice I'd eventually want to make.

Mark's polo shirt was neatly tucked into his slacks which were held up by a thin leather belt. He had on a Rolex watch and Bally leather shoes—both good indicators of a customer's possible wealth.

Mark chose to sit and talk with me, rather than dance or go to the dreaded TV room. We scooted into a booth around the dance floor. Only one portion of the club was devoted to dancing. Comfy booths were arranged in an L-shape around the dance floor. Across the room, a small bar sold overpriced watered-down juices and non-alcoholic beverages. Another section of the stinky club contained bar-sized pool tables.

"Can I buy you a drink?" Mark asked.

Oh, good. He was willing to spend money on me, which was rare. "Yes, cranberry juice, please."

Rather than wait for the waitress, Mark excused himself, walked to the bar and returned with juice for me and a Coke for himself.

"Where are you from?" His small brown eyes looked beady black in the dim lighting.

"From around here." For safety purposes, I stuck to vague answers. "What about you?" I sipped my drink.

"My family has a big plantation in the Philippines. That is where I grew up, but I moved here to start my business."

Each time he turned his head toward me, he reminded me of a meerkat peering out of its hole. "What type of business do you do?" I was hesitant, as usual, to spend too long with a new guy. Knowing what type of work he did might ease my fears of being jilted at the register.

"My brother has a successful box business in the Philippines, but I did not want to do that. I came here and started a printing business. I print stationary and letterhead for banks. I have several big clients."

"How did you get started?" I liked money and thought about starting a business one day in the future, so I had a genuine interest in this topic.

"I bought printing machines from Germany. It's expensive equipment, but it's the best there is. I went there to purchase it. When it was delivered here, I opened my business."

I wanted to ask how he found his clients in order to gather ideas for my own future ventures but I decided to let him steer the discussion. I figured if he thought I was interested in him then he would tip me at least twenty bucks.

"What do you do?" he asked. He folded his hands together and rested his elbows on the black Formica table top.

Besides this? I thought snidely.

"I'm going to college. In fact, as soon as I finish my physics, anthropology, and math classes, I'll be ready to transfer to a four-year university."

"Good." He nodded. "How are your grades?"

I'd never been asked that by a client before. "I get mostly A's and B's. In high school, I graduated in the top four percent of my class."

"Good." When he grinned, his island-dark skin revealed deepening age lines. "Do you have any children?"

This felt like an interview. While I normally hid the truth, I somehow allowed it to escape my pink-painted lips. "I have one son. He'll be two in October."

He looked off to the side for a moment. "So, he's not yet two?"

"Yes."

"Who's watching him right now?"

"My mom." I sipped the last of my juice. "Sometimes I have to get a babysitter, but usually she watches him."

He nodded again. He opened his mouth to speak, but stopped himself. After an awkward silence, he asked, "Do you want another drink?"

"Yes, thank you." Puzzled, I watched him walk away. This was a first—a client who paid for not only one, but two drinks.

When he returned, he sat down across from me, so we were eye-to-eye. "I would rather go get the drinks and tip you than tip the waitress for doing nothing. Are you married?"

"No," I said. "I made one mistake, not two."

He laughed and we talked about a myriad of mundane topics concerning my school and his work. Although flirty, he was friendly, not at all what I was used to from clients in this underground hostess club. I imagined this was more like the dialogue Geisha girls or high-end hostess girls in Japan had with their clients, but then again I had never met one.

After an hour, Mark clocked me out, paid the bill, and wrapped my tip inside a slip of paper with his phone number. Even though I hoped he had given me at least twenty dollars, I knew I wouldn't feel bad if he hadn't. That was the easiest hour I ever worked as a hostess, and the conversation was actually enjoyable.

Without looking at it, I put the tip into my purse, gave him a hug good-bye and went into the restroom. In the locker room, I sat down to organize my tips, arranging the dollar bills in the same direction. I pulled out Mark's tip and unraveled the note which is when I discovered the hundred dollar bill. My eyes widened and my jaw dropped. Without a second thought, I put Mark's phone number next to Hiroki's, closed my purse and finished out my shift in a much better mood.

I shared my excitement with Yessenia. She told me a high-powered Japanese millionaire—we verified his status with the other girls—had given Yessenia his phone number along with a large tip. How much she wouldn't say. The millionaire was frequently seen in his double breasted suits accompanied by other suited men, presumably business partners or clients. He had a towering presence and liked to throw his money around. Yessenia, whom he agreed looked like a cross between Cindy Crawford and Julia Roberts, was his current favorite because he thought she exuded a high-society vibe.

After driving home, Yessenia parallel parked her car on the street and we chatted as we walked along the dark pathway to our apartment. Ours was the third unit in a fourplex built between a parking lot and another fourplex. The building had a 1970s-style wood shingle roof and was painted beige with dark brown trim, making it blend well with the eucalyptus trees surrounding it.

We strolled past the front unit occupied by the manager and her family, and past the unit occupied by a single-mom whose autistic daughter loudly pounded on the keys of their piano at all hours of the day. Yessenia and I stopped at our front porch.

We entered and I shook off a chill that made my hairs stand on end, which I attributed not to a change in temperature, but to the tale of our apartment unit's history.

When Yessenia and I had moved in the year before and she'd complained to the manager about the neighbor's daughter running up and down the stairs next door, the manager told her the story.

"It's not your neighbors," the manager said.

"Then what is it?" Yessenia asked.

"Your apartment's haunted," the manager explained. "A young lady hung herself over the second-floor railing many years ago. Ever since then, tenants have complained about invisible feet walking up and down the stairs. I've had to repaint the wall over the staircase many times, too, because the strange impression of a portrait reappears."

Out of fear and discomfort, Yessenia let my brother Kirk have the second upstairs bedroom, so she wouldn't have to use the stairs. Nor did Yessenia want to share a room with me and my wild toddler; she opted to sleep on the couch. But before becoming her bed at night, the living room couch was the social center of our place.

It was almost three in the morning when Yessenia and I entered our apartment, changed into our pajamas and sat down on the couch to talk as we often did after work.

"Boom, ba ba boom, boom, ba ba boom," Yessenia hummed.

I raised an eyebrow. "We should play some music and dance."

"I'm too tired."

I placed a hand on my heart. "*Aww…you've lost that loving feeling, o-oh that loving feeling,*" I serenaded her.

She giggled. "You're such a dork."

"You know you want me." I jumped up and turned on the radio, careful to keep the volume low enough not to wake Jacob, my mom, or Kirk.

When a familiar tune came on, Yessenia stood up and dramatically strutted across the carpet as though it were a catwalk. "*I'm too sexy for my shirt, too sexy for my shirt, so sexy it hurts!*" she sang along.

It wasn't long before we were rolling around on the carpet, laughing so hard my stomach cramped. Since high school, she and I often entered this state of delirium.

"My face hurts!" I said "Oww! My smile hurts. Stop making me laugh." This only made the infectious laughter continue.

She intentionally snorted in between her laugh. I reached over and tackled her. We wrestled around until our hair was tangled and we were two sweaty messes.

"I seriously need to go to bed." I sat up, wiped the tears of hysterics from my eyes, and looked up at the clock. "Oh my gosh. I have school in a couple of hours." These random bouts of late night silliness kept my spirits up.

* * *

After my morning classes were over, I walked to the college cafeteria with Kloe, a friend I'd made at school. She was what I called a "lifer"—a student who had no direction in life, had been going to community college for too many years, but kept up the charade so long as her mommy and daddy were paying for her tuition and her car. None of that mattered to me. I enjoyed eating with her rather than by myself.

"Have you had the curly fries?" Kloe asked.

"No, why?"

"It's only a couple of dollars and they load up a pile of 'em on a big ol' plate. Wanna share one?"

Knowing I only had a couple of dollars in my wallet, I agreed.

We sat down on stiff plastic chairs and smothered the pile of seasoned fries with ketchup.

She wiped her mouth. "So, hey, me and the girls are gonna head out to a club tonight, wanna come? The DJ who's spinning is totally awesome. One of my friends knows him so we can get in free."

"Sounds cool, but I don't have anyone to watch my son," I lied. I couldn't explain why I had a night-only job to anyone; Jacob was a convenient excuse.

That was the last time Kloe invited me to come along. I figured she had grown tired of my excuses and decided I wasn't any fun, which I'd have to let her believe.

* * *

Yessenia and I had a slow night at work—neither of us made much money. These nights were becoming more frequent. When we arrived home, we sat and discussed our options.

"How do the other girls do it?" I asked. "They get more minutes."

"They're sucking dick." She laughed. I could tell the late night silliness was going to kick in again.

"Eww. Seriously though."

"They're doing hand jobs in the parking lot."

"Come on, I need your help," I pleaded.

"Hell no, I ain't gonna help you get it on." She hopped up and down on the couch.

"Yessenia, quit it." I sighed. Arguing with her never got me anywhere. "We should call our customers. How do the other girls do it?"

She rolled her eyes. "They...call them."

"So, should we do it?" I asked.

"I'm not going to talk to them."

"Well, we don't have to talk, but schedule times to meet, right?"

"Yeah right," she said. "You believe that?"

"What?"

"Sucka."

"Don't you have the millionaire's phone number?" My income had been dwindling. If I could pay the bills for two more years I could earn my degree. I thought of Hiroki's fifty-dollar tip and Mark's hundred-dollar one. "Just think, no more corner grinding. Want to call?"

The corner of her lips upturned. "May-be."

Something rustled outside, like leaves crinkling underfoot. Our eyes widened. I leaned in close to her. "Did you hear that?"

She nodded and went silent. Twigs snapped outside our floor-to-ceiling living room window, only a couple of feet away from us.

Yessenia stood up and tiptoed to the window. The only separation between her and the outside darkness were the hanging vertical blinds.

I shook my head and waved my arms at her. It was like a bad horror flick, the kind where the chick traipses stupidly into the room where the murderer is hiding.

Too late for me to say anything, Yessenia thrust open the blinds with one sweep of her hand. They clinked against each other and the metal chain. When she turned to me, I saw the color drain from her face.

"There's a guy there. He's standing at our window."

I grabbed the phone and dialed 9-1-1.

"Is he still there?" I asked.

"I don't know."

"Did you see what he looked like?" I relayed the operator's questions.

"No, I was looking down. I saw his shoes and saw him back up and run."

When the cops arrived, they confirmed there were large, fresh footprints outside our window. After checking the perimeter, they advised us to lock our doors and windows, and to call them back if the prowler returned.

"Oh shit," I said. "Someone heard us talking about our jobs. I can't believe we're being spied on." I paced the living room.

"Do you think it could be Jacob's dad?"

"I don't know," I said. "I don't think so. Someone from work followed us." As if that was any consolation. "Besides being disgusting, this stupid job's dangerous."

She rocked back and forth on the couch. "I'm not sleeping out here tonight."

"We better keep a closer watch in our rear-view mirrors on the way home from work."

Although the prowler didn't return—it was an "isolated incident"—he caused Yessenia and me to be more aware of our surroundings. We always checked to see if anyone was following us after work, took alternating routes home, and became even more guarded with our personal information.

We grew paranoid.

CHAPTER SIX
ARRANGED MEETINGS

JUNE 1998

I SAT ON OUR living room carpet and unraveled rubber bands and paper clips from stacks of money.

"What are you doing?" Yessenia asked.

A mound of cash surrounded my feet. "Counting." I placed each twenty in the same direction and flipped through the piles, one crisp bill at a time.

"No, I mean with that."

"The briefcase? That's where I put my money."

"Why?"

"So I can lock it up."

My sixteen-year-old brother, who was on the couch listening to us, laughed. "Oh yeah, that's going to stop someone from stealing it. I could break it open if I wanted to." With his shoulders broadening, Kirk's five-foot-six-inch frame didn't look as scrawny as it had only last year—his jeans no longer looked baggy. Done with the shaggy-bangs look, he now spiked the top of his dark brown hair up with gel. Like me, he preferred his humor dry.

"That's because you're a thief," I said.

"Don't be jealous of my fine skills," he said. "So what makes you think someone wouldn't walk off with the whole thing?"

"I hide it under my bed." I refused to look up to see the laughter I knew was in his eyes.

"Stu-pid." He chuckled. "You watch too many spy movies."

"It's easier to keep track of," I said. "I'm paper-clipping it in stacks of hundreds."

"Why don't you put it in the bank?"

"Or in your dresser drawer or something?" Yessenia added. The two of them liked to join forces against me far more than I liked to admit.

"It's not a good idea to put it all in the bank," I said. "Someone could find out about this job. That's why I pay for everything with money orders or cash."

My brother rolled his eyes. "Mmm hmm. Thought so. You're such a dork. Like Scrooge, you like to sit and play with your money."

"Whatever," I said. "I need a five-thousand-dollar down payment to buy a car."

"You don't need that much," Yessenia said.

"I do if I'm going to qualify for a loan and be able to afford the payments." Besides, it felt good to be able to physically hold the results of my efforts.

*   *   *

The paper with Hiroki's phone number shook in my hands. I dialed the number but hung up when I lost my nerve. I tried again, hoping to get his voicemail. I didn't.

"Cassie," Hiroki said. "Good to hear from you."

"Yeah," I said. "Uh, I was wondering if you were going to Flamingo's this weekend." I bit my lower lip.

"When are you working?"

"Friday and Saturday." I tapped my foot and played with the phone cord.

"Friday isn't good for me." Hiroki had a no-nonsense approach, very business-like. "But I can meet you at eight on Saturday night."

That was it. The call was over. It was easier than I thought it would be. I phoned Mark, who kept me on the phone for five minutes engaged in small talk before he agreed to meet me on Friday night.

"Make sure to clock in at 7:30 PM," Mark said.

"You want me to clock in even if you're not there?"

"Yes. Don't worry. I'll be there."

I did worry.

On Friday night, not wanting to get yelled at by the owners, I was too hesitant to clock myself in. Instead, I hid in the locker room until Mark arrived.

"Hello again, Cassie." Mark hugged me. "Good to see you. You look pretty."

I glanced down at my simple black slip dress with lace fringe and spaghetti straps. "Thank you." I forced a smile and followed him to a booth where we spent the next hour talking about work, school, and my son.

"So you are almost done with your semester?" he asked. "Have you thought about starting a business when you finish college?"

"No. I start summer session soon." I twirled a strand of hair around my finger. "I don't know for sure what I want to do after I get my bachelor's degree. I know my dad's parents don't think a degree is such a big deal unless it's a master's or higher. Or unless I become a doctor or a lawyer or something like that."

"Is that what you want?"

"No, I don't think so. At least not right now."

He stared at me for a while and smiled. "What grades did you say you have in school?"

"Mostly A's and B's."

"Good." Mark looked down at the gold Rolex on his wrist. "Well, Cassie, I have to go. I enjoyed our time tonight." He placed a hand on my hand. "Do you want me to come next week?"

"Is Friday night, same time, good for you?"

"It is. Do you want to see me again?" He stared into my eyes. His smile made his wrinkles deepen showing his age to be around fifty. I was only twenty.

My stomach tightened. "Yeah, I had a good time. Did you?"

"My pleasure, Cassie." He gave me a long hug goodbye. Same as he did the first time we met, he handed me a hundred dollar tip. That's when I figured I'd made the right decision to phone Mark. I copied his phone number into my address book.

The following night, Hiroki showed up right on time. He didn't hug me hello, but did touch my hand occasionally during our conversation in the TV room. Unlike Mark's personal questions, Hiroki mostly talked about himself and his job in the banking industry.

"Do you know much about finance?" he asked.

"Well," I said. "I've been investing since I was sixteen when I bought my first certificate of deposit."

Hiroki nodded. "Good, good. Have you heard of the financial triangle of risk?" He took out a pen and pulled a napkin out from under his soda. "Let me show you how it works."

I felt like I was being talked down to since I already knew basic finance, but I feigned interest.

At the end of our visit, he gave me a brief hug and slipped me another fifty dollars. "If you give me your cell phone number," Hiroki said, "I'll contact you when I'm available."

"I don't have a cell phone, but I'll give you my pager number." I wrote it down on one of the slips of paper by the register. He put it into his pocket, nodded, and left. I realized Hiroki didn't smile nearly as much as Mark. That, and his lack of interest in my life as opposed to Mark's intense curiosity about it, should have hinted at what I could expect from each of them in the future. But back then, I could only think about the present.

*   *   *

I cradled the phone with my shoulder while I lay on my carpet in the bathroom, my knees bent and my feet pushed up flat against the wall. Except for a nightlight and the glow of the living room lamp from underneath the door, it was dark. I didn't want to wake Jacob so I kept my voice just above a whisper.

"So what do you think?" I asked. "Do you think it was a mistake?"

Jason was quiet for a moment before he asked, "What do *you* think?"

"My tips double when I have these arranged nights with Hiroki and Mark." These were secrets I shared with no one but Yessenia and Jason. Even though I'd been dating other guys, Jason was the only one I stayed up all night on the phone with.

"There's your answer," he said.

I giggled. "You always seem to do that."

"Do what?"

"You answer my questions with questions and I end up answering my own questions."

"Do I?"

"You're doing it again."

"What, hon'?"

I didn't know what to say. I had an urge to be in his powerful arms, to nuzzle my face against his chest, to be held. I wanted him to come over but knew he couldn't. Although I could sneak out to someone's house on occasion without disturbing Jacob when my mom or Yessenia knew, I did not bring men around Jacob. I somehow knew it was better that way. After they divorced, my mom and dad didn't bring strangers around us until my dad decided to remarry and it was time for me, Kirk, and our older sister Amber to meet our new stepmother.

But Jason and I were only dating, we weren't having sex, and we weren't exclusive, so it wasn't time for him to meet my son.

"I wish I could be with you right now." I sighed.

"You haven't tired of your boy toys yet?" Jason asked.

"Come on, you know I don't do anything with any of them. We go to dinner, or the movies, or shoot pool." Unlike the other men I dated, Jason was okay with hearing the details of my dating life even when it didn't involve him. I wasn't sure if it was a massage therapist thing or what, but Jason was deeply philosophical, emotionally mature, and intensely passionate—all qualities which I hadn't yet found in other men. "I go out and have fun. I don't hang out at my place with those guys. Most of them don't even know where I live."

"Are you sure about that? They don't spend the night?"

"I told you I haven't had sex with anyone since Jacob's dad. I'm a born-again virgin." I laughed.

"I'm only teasing. You don't need to prove anything to me. I know you're going through this phase. I completely understand. I'll give you your space."

"How come you're so awesome?" I turned over on my side. "I miss you."

"I miss you, too." He paused. "When are you coming over again?" I'd only been to his apartment once, and the most that had happened was that he gave me a great massage.

"When do you want me to?"

"I always leave that completely up to you. I know you have to work at night and you have school and your son. I don't have those responsibilities."

Sometimes I wished I didn't, either. I wondered what a carefree life felt like.

* * *

In addition to Hiroki, I gave my pager number to Mark, so they both could leave voicemail messages to confirm, to cancel, or to alert me to their arrival at the club. That was how they signaled to me to stop entertaining other men and clock out so I could focus my attention on them.

One time, in order to make the drive into work more profitable, I scheduled Mark and Hiroki on the same night. What a stupid idea that was.

I sat in the TV room with Hiroki, dressed in his usual suit slacks, button-up dress shirt, and simple suit jacket, when my purse vibrated. I ignored it and listened to Hiroki's dilemma: he had received two competing job offers for bank president positions.

Hiroki, born in Japan, continued to talk in perfect English without any hint of an accent. He didn't need a listener. He didn't pick up on any social cues of disinterest no matter how poorly I hid them.

The dim recessed lighting reflected off the black loveseats, off Hiroki's large round glasses, and off of his nearly bald head. I wondered why he didn't get rid of the comb-over and go bald. Sure, he had money, but with his below-average looks and nonexistent social skills, I figured he probably wasn't popular with ladies outside of Club Flamingo.

"What do you think, Cassie?" he asked.

I had assured all the men in the club that my real name was Cassie; they had no idea my name was really Miranda. I felt safer hiding behind a fake persona, especially after the peeping tom incident.

"Have you listed the pros and cons of each?" I mirrored his serious countenance. "You should make a couple of columns and list the pay, the benefits, the drive time, et cetera."

"Yes, I thought about creating a list."

My purse hummed again. I discreetly peeked inside. Damn it, Mark was early. But Mark did tip more than Hiroki and seemed more committed to our business relationship. He came to the club more often and spent more time with me. However I didn't want to insult Hiroki so I smiled and nodded while he continued to talk.

Background noise from the big screen televisions at the front of the room caused me to stare at Hiroki's lips to understand some of what he was saying. I don't think I ever paid attention to what movies played on the large screen. Probably nobody else did, either. The stuffy air of the confined space of the TV room, which wasn't built with ventilation in mind, overpowered me.

"Are you hot?" I asked. The air, heavy with humidity from the talking, breathing, and sweating of the couples on the couches, pressed down on me.

"Yes," Hiroki said. "Do those windows in the back open?" We turned our heads to see a customer struggling to lift open one of the four windows, which were stuck more often than not.

"Not easily." I fanned myself with my hand. Mark buzzed me a third time. With a guaranteed easy hundred dollars, I'm sure he figured I should run to his side and he was right. I had to get away from Hiroki.

"They should have fans in here," Hiroki said.

I squirmed, my legs glued with sweat to the leather sofa. I slipped my hand inside my purse to quiet my pager. "I think my babysitter is trying to get a hold of me." Both of my regulars knew I had a little one to support, which fortunately didn't affect their interest in me. "Plus, I need to use the restroom," I added.

To him, this meant I would need to use one of the payphones in the women's locker room, and would disappear into the black hole bathroom like many other hostesses, for an inordinate amount of time on his dime.

Hiroki pulled his glasses off and wiped the bridge of his nose with a napkin. "We should clock out."

"When will I see you again?" I batted my mascara-laden eyelashes at him and smiled.

"Next week. I need to talk to you about something. I'll page you to let you know."

We locked eyes in a mock intimate way.

"Good luck with deciding which job to take. Either place would be lucky to have you." I squeezed his hand as he led me out of the television room. We hugged good-bye and parted at the counter.

I spotted Mark. Uh-oh. Was that a look of jealousy on his face? I feigned extreme happiness and rushed over to welcome him with a hug. He stiffly hugged me back. I clocked in and we settled into one of the padded booths around the dance floor, our usual spot.

He fidgeted with his Rolex, pursed his lips together, and stared at me. I couldn't tell whether he was smirking or scowling.

"What took you so long?" he asked.

"My pager's in my purse. I didn't hear it."

He didn't blink for a long moment, as if he were trying to discern the level of honesty in my face. His composure changed and he smiled.

"Cassie, Cassie, Cassie. It's good to see you again." He intertwined his fingers with mine. "Next time, clock in and wait for me, even if I'm late, so no one else can clock you in and I won't have to stand around waiting for you."

He was still under my spell. Everything was under control. Note to self: don't overschedule again.

* * *

Although we both had expressed an aversion to the idea of meeting clients outside of the club, Yessenia urged me to accompany her on a lunch date with her regular, the millionaire.

"So you phoned him, huh?" I teased. "Weren't you saying the other day—"

"Whatever." She rolled her eyes.

"Are we going to get money for this?" I asked. Since we had never met anyone outside of work, we didn't know the protocol. It was awkward enough to run into a customer in the parking lot on the way into or out of the club.

"I think so," she said.

"Does he know I'm coming?"

"He knows," she said. "I pointed you out to him last night and he said it was fine to bring you along. Anyway, I'm not going by myself."

We arrived at the Regent Beverly Wilshire Hotel in Beverly Hills, and waited in the posh lobby for her client. The furniture looked like it belonged in a dead person's mansion. Every floor tile was waxed and every brass surface shined like gold. Potted trees and flowers reflected the chandelier lighting. The concierge and bellhop workers were dressed in suits, not the typical hotel attire. The air conditioning gave me goose bumps, but kept the area feeling fresh and crisp.

"This is fancy, and cold." I slipped my sweater on over my gray and black flowered cocktail dress.

"Yeah, I don't know why he picked this place." She rubbed her bare arms. "At least it's not far from work."

A tall Japanese man in a dark double-breasted three-piece suit approached. His shiny leather dress shoes squeaked across the floor. His full head of black hair was lightly slicked back. Although older, his tanned face was handsome. He had a chiseled chin, high cheek bones, and broad shoulders—or were they shoulder pads? I couldn't tell. Even though I'd only seen him in the dim hostess club lighting, I knew it was Yessenia's client, the millionaire.

"Lacy." He gave her a polite hug hello. Lacy was Yessenia's work name. "Hello Cassie." He nodded to me. "Let's go upstairs. I have some clients meeting us for lunch."

I whispered to Yessenia, "I didn't know there were going to be more people coming."

She shrugged. "Neither did I."

He walked alongside her. With Yessenia wearing low heels, her height nearly matched his. I followed behind and listened to their conversation.

"Do you know why I chose this hotel?" he asked, his tone arrogant.

"No, why?" Yessenia's long, blond-streaked curls bounced against her back as she walked.

"Have you seen *Pretty Woman?*"

"Yes."

"This is the hotel where Julia Roberts's character, a prostitute, slept with Richard Gere after he picked her up off the street." He pointed to memorabilia on the wall from the movie. "You look a lot like her which is why I picked this place." He smirked.

I saw her cheeks redden and her fists clench at the mention, not of her doppelganger Julie Roberts, but of the movie *Pretty Woman*, the story of a millionaire who had sex with a prostitute then fell in love with her.

Yessenia and I walked around a large round table in an otherwise empty restaurant. It seemed like the place had been opened early for us. Several other well-dressed Asian businessmen entered, nodded at Yessenia and me, and sat down at the table, which left none open for Yessenia and me. The millionaire motioned for us to sit by ourselves at a round table next to theirs.

After the waiter took our lunch orders, the millionaire spoke in a foreign language with the other Asian men. They went from serious conversation to laughing and glancing at me and Yessenia, and back to serious negotiation. I had no idea what they were talking about, but each time they chuckled and looked at us, I uncomfortably shifted in my seat and looked away.

The waiter brought our food. He set a bowl of ravioli in front of Yessenia.

She moved the large pasta squares around the scant white cream sauce with her fork. "What's this?" she whispered to me. "I'm not going to eat it."

"Ravioli. Isn't that what you ordered?"

"I didn't know it was going to look like this. Where's the red sauce? This doesn't look like the cans of Chef Boyardee we used to eat at home."

I didn't think so, either. She ate one bite then pushed the bowl away.

The Asian men in high-powered suits ate, drank, and talked, but not to Yessenia or me. Only on occasion would one of the men finish a sip of alcohol and smirk at us or wink; otherwise, we were ignored. I felt like we were pretty little table decorations in the background for their viewing pleasure and the objects of their seemingly condescending jokes. I was glad when it was time to go. We picked up our purses and lingered for a few moments, waiting to be paid.

Yessenia's millionaire squeezed her shoulder and told her he'd see her later at the club if he could. He turned and followed the other men out, leaving us standing there by ourselves.

"I didn't know he wasn't going to pay us," Yessenia said on the way to the car.

"Yeah that sucks," I said. "We don't need to be going out to lunch with these guys for free. Next time—"

"There won't be a next time."

"Well, we'd better make sure we have an explicit agreement if we choose to meet anyone else outside of the club."

*   *   *

The next weekend, Yessenia didn't feel like going in to work, so I drove myself.

I took my position on the red couch and went about my night. Yessenia's millionaire entered the lobby with an entourage of businessmen. Like usual, he was dressed in a sharp three-piece suit with tie and matching handkerchief neatly folded with only a triangle peeking out of his coat pocket. I imagined that his walk-in closet at home looked like a tailor's store with rows of hanging suits, a wall of nearly identical ties and handkerchiefs, and racks of matching shined shoes.

I became confused when he approached me and asked me to clock in. Maybe he wanted to talk to me about Yessenia? On one hand, I needed the money. On the other hand, I felt like I was betraying her. This was her reg, not mine. Not that I had a choice in the matter. I couldn't afford to lose my job, which could happen if I were to decline.

I was relieved when he immediately led me to the TV room—fewer girls to see me with him.

Small talk came first. His wandering hand came next.

I nearly jumped at the sensation of his cold fingers on my bare thigh. I nudged his hand away. His hand returned and slid further up my leg, to the edge of my miniskirt. I grabbed his hand, lifted it up, and smacked it down onto his dress slacks.

He chuckled. He clocked me out, tipped me, and we went our separate ways.

Later that night, I told Yessenia what happened.

She stared at me in disbelief. "What were you doing with my regular?"

"What was I supposed to do? He clocked me in."

"You could've said no."

"Do you want me to get fired? It's not like I enjoyed it when he groped me."

"Groped you? That doesn't sound like him. He's never tried to touch me before. He's always been the perfect gentleman. How do you even know it was him?"

"How could I *not* know it was him? I had a whole lunch with him. I'm not lying to you. He touched me and laughed like it was a game to mess with us."

"That sucks. I guess he's not my regular anymore. There goes my money." She stormed out.

CHAPTER SEVEN
CAR FAIRY

EARLY JULY 1998

"I LIKE THE SMALL of your back," Jason said as his fingers caressed my bare skin. "That's the sexiest part of your body." In addition to his freelance massage therapy, Jason did personal training and had powerful arms and hands. I melted every time he kneaded tension from my muscles.

"Gee, thanks, only that? Nothing else is attractive to you?" I rolled over onto my back, glad to be with Jason again. Jacob was asleep at home which meant I could stay at Jason's apartment until six o'clock in the morning. That would leave me with enough time to slip back into my own bed before Jacob awoke. Of course, that also meant I'd have to survive tomorrow without a good night's sleep. Jason was worth it.

"You know what I mean." He kissed my stomach. "Now I need a cigarette. Do you mind?" He pulled his brown hair back into a ponytail and put a t-shirt on over his smooth chest.

"Go ahead." I stroked his clean-shaven cheek and planted a series of kisses along his neck, from chin to ear. Besides Jason, I hadn't dated any other man who smoked. At least his cloves smelled better than regular cigarettes.

"Now I'm gonna need two." His voice, like his mannerisms, was calming and gentle. He left me in his bedroom, one of two master suites on opposite ends of the apartment he shared with a roommate who usually wasn't home.

The sliding glass door opened and shut. He had his cigarette on the patio. He knew I didn't like the smoke.

I glanced around his room. Dim color-changing lights tinted his walls light blue, then pink, green, and purple. Ambient music, his place, and his presence lulled me into a state of relaxation I had rarely experienced outside of a Yoga class. He had a welcoming charisma about him. For me, the only thing in discord with the room was his pet snake in the terrarium on his dresser.

We'd been dating for a couple of months, but we weren't exclusive. I made a point to tell him and all of the other men I met off of the Internet that I wasn't ready for a serious relationship.

I remembered when I delivered my typical straightforward speech to Jason on our second or third date. We were shooting pool at a bar around the corner from his place when he asked, "What kind of relationship do you want? I know you're dating these other guys, so what are you looking for?"

"I tell everyone the same thing," I said, "We can go out on dates and have a good time, but I'm not going to have sex with you. I don't want a relationship yet, I'm not ready."

He sunk the blue ball into the corner pocket and laughed. "Not ready? How's that?" He shot again. The cue ball rolled past the red.

"I'm still recovering from a bad relationship." I bent seductively over the table, reached my right elbow back and pumped my arm forward, but missed my shot. The cue ball bounced off the green felt edge. "It wouldn't be fair to you or anyone else. So, let's not get too attached and just have fun."

Jason reached for his beer. "How do most men act when you tell them that?"

I shrugged. "I mean it." I chalked my stick. "Whenever a guy breaks the rules, I break it off."

He raised an eyebrow and took his shot. The yellow ball dropped into the side pocket. "Pretty strict dating rules. So you think you're in control?" He shot again, missing his green ball.

"What do you mean?" I flipped my hair behind my shoulder. "Trust me, I'm not a prude or a saint, but I always quit before I hear the crinkle of the condom wrapper being opened—to more than one man's disappointment."

He smirked and finished his beer. "I bet."

"What are you saying?"

"Nothing. Other than that you're more like a man than a woman when it comes to dating. That's all." He pointed to the table. "Your shot."

"What are you talking about? Guys only care about sex. They don't care about relationships. How am I like a guy?"

"Do you care about these men you're dating? Or are you using them for fun?"

"They have fun too." I rolled my eyes. "What's your point?"

He chuckled. "Miranda, do you hear yourself?"

I gripped the cue stick in my hand and considered smacking him with it. Nobody challenged me. "Whatever. Let's finish this game and call it a night." I shot at my striped red ball and ended up hitting his green one into the side pocket instead. I clenched my teeth.

"If that's what you want." Jason shrugged. "But you never answered my question."

"What question?"

He winked. "I only asked what kind of relationship you were looking for." With his cue stick, he hit his orange ball into his purple one, knocking both into separate pockets. A couple of shots later, he had won the game.

All of my balls were still on the table.

The reason I didn't let our budding relationship end there that night, was because I realized Jason understood me better than I understood myself. He saw through the bullshit I didn't even know I was using, so I trusted him. He was the only one of my romantic interests who knew about my hostess job.

Jason returned from his smoke and sat next to me on the bed. "Want a stick of gum?" He held out the pack.

"No thanks." I sighed. "I need some advice."

"Sure. What's up?" He brushed the hair from my face and kissed my neck.

"I'm thinking about seeing my customer Mark outside of the club. He knows I need to buy a car by August, before my fall semester. He says he wants to help me out by giving me at least two hundred dollars each time I go anywhere with him."

"You mean you want to escort?"

"No, I wouldn't have sex with him. He asked me to go to the track. He bets on horse races a lot."

"Miranda, being an escort doesn't mean you have to have sex with a man; otherwise, you'd be a prostitute." His fingers tickled my cheek. "So, what's the dilemma?"

"I don't know if I should. I don't want to lead him on or anything. I don't want him to think more than my time is for sale."

"It seems like he knows what he's in for. He's a big boy. If he wants to be stupid enough to pay you for nothing, then let him. If not you, then another girl will take his money."

This made sense, but deep inside, a part of me wished Jason would object out of concern. I wanted to know he cared, but I never told him.

*　*　*

I couldn't make up my mind about meeting Mark outside of the club and kept talking the issue over. I sought Yessenia's counsel.

"Should I go out with him or not?" I asked.

Yessenia wrapped strands of her hair around curlers and stared at herself in a mirror, not paying any attention to me. "Do what you want."

"But I don't know what do to. What do you think?"

"How should I know? It's up to you."

"But I can't decide. I need more money to buy a car before August when I have to transfer."

"What you do for money is your business."

"That's rude. I'm not talking about doing anything other than meeting him outside the club for money."

"Ri-ight."

I threw my hands in the air. "What's that supposed to mean?"

"Take it however you want."

"What's your problem? Aren't you worried about paying bills?"

"Not really." She clipped another curler into place.

I stood there for a moment. "Jason thinks I should do it."

"Then do it."

I didn't understand how she was so blasé about everything. Did she withhold comment because she didn't have an opinion or because she didn't want to tell me? She was so aloof. I wondered why I tried so hard to connect with her. Probably a lot of it had to do with our shared past, our shared job, and our late night silliness. I only wished she were more interested in my life.

"Okay, I will," I said. "I'll make extra cash to get my car sooner."

"That's good." Yessenia clipped the last roller into place. "I might see Gary."

Gary, her new Japanese customer, was tall, socially awkward, and extremely wealthy. How hypocritical of her to give me a hard time when she herself was planning to do the same.

*　*　*

The first time was the worst. Mark insisted he drive to my house to pick me up which required a lot of trust on my part. He seemed harmless. I reasoned he was short enough that I could take care of myself if need be.

What to wear? It wasn't nighttime so a miniskirt, tank top, and heels seemed inappropriate. Nevertheless, jeans weren't nearly as attractive, and I felt I was being paid to keep him company and to look cute. I opted for a spring dress.

When I saw Mark arrive with a bouquet of flowers in hand, my stomach dropped and my mood darkened—while I was treating this as a business arrangement, he was acting like it was a real date. Mark had dressed up in black slacks, black belt, shiny black leather shoes, and a gray polo, much like he wore to the hostess club. Large glasses hid his round chestnut face.

He stood on my doorstep as though he expected me to let him in. Instead, I told him the house was a mess and to wait outside a minute while I put his gift in water. Later I could either throw the bouquet away or put the flowers on the dinner table.

Mark seemed a little miffed and tried to stare at me through the crack in the door. I hurried outside; I didn't want him standing on my porch for my neighbors to see.

He smiled. "Cassie, it's so good to see you. You look beautiful."

"Thanks." Although I didn't want to, I grabbed his hand and rushed him along the pathway which led to the street where he was parked. On the way I wondered whether he'd have a Mercedes, a BMW, or a Jaguar.

He pulled his keys out of his pocket and unlocked the doors to a plain green van. I hid my disappointment and inconspicuously tapped my foot while he insisted on opening my door. Letting my hair hang about my face, I prayed nobody would see me getting into a middle-aged Filipino man's minivan, which he explained he used for his printing business. At the same time, I couldn't let my displeasure show. I fiddled with my purse as an excuse to keep my head down until we drove out of the neighborhood.

Thankfully, nobody I knew followed horse racing which permitted me to hold my head up high as he led me through the gates, hand-in-hand. He had a private booth, separated from the masses on the bleachers. With the *Daily Racing Form* in front of him, Mark taught me how to handicap the races.

"Don't rely on what the experts say," he said. "You'll never make money betting that way. The longshots are where the money is."

"What's a longshot?" I asked.

"The underdogs."

"Oh." I nodded my head, pretending to care.

"See here." He pointed to a page in the racing magazine. "Bob Baffert, he's a good trainer, but the jockey's important as well."

"Jockey?" My family wasn't into sports.

"A jockey is hired to ride a horse for a race. Desormeaux, Silas, Stevens, and Pincay are all great jockeys." He pointed to the field below, where several men in white caps and checkered shirts trotted their horses to the start line.

I squinted. "Those guys look so little."

"They are. The smaller and lighter the jockey, the faster the horse."

"So you pick the horses based on the trainer and jockey? It doesn't sound too hard."

He laughed. "Well, you look at the horse, too. Has it raced before? What was its time in other races? How long has it been since its last race? See what the track conditions are, if the horse's blinders are on, and study their starting position."

I stared blankly at the black-and-white print. "Sounds complicated. So there's one race and you pick one winner?"

"No, there are a series of races. I pick the ones I know I can win." His face brightened like a kid on Christmas. "And, guess what?" He raised his eyebrows and his voice quivered with excitement.

"What?"

"There's going to be a big one today. I have a good feeling about this one, which usually means a big win for me. The predictions in the paper, which many people rely on, are wrong."

"You must have been doing this for a long time to be so good at it." I made a conscious effort to smile and sweeten my tone of voice—not to be flirty, but to flatter him. I figured flattery was a safe strategy for maximizing my tips, without putting me in an uncomfortable position where he might feel I was offering more than companionship. "How do you bet?"

"The trifecta. We'll pick the first, second, and third place winner. You can help me choose. If we win, we'll split it."

Sounded good to me. I had an investment of only my time, with the potential for substantial returns. No one knew I was here. No one to recognize me. Complete anonymity.

A man, a taller and rounder version of Mark, entered our booth. Through Mark's muffled cell phone calls and the wide grin stretching across this stranger's face, I guessed that Mark must have been bragging about me to his friend. His friend apparently wanted to see for himself.

Mark introduced us, and I allowed his friend's name to go right through both ears. That had developed into a habit of mine—forgetting names on purpose. I met so many men at Club Flamingo and I preferred not to associate their names with anyone I knew on the outside. This defense worked great until it become so automatic that I began to have difficulty remembering names when I wanted to.

Mark's friend giggled like a schoolgirl. He began every other sentence in English then switched to their native language Tagalog, which sounded to me like a strange series of clicks.

After the first race ended, Mark whispered something to his friend. His friend nodded and left. I figured Mark wanted some alone time with me, and would fill his friend in on the details later.

We didn't win much money, but as Mark pointed out, I had still won. True to his word, he handed me two freshly minted $100 bills. All I had had to do was smile and act completely interested in whatever he wanted to talk about.

* * *

Life became uncomfortable at my house. My little brother Kirk, now a senior in high school, knew what was going on and it amused him to no end to see strange-looking old men bringing roses to the front door as they picked up me or Yessenia. A few hours later, we'd return. My brother even watched us hug our clients good-bye then teased us about it.

Since word was getting around at Club Flamingo that Yessenia and I refused to go further than mild grinding and hand-holding, our earnings dwindled. This made it more important for us to continue to escort. Everything started out as a business arrangement: we were paid for dates with these men, but it wasn't long before we ended up feeling we were being paid to pretend to be their girlfriends.

I told myself this was only temporary; I would graduate with my bachelor's degree in about two years. In the meantime, I was saving for a car.

With her money, Yessenia bought a white foo-foo dog to complete the stereotype. Missy was the cutest little thing; nevertheless, she made me hate her when she chewed up my toddler's toys.

Yessenia's response to my anger? "Don't leave Jacob's blocks and toys out then."

In Missy's defense, I witnessed Jacob putting one of his pacifiers into her mouth.

I ran across the living room. "No, no, no, Jacob. Don't give that to the dog."

"I share," Jacob explained.

Missy chewed on the squeaking pacifier.

How could I get mad? I hid the smirk on my face and lifted Jacob into my arms. "You are so cute." I kissed his cheeks while he twisted, trying to squirm away. "Mommy loves you."

"No more." He giggled.

I kissed him again before letting him down. I yanked the pacifier out of Missy's mouth. Her teeth had punctured the rubber end. Not that it mattered. I had to break Jacob of the habit anyway, since his pediatrician warned it could affect his teeth.

"Hey, Jacob," I said. "Are you a big boy?"

"Yeah." He jumped up and down.

"Do you know what big boys do?"

"What?"

"Big boys don't use pacifiers. Do you want to be a big boy and throw away your pacifiers?"

"Okay, Mommy."

I tilted my head, but didn't question his sincerity. "All right, let's go throw it away. But, since you're a big boy, you can do it all by yourself." I handed him the dog-slobbered remains and walked to the kitchen trashcan, which Yessenia and Kirk hadn't taken out like they said they would, probably to piss me off. "Go ahead, throw it away."

Without a second thought, he dropped it in. "I'm big boy." He grinned.

Might as well continue the streak of good luck. "Why don't you go find your other ones? Go bring Mommy all of your pacifiers."

He took off running. To my surprise, his pacifiers were deliberately hidden around the house. I had assumed they were lost when I found them in the couch cushions and toy box. I was wrong. Jacob ran to each location, reached his hand in and pulled them out. He returned to the trash with four, two more than I thought he had. One by one, he threw them in.

Today was a good parenting day, I thought.

* * *

I watched Yessenia pack up her duffle bag and her dog's toys.

"Where are you going?" I asked.

"None of your business."

How rude. "Seriously, Yessenia. Where are you going and why are you taking Missy? You never take her overnight when you go to Joe's place."

"Gary is picking me and Missy up and we're going down Gary's place in San Diego for the weekend."

"What the hell? Are you crazy? Are you sleeping with him? Does Joe know?" I couldn't imagine her boyfriend agreeing to this.

"Gary says he's going to be Missy's Godfather."

"What are you talking about?"

"He's going to pay for Missy's shots and pay to get her fixed. I can't afford it, and can't get her licensed until I do it. He offered to take care of it. Besides, he'll be working most of the weekend while Missy and I stay in his penthouse apartment overlooking the bay, alone."

"What if he expects something from you?"

She shrugged. "I'm not worried about it."

I wish I could've said the same. We'd both been compromising our safety and a little bit of our dignity from the moment we agreed to meet anyone outside of Club Flamingo.

* * *

Every time I heard Mark knock on the door, I cringed and had to psyche myself up to open it and appear happy to see him. After a while though, the visits became routine and at one point, I even allowed my son Jacob to come along on a trip to the Del Mar Racetrack. I laughed at the sight of Mark struggling to hook Jacob's car seat into his car. Obviously, it had been a number of years since he had done this with either of his two children, one of whom was about my age.

Looking back, I realize how stupid it was to allow my son to have any interaction with the temporary men in my life, especially my clients. At the time, the boundaries between what was appropriate and what was not had already blurred, and I was too immature to know the difference. Putting myself at risk was bad enough, putting Jacob at risk was far worse.

Together, the three of us drove down to the Del Mar Racetrack. The dark blue ocean sparkling out my window mesmerized me, temporarily removing me from the front seat of my client's van. Jacob kicked my seat from behind. I began to wish I hadn't brought him along. Unable to do anything about it, I directed his attention to boats along the coast.

"Yeah, that's a big ship," I said. "Oh, look at the clouds. What animals do you see?"

"Um, uh," Jacob said, "I see a…a dog!"

"Where?"

"Right there." He pointed.

"We're here," Mark exited the freeway. "I'll drop you two off at the gate while I park."

I adjusted my sleeveless cropped sweater top and lifted the cuffs of my blue lounge pants so my stilettos wouldn't get caught in them.

Once in the gate, Mark led us through an underground tunnel. We walked under the racetrack to get to the grassy infield. After we set foot on the other side, Mark tapped Jacob on the shoulder.

"There's a playground over there." He pointed. "You can swing and slide."

"Yay!" Jacob bounced out of my arms.

While he played, Mark and I sat on a park bench, studying *The Racing Form*. He let me pick out my favorite horses and he placed our bets. When he returned, we watched the scoreboards and listened to the crackling voice of the announcer to hear the results.

Mark's eyes widened. "We won! You did it."

He cashed out the ticket and returned with a grin. "Guess what, Mia?"

Because my pager's voicemail announced my name as "Miranda," Mark no longer believed my working name "Cassie" was my real name. He knew I was Miranda and refused to call me Cassie anymore. It took some effort on my part to get him to say "Mia" instead. I convinced him Mia was the nickname only my closest friends used. A clever lie, yes, and it worked. To have both my client sweetly calling me Miranda and to have boyfriends passionately calling out Miranda while kissing grossed me out.

"You did it." He grinned. "You won your first trifecta. Mia, Mia, Mia, you did it."

"Really? Wow. What did I win?"

"You won over $400." He handed me four beautiful C-notes and wrapped his arms around me. "See, I told you you'd figure out how to pick the winners." He beamed with pride.

I stiffened at his touch. He didn't notice.

Mark insisted we let Jacob go on the pony ride in the center field. He took a lot of pictures with his telephoto lens. I didn't realize how many he shot until he returned the following week and handed me a stack of processed 5x7s.

There's me in a white crop top, with my bare midriff showing and Jacob in my arms. And there's another of me walking next to Jacob's pony. And another. The shots felt intimate, the kind a boyfriend or husband might take.

"Do you like them?" he asked.

I threw up a little in my mouth. My stomach burned with acid. "Oh, yes. Thank you. They're great." Actually, something felt terribly wrong. I felt dirty and ashamed. A client shouldn't be spending quality time with me and my son, like a family. It didn't feel right.

Mark wrapped his arms around me again.

I fought my gag reflex, hugged him back, and pulled away with a plastered smile.

* * *

At Jason's place, he and I lay in his bed nude—even though we still hadn't had sex—talking. Actually, he listened to me complain.

"If the guy creeps you out so much," Jason said, "stop seeing him."

"I can't. I need his money."

"Sounds like you have a problem."

"I know." I leaned my head against his shoulder. He wrapped a comforting arm around me. "I thought I could do this, you know, the job and going out with clients until I finish school, but now I don't know. It makes me sick to my stomach."

"Get another job."

"I can't find another job that will pay me enough to support Jacob and go to college."

"Then quit college."

I scowled. "No way. Then it would be way too hard to get a good job."

"Take less classes so you can work more at a job you can stand."

"But I have to finish my bachelor's degree in two years."

"Why?"

"It will get too expensive to go to college if it takes longer." I looked down. "I need to be done with all this stress and worry. I've been so depressed about everything lately."

He moved his hands across my back, rubbing away the tension. "I don't know what to tell you."

Knowing he cared helped me more than he knew.

*   *   *

I decided to see how far I could push Mark. If he didn't like it, he could stop seeing me, and I'd lose no sleep over it. Besides, he was paging me more than once a week. It was a chore having to return his calls. After all, I wasn't getting paid to talk on the phone and I had become accustomed to being compensated for my time.

During one such conversation, I said, "As you know, I'm transferring to the university soon. I'm going to have to buy a car by August. Otherwise, I can't get to school. I thought about a cheap used car, but it has to be reliable and safe because of Jacob. I don't want something that's going to break down which means I need to buy a new one, but I don't how I'm going to make the payments."

Through the phone, I sensed Mark's smile. "I can help you out."

I had hoped he would offer. "You don't have to."

"Of course I don't. How much do you think your payments will be?"

I had already done the calculations numerous times. "About $400 to $500."

He paused. "I'm already giving you $200 each time I see you. What if I give you $400 once a month for your car payments? Would that help?"

"You have no idea how much that would mean to me. Thank you." I hoped he didn't expect anything extra for the car payments.

Years later, I learned the truth in the saying "nothing is free." At the time though, I naively felt the aphorism was for suckers. I thought by taking Mark's money for car payments, I was doing my mom a favor. Whenever I borrowed her car to get to school, my mom had to take two or three buses to work, sometimes waiting for long periods in between buses in shady parts of town at night. It wasn't fair to her; however, if she knew where I was getting the money from to buy my car, she likely would have insisted I continue to borrow hers.

I didn't want her to know. I wanted to prove I was independent. I never stopped to consider how dependent I was becoming on Mark.

CHAPTER EIGHT

SHOES AND STRIPPERS

JULY 1998

YESSENIA AND I WERE late for work.

"You're not ready?" Barefooted and still in jeans, neither was I.

"No," Yessenia said. "Go without me."

"I don't want to go by myself." I leaned against the wall, slipped out of my pants, and zipped up a miniskirt. "Come on, we need to pay rent."

"Fuck." She threw down her brush. "I hate this fucking job."

"Me, too." I put on my heels. "I've been canceling real dates to go out with Mark."

"You talk to him too much on the phone. Is he your boyfriend now?"

"Screw you." I narrowed my eyes. "I hate talking to him on the phone, but I need him to keep paying me. I hate pretending to be happy when I see him. I hate the jerks at work who try to grope me."

She didn't respond, but stared in the mirror and applied more makeup.

*   *   *

In a small office room, my mom and I sat across from a Catholic priest from our church. The air conditioning gave me goose bumps. Jacob, who I dressed in a Polo shirt and gray slacks, fidgeted on my lap and yanked on my long hair. I tapped my foot against the carpet.

"So, you're sure you're ready to make the commitment to raise Jacob according to the faith?" the priest asked.

"Yes." I nodded. Like a magnet, the collar of his black robe drew my eyes to it. I attempted eye contact with the priest, but couldn't pull my gaze away from the white square on his collar. My sweater seemed to tighten around my neck. The walls enclosed me in an increasing panic.

"Do you understand what this means?" he asked. "Have you shown commitment to living your life according to the teachings of Christ?"

If you don't count my night job. I looked down at Jacob, the child I had given birth to out of wedlock. I hadn't attended church for a while because disappointed glares from my former church friends and my own guilt made it very uncomfortable to be there. Regardless, Jacob was the reason I was now ready to resume my church attendance. "Yes." I pulled my hair back with a hair tie. "I mean, I've made mistakes, as all people do."

My mom interrupted. "Miranda's been raised in the church. She was baptized, had her first communion, made her first confession, and was confirmed." She smiled and continued. "She used to sing in the church choir, was a lector, and...weren't you in the youth group?"

I nodded. "Yes, I went to youth group every week and church every Sunday at 7:30 in the morning."

The priest stared at me. My soul felt exposed and I looked away.

"I've chosen Jacob's Godparents," I said. "They're friends of ours. They're both Catholic."

Jacob grabbed my tennis shoes and knotted my laces.

"So you've been attending weekly mass again?" he asked.

I nodded. I did attend...when I actually woke up in time, which truthfully wasn't often.

"You've completed the baptismal parenting classes?" the priest asked.

"Yes, I went with her," my mom said.

I glared at her. Her answering for me like I was still a child annoyed me. Jacob squealed and made growling noises. I handed him a sippy cup of juice to quiet him.

The priest bowed his head and paused for a while, deep in prayer. "We will be happy to welcome Jacob and your family into our parish. You can call the office to schedule the baptism as soon as you feel ready."

"Great." My mom stood up and shook his hand. "Thank you, Father."

I smiled, but my heart sank. I was a liar in God's presence. How could I in good faith be a hostess dancer and escort at night and still attend church? At that moment, I decided it would no longer be appropriate for me to receive holy communion during mass—at least not until I could quit hostessing, confess my sins, and complete my penance. My soul might be scrubbed clean and I could once again feel at ease in the church pews instead of like a stranger.

Reflecting on this, years later, I think it was the disconnection between the values I was raised with and those I needed to live by which caused my increasing discomfort. As a "sinner," I began to see that many other parishioners swore by the doctrine of their faith but left those values behind on the church steps every Sunday. Pure hypocrisy.

To me, faith would come to mean faith in myself.

* * *

At Club Flamingo, I sat next to Yessenia on the red couch and asked, "How does my makeup look?"

"Nobody's looking at your face." She crossed her arms.

I was approached by a suit. "What's your name?" he asked. "Would you like to dance?"

Either he was new or was more polite than most. "Cassie. Yeah, let me clock in."

On the dance floor, he gave me a brief history lesson. With an arm around my waist, he asked, "What do you think of being a taxi dancer?"

"A what?" I strained to hear him over the music.

"You know, a dime-a-dance girl." He smiled.

Was this man speaking English? "What are you talking about?"

"You've never heard the term taxi dancer?"

I shook my head.

He laughed and pulled back a few inches in order to look me in the eyes. "Many years ago during the 1920s and 30s, dime-a-dance girls made a decent living dancing with men who'd pay a dime per dance, especially during wartime."

That must've been when life was simpler, two cents for a loaf of bread.

"By the 1960s," he said, "these clubs were mostly gone, but fortunately this one's still here."

Yeah, fortunately. I let him talk, knowing it would extend our time together. It was much more pleasant to chat than to submit myself to grinding, like every other man that night was trying to do.

Our time ended too soon and he shorted me on the tip.

When we arrived home that night, Yessenia and I sat on the couch and I counted my earnings. There wasn't enough to pay rent.

"I don't know how much longer I can do this," I said. "I'm not making enough to pay the bills."

"There are other jobs we could do," Yessenia said.

"Like what?"

The corners of her lips upturned. "We could strip."

"Are you kidding me? There's no way I could do that."

She shrugged.

"Would you?" I asked.

"Exotic dancers make more money and don't have to put up with half the shit we do."

"What are you talking about? They take off their clothes. That's way worse."

"Is it? Strippers don't sit around on red couches waiting for men to clock them in and grind on them."

"They dance naked." I stuck out my tongue. "Ewww. How is that any better?"

"You don't know anything about exotic dancers."

"And you do?"

"I've been talking to a few online."

I raised an eyebrow.

"I'll get more info," she said.

Yessenia and I began entering adult chat rooms on the Internet to find out more about exotic dancing and local clubs.

Finding other dancers online wasn't as easy as it sounded. We went in and out of many adult chat rooms, hoping to connect with someone. We got a few nasty surprises.

For instance, Yessenia was bragging about how much she loved her dog Missy while in the "Dog Lovers" chat room. A barrage of questions was hurled at her.

"How much do you love your dog?"

"I love her a lot," she replied.

"Do you let her lick you?"

"Yes…I guess so, why?"

"Who's better, your dog or your boyfriend?"

"What are you talking about?"

After hearing their detailed explanation of bestiality, Yessenia freaked out. It took her days to get over her disgust.

Meanwhile I went into the "Millionaires Seeking Young Women To Spoil" chat room, and who could resist going in there—for curiosity's sake? I hoped to find a dancer or two.

After entering, I silently observed the conversation and got bombarded with private instant messages from men. Since I figured most people online were a bunch of liars, I ignored them.

However, one man's screen name had me wondering: what did he mean by "SlaveToWomen"? Would he clean my house? Cook gourmet meals? Wash my car?

"SlaveToWomen" turned out to be Tony, a handsome Frenchman in his forties with dark skin, dark hair, and dark piercing eyes, who got his kicks by purchasing things for young, attractive women. Even though I made my living off men of his kind, I hadn't allowed men from the Internet to buy anything for me.

Tony told me a lot about strip clubs and he offered to take Yessenia and me to several of them.

"Do you want to go?" I asked Yessenia.

"Seriously?" she said. "Is this an escorting thing?"

"No, but you're the one who suggested we try exotic dancing. Tony said he'll take us to some local strip clubs to check them out. He'll pay for it."

Yessenia and I arranged to meet him at the mall. We explained where we'd be and what we'd be wearing.

She and I browsed a shoe store while we waited. I peeked at the price tag on a pair of stilettos and set them back on the display shelf.

"I like these but I don't have any money," I said to Yessenia.

"I will buy them for you, Miranda," said a voice behind my back.

I turned around and Tony, who looked exactly like his photo, was standing there. "No, thank you," I said. "It's okay."

"I insist." Tony smiled.

"Are you sure?" I asked.

Yessenia looked at her watch, threw me a dirty look and walked out of the store.

"Do you like the strappy shoes or the stilettos?" I asked.

"Try them on."

I adjusted my miniskirt hemline then walked up and down the center aisle, my personal runway. I struck a pose. "Which ones are cuter?"

"Both are sexy," Tony said, with his thick French accent. "Get both."

With a bag of shoes in my hand, I found Yessenia sitting down outside the store and we followed Tony to his classic convertible. Its soft cover top was down. I thought, one day, mine might be too. I cringed.

"This is a nude club." Tony parked the car. "I have to pay to get in, but I'm sure you two can get in for free if you tell them you want to check it out to see if you want to work here."

I followed Yessenia to the window at the front of a nondescript building in a strip mall. The only difference between this one and the building next door to it was the club's neon lighting along the blacked-out windows.

"Are you hiring?" Yessenia asked through the cashier's window.

The man behind the glass took a good look at our bodies. "Can I see your IDs?"

We slipped them through the opening.

He compared us to our pictures and handed them back. "Okay, I'll buzz you in. Ask to talk to the manager."

It was simple. We did so and were granted entrance to a square room, not at all the glamorous interior I expected to see like in movies. As our eyes adjusted to the darkness, I saw two raised rectangular stages. A young nude Hispanic woman crawled across one, arched her back and opened her legs in front of the men seated around her stage.

Couch seating lined the entire room which was painted black. Men leaned against mirrored walls lined with purple and blue neon lighting. A few bikini-clad dancers were air grinding mens' laps to the beat of the music.

"I can't do this," I said to Yessenia.

I felt a hand on my shoulder; it was Tony. "Why don't you sit down and watch? See how the girls work."

I took Yessenia's arm and scooted next to her on a couch. Tony left us there and headed to the stage seating for a closer vaginal inspection.

"These girls aren't even cute," Yessenia said. "We could totally make money here."

"But they're nasty." I pointed her attention to a plump girl who was allowing a man's hands to guide her hips. "There's no way I can do this."

"Would you rather date Mark?"

She had a point. "But look at them."

A flat-chested Asian dancer on the other stage pulled at her nipples.

"She probably has to do that since she has no boobs." Yessenia laughed. I felt ashamed to find myself laughing, too.

The next club we visited, a topless bar, was not as easy to enter because we were under age. Tony introduced us to the manager who recognized him.

"They're not twenty-one yet," Tony said, "but they will be soon. They're considering working here. Can I show them around?"

The pudgy manager ran his fingers through his hair and slowly looked us up and down. "Nice bodies, pretty faces. You two would do well here. Here's my card. Let me know when you're old enough to audition."

We smiled and giggled. I twirled a strand of my hair.

He granted us access to the large, elegant club. Plush velvet armchairs rolled along the clean carpet up to round glass tables. Spotless mirrored walls reflected the multi-colored neon lighting. Intimidated by the Amazonian women with huge implants and toned bodies, I slunk into a chair at a table several feet back and focused my attention on the fairly well-lit stage.

"That's good this place isn't as dark as the last one," Yessenia said.

A spot light randomly floated across the stage, at times showing the dark-tanned skin of the hot blonde positioned there before returning her body to a red tone.

"I don't like how bright the light on stage is." I thought of the deep stretch marks along my stomach and thighs—thanks to Jacob— as well as my pale skin.

"It's good for you two." Tony smiled. "It shows how old some of these women are compared to how young and beautiful you two are."

"I would only do this if I could hide from that stupid light," I said. "White lighting is not flattering."

"It wouldn't bother me." Yessenia counted the three men at the stage. "It's dead in here. How are the dancers making any money?"

"Darling, the money isn't on the stage; they make money from the private dances. Come, I'll show you the dance area." Tony led the way to a smaller section of the club.

Long padded benches were separated from the main area by short walls topped with frosted glass. We sat at a nearby table and watched two long-legged dancers with voluptuous breasts—barely covered by triangles of fabric—give air dances to men in suits.

They danced way slower than I'd ever seen anyone dance before. With slithering hypnotic movements, they kept time with every other beat of the song. They played with their hair, ran their manicured nails along their bodies, and posed like models at a photo shoot.

The men stared intently at the strippers' every move.

"The dancers are hardly making any contact with the men." Yessenia smirked. "I could totally do that."

"Look how tall they all are," I said. "I'd be the shortest one here."

"Love, not all men want the same thing." Tony put his hand on my shoulder. "Everyone here looks the same, like Barbie dolls with wrinkles. You heard the manager. He said you two would do well."

I wanted to believe him, but the sight of these sexy women killed my confidence. "I don't know. See how huge their breasts are?"

"Maybe I'll get implants." Yessenia grabbed her full C-cups.

"No," Tony said, "those bad boob jobs are no comparison to natural ones. You two have gorgeous breasts."

Yessenia straightened up and looked down at her chest as if about to take hers out for an accurate assessment.

I turned back toward the stage at the blonde leaning against the shiny brass poles. "Everyone here is blonde," I said. "I'd have the darkest hair."

"Variety is good." Tony's wandering eyes gave me the creeps. I felt like one of my dad's friends was checking me out. "Why don't you follow me?" Tony motioned. "There's another room I want to show you."

In the other room, a rowdy crowd of standing men whistled and called out sexual obscenities to the young girl wiggling around on a small stage. Somehow this attention encouraged the dancer who grabbed at her small perky breasts. She dropped to all fours for some doggie-style air-fucking.

"I'm going back to the other room." I averted my eyes. "It's quieter."

Yessenia followed me, while Tony stayed behind in a trance.

"This place is way classier, don't you think?" Yessenia asked. "The last place was a dump."

"It was darker," I said. "Nobody would recognize us there."

"Look at those platform stilettos." Yessenia pointed. "I don't know how they dance in them. I can't even walk in heels. I need to practice before we audition."

Audition? I hadn't committed to the career change yet. "I need at least a year to get in shape." I pulled up my skirt and pointed to my stretch marks. "Ugh."

"Come to the tanning salon with me. With a tan, no one will see those."

The next day, upon Yessenia's intuitive hunch, we went on the Internet and created a fake screen name to find out more information about Tony who had been offering to take us to another strip club. She didn't use her 'Destiny' profile and I didn't use my 'Sexy Serenity' profile when we went online, because she suspected Tony was hiding something.

We baited him well. Our fake persona identified herself as 5'5", 115lbs, blonde, blue eyes—a nymphomaniac dancer who was in search of real offline sex. We found Tony hanging out in his usual locale—the "young women to be spoiled by older men"—chat room. There we waited.

Within moments "Slave to Women" initiated contact. Ten minutes later we were engaged in an online sexual conversation where Tony detailed what he wanted to do to our beautiful and willing "Jenny."

"I will chain you up by the wrists," Tony typed.

"Oh really? Where?" We responded with hesitation.

"At my house, I have lots of toys. I have a tall hook with a chain."

What the hell did he say? "Have you done this before?" we typed.

"Yes, many times."

I hope he's joking. "Sounds interesting. What will I be wearing?"

"I'll chain you up naked by your wrists. You'll only be allowed to wear heels, and I'll pull the chain tight enough until your toes can barely touch the floor."

At this point Yessenia and I were seriously concerned about this guy, but we continued the charade to see what else he would say. "Then what?" we typed.

"Since you've been a bad girl, you'll be punished."

"How have I been a bad girl?"

"You haven't done what I've told you to do."

"So if I've been a bad girl, what are you going to do about it?"

"You need to be punished."

"How?"

"I'll spank you and whip you until your nipples get hard. Then I'll bend you over and fuck you in the ass."

"Ouch, that sounds painful. I'll scream." I kept Yessenia from adding, "You sick fuck."

"No one can hear you down there. A little bit of pain will turn us both on. I'll stop after you beg me to stop."

"I don't beg." Yessenia and I strongly felt Tony wasn't merely engaging in perverted online sex, but was being completely honest with one whom he believed was into the same S&M thing and with whom he was told he might be meeting for a real sexual encounter.

"Bad girls who don't do what they're told will be punished," he said. "I have other ways to hurt you and make you scream for more."

"What if I tell you to let me down and untie me?"

"When we meet, I'll show you what I do to bad girls who refuse to listen."

At that point, Yessenia and I envisioned a serial killer with a dungeon hidden from view of his neighbors who kidnapped women and buried their bodies under his house. I agreed with Yessenia and typed out, "You're one sick puppy. Go fuck yourself." We logged off and deleted the fake screen name, then blocked Tony from ever contacting us again through our screen names "Destiny" and "SexySerenity." From then on, I never answered his calls.

As far as strip clubs, Yessenia and I would have to research them on our own.

*   *   *

Against my better judgment, I drove up to Hollywood with Yessenia to shop for "stripper shoes"—clear, crystal-like, slip-on platform stilettos—the exact pair we saw on most of the dancers.

We wanted to fit in, so we figured we should dress like we assumed the dancers might—based on what we had seen in movies like *Strip Tease*.

In her cleaned, jizz-free powder blue miniskirt and halter top, Yessenia led the way. Not to be outdone, I sported tight, low-cut, navy pin-striped pants and matching backless halter top which showed a fair amount of cleavage along with my entire midsection. Somehow, I thought nothing of my choice of attire and was proud to complete my outfit with strappy black heels. My long hair flapped against the bare skin of my back.

I walked in sync with Yessenia along the celebrity stars embedded in the Hollywood Boulevard sidewalks.

Each block was comprised of rows of clothing stores, tacky souvenir shops, touristy museums, and a variety of restaurants. Every few steps, there was another golden star under my feet, usually imprinted with a name I'd never heard of.

Smells from the Asian BBQs, the hamburger joints, and the Mexican cafés blended together with the smog.

Parallel-parked cars lined the street bumper-to-bumper in both directions, at coin meters, and a few in loading zones where they shouldn't have been. Occasionally I'd see a homeless person covered in rags around a corner, or a group of businessmen and -women out for lunch, or a street performer painted in silver performing "the robot" to a small crowd of tourists, or the performers dressed liked superheroes posing for pictures for tips. It was an eclectic scene.

We glanced to the right and left, trying to decide which shoe store to go into first. A car honked, startling us. We stopped and turned to face the commotion, expecting to see some road altercation. Instead we were greeted by a good-looking man in his early thirties, the driver of a BMW. He leaned over toward his open passenger window, but his words were lost in the purr of his motor.

I bent down slightly to see him. "What?"

"I asked how much." He called out, louder than before.

My face contorted. "What did you say?"

"How much?"

I turned to Yessenia. "What's he talking about?"

She walked towards the car. "Excuse me?"

"How much do you two charge?"

Wow. Here, on Hollywood Boulevard, in the blaring sunlight, we were being propositioned for sex.

"You asshole!" I screamed. "We're not prostitutes."

He honked again and drove off yelling, "You look like it!"

My jaw dropped.

"Fuck him." Yessenia continued up the sidewalk.

We brushed it off as a freak incident. Looking back, I chuckle at how clueless I was. Most would assume a twenty-year old with a child would have been more worldly and knowledgeable than I was.

Yessenia paused at the window display in a shoe store. "These shoes look big enough for my size tens."

"Your feet aren't big. You're five-foot-nine, what do you expect? I wear size seven or eight and I'm barely five-foot-four." I followed her inside where we were met with strange stares. I wondered if the men who worked there had overheard our earlier escapade.

Nope. As it turned out, that shoe store sold large shoes because they catered to transvestites. Dressed in hip-hugging jeans and a floral pastel-colored top with bright red lipstick, the lovely young salesman directed us to the store across the street.

At the second store, Yessenia almost tripped while trying on a pair of platform stilettos.

I felt as though I would fall over or stumble on the slightest carpet crease. "Oh shit, Yessenia," I said. "It's scary up here. These are dangerous."

"We can't start dancing without them."

We each bought a pair of shoes. Unlike the pleats and polo shirts that I had to buy for the department store, hopefully this would be a more flattering work uniform.

"Does your brother still have his disco ball and strobe light?" Yessenia asked.

Memories of my innocent high school parties came to mind. "Yeah, why?"

"You know my long mirror?"

"Yeah, why?" I didn't see where she was going with all this.

"When we get home from work, we'll practice downstairs."

"Hell. No. What if my mom or brother sees us?"

"It'll be dark. We'll keep the music low so they won't hear us."

*   *   *

Weeks passed and we still hadn't worked up the nerve to put on our new stripper shoes. I did, however, pair the strappy shoes Tony bought me with a number of cute outfits.

"You should burn those shoes," Yessenia sneered.

"But I like them," I whined and turned away from her glare.

CHAPTER NINE

DANCING FOR DOLLARS

END OF JULY 1998

THE OWNERS OF CLUB FLAMINGO had what they considered a brilliant idea for increasing business—a weekly lingerie contest.

Two middle-aged coworkers, dressed in blue Dickies and striped mechanics' shirts with their first names embroidered on the pockets clocked in Yessenia and me. The four of us scooted into a booth around the dance floor. My date for the hour sang along to the 70s love songs the DJ played. He had a great voice; however, he was as old as my father. I had to force myself to smile with adoration while he serenaded me.

The music stopped.

"All right ladies and gentlemen," the DJ said. "Tonight, at Club Flamingo, it's lingerie night. That's right, you heard me—a hostess will dance for you in lingerie. But if you want to see the dancer, you must have a girl clocked in. So guys, go clock in a girl, get your dollar bills out, and get ready to show your appreciation. Let's welcome Isabelle."

A lingerie contest? Great. The customers are going to be even more difficult to deal with after this.

We turned our heads and saw a dark-haired Mexican girl standing on the dance floor in a short black satin robe. Her long curly hair hung down to her lower back. Her face was heavily made up and her fake eyelashes accentuated her big brown eyes. She couldn't have been much older than me.

Music blared out of the speakers and the disco ball mounted on the ceiling projected rainbow sparkles across Isabelle's bronze skin. She threw her robe to the ground to reveal the strangest lingerie I'd ever seen. It resembled a low-cut wrestler's uniform, but with a bikini bottom-half. Black straps came down from her shoulders, barely covered her breasts and ended below her belly button where they attached the bottom piece. I wondered how she had wiggled into the costume.

Isabelle gyrated around the booths. She performed a fast club-style dance and shook her stuff without ever making contact. Men threw dollars on the ground.

Having checked out strip clubs with Yessenia, I knew Isabelle's fast dancing was not at all like a slow stripper sway. Her grin was big and goofy. I thought her outfit was hideous. It was like watching a trashy talk show on TV. You know it's wrong that the guests are punching each other, yet you can't pull your eyes away from it. Of course I had to admit Isabelle had more guts than I did; she was far more comfortable in her own skin than I was in mine.

The men didn't seem to care about the quality of her dancing and couldn't keep their eyes off her.

I took a mental note. Apparently, outfits and dance moves didn't matter as long as the woman was scantily clad. Fantasies took over from there.

Back in the locker room, girls talked about the new lingerie contest.

"Damn, did you see all the money Isabelle made?" one girl said.

"Shit," another said, "I should enter the contest next week."

"Not me," a third said. "I couldn't get my fat ass into lingerie in front of everyone. I'd have to tuck in my rolls. You go ahead."

"Shut up. You're not fat. If I do it, would you? We could shake it together."

Laughter erupted.

"I hate that place. I hate that contest. I hate those stupid girls," Yessenia said to me during the drive home. "They're selling themselves short."

"Why are they doing this?" I asked. "That trashy contest gets the guys so worked up that they just want to grind the hell out of us."

"I don't want to go back to Flamingo. I hate it there. I'd rather strip," Yessenia said. "Besides it would be the ultimate 'fuck you' to my dad who already thinks I'm a slut."

"Come on, don't believe anything your dad says."

She shrugged. "Did I tell you I almost modeled? Several photographers have offered me free headshots if I'd let them add my pictures to their portfolio. My dad wouldn't let me. He said, 'Modeling is selling your body for a living. It's a form of prostitution and would bring shame to the family name.' Well, you know what? Fuck him."

"It doesn't mean you need to strip."

"Because I choose to, doesn't mean you have to."

"I need money more than you. I have a kid to support. What about waitressing?"

"Why? Men already gawk at me. I might as well get paid for it."

Client dates, hostess dancers, lingerie contests. Could stripping be any worse? I'd condemned the entire adult entertainment profession since high school yet here I was, entertaining adults. Why not go all the way?

"Okay, fine," I said. "Let's strip."

Yessenia raised an eyebrow. "Are you being serious? You're actually going to do it?"

I nodded but wasn't sure if I'd have the nerve to follow through.

*　*　*

Yessenia and I spoke to the owner of Club Flamingo in his office, the first time we had seen the room since the day we were hired. It was more my idea than hers. Out of fear of not being able to support my son, I wanted to keep this job open as a backup plan in case stripping didn't pan out.

"We need some time off for a while," I said.

He narrowed his eyes. "Then go home tonight."

"Not just tonight. We need to take a couple of weeks off."

"Why so long? I have plenty of girls who want to work the shifts I give you two."

"I'm burnt out," I said. "You know we both get a lot of minutes. After a break, we'll be ready to come back and make money."

He shrugged and agreed.

On our way out, we grinned and waved to the girls who sat on the red couches like dolls on a store shelf. Their eyes seemed to question where we were going and why we looked so smug. I enjoyed descending those creaky wooden stairs. Hopefully it would be for the last time.

*　*　*

Tropicana, a bikini bar on Western Avenue in Hollywood, was known for its mud and oil wrestling. Back in the 1980s, it was a popular joint. Mötley Crüe had frequented the place and Madonna supposedly had her bachelorette party there.

But it was a seedy joint by the time Yessenia and I walked through its doors on Wednesday, July 29, 1998. On the end of a street bearing no Hollywood glamour, in the wrong part of town full of buildings that had seen better days, the club and its brightly-lit sign could be seen from the 101 freeway.

We didn't know what to expect when we approached the front door. A heavyset Hispanic male with a shaved head, goatee, and diamond stud earrings stopped us. Bulky biceps peaked out of the sleeves of his polo shirt labeled "Security."

"IDs, ladies," he said.

"How do we get a job here?" Yessenia asked.

"Gimme your IDs and I'll go talk to the manager." The beefy security guard took our ID cards and went inside.

"I'm nervous," I said.

"We're only getting some info and checking it out."

The security guard returned and handed back our IDs. "He said you two can audition. Who's first?"

"Audition?" we asked in unison.

"We only wanted to look around," Yessenia said.

He tilted his head, chin up, and crossed his arms, looking quite menacing. "I told him you two wanted to work here."

"Can't we come back another time?" Yessenia asked. "We didn't bring anything to audition in."

She and I looked at each other. We were wearing miniskirts, tank tops, and heels, the same outfits we wore at Club Flamingo.

"What you have on is good enough. Trust me. You look hot. If you want to work, I suggest you go in now. He's in a good mood. Who's first?"

My eyes widened in fear. "Can't we go in together?"

"No. One at a time."

Yessenia and I huddled close together. "No," she whispered to me. "I'm not doing it today. I'm leaving. Let's go."

"But it took us over an hour to get here. We might as well try." Why was I convincing her to do this? "Come on, this was your idea. You're the one who wanted to come here."

"Whatever." Yessenia turned toward the security guard and followed him. I could sense an attitude in her walk, which made her appear more confident.

I was alone in the cold. I shivered.

What was taking so long?

Finally, they returned. There was a look of fear and shock on Yessenia's face. Before I could ask her what happened, the security guard pointed to me.

I followed him into a large room which looked more like a living room than an office. There were plush couches, tables, lamps—the whole deal. The security guard walked back out and shut the door. Confused, I looked around until I saw the manager seated in an armchair. Dim lighting shone down on his face reminding me of Al Pacino in *The Godfather*.

"Come here." He motioned toward his end of the room.

I did as he instructed.

"What's your name?" he asked.

"Miranda."

"So you want to work here?"

"Yes."

"Have you ever danced before?"

"I've done hostess dancing."

"You've never stripped?"

I felt inadequate, ashamed and out of place. It was like he saw me as nothing more than a little girl wearing her mother's heels. I thought of Jacob. Sucking in my stomach, I straightened my posture, gathered my wits and pumped up the charm. "No, but I've been to plenty of strip clubs. I love to dance." I smiled.

He was quiet for a moment. "Okay."

Am I hired?

"Take off your clothes," he said.

Those words alone made me feel nude in his presence.

"Excuse me? Everything? Now?" I wanted to run, hide, and puke. "I'm not wearing a bikini or anything."

Fuck you, Yessenia. Bitch didn't warn me.

"You can leave your bra and panties on." He noted my hesitation and dimmed the lights.

Bills to pay, baby to feed, college to finish, I repeated in my head.

"Walk across the room and back," he said.

Walk? I can walk. I can do this. "Okay." I took a deep breath.

Shit. I had on granny panties, not at all attractive. I winced.

He cleared his throat and leaned back in his chair.

Don't cry. What's the worst that can happen? I don't get hired. That's okay. We can go back to Club Flamingo. Mark and Hiroki don't know about this. Everything will be all right.

"Go ahead," he said.

I turned around. With my back to him, I took another deep breath, lifted my tank top up and tossed it on the floor. The air was chilly on my skin, but heat overcame me from the cheeks down. I stood still and tried not to shake from fear.

I was crying and screaming inside at the same time. *Don't do it. Fuck it. Do it. It's too late now. Yessenia's waiting for me. She must've done this. It'll be over in a few minutes.*

I placed both hands on the elastic waist band of my skirt and pulled it down, which revealed my ugly white cotton panties.

"Now walk across the room and back," he said.

He didn't tell me to get dressed again and leave. He didn't say anything about my undergarments. *That's a good sign. Maybe he can't see the cellulite on my butt. That's a plus. Don't go too fast.*

I placed one heel in front of the other and slowly made my way across the room.

Act sexy. Feel sexy. Pretend. I'm an actress. Steady. Damn it. I feel my thighs jiggling. That's not good.

I reached the end. I swiveled in place, lowered my gaze and seductively stared into his eyes from across the room.

If I get him to look into my eyes, he won't be judging my body so harshly. Good, he's looking at my eyes. Shit. He's checking me out. Staring at my breasts, my naked stomach, my bare thighs. Walk, walk. Don't trip. Don't let him see how I'm shaking with fear. Almost there.

I reached my starting point and stopped. Unable to move, I stood there like an idiot.

"You can get dressed now."

Did he chuckle at me? Shit. He thinks I don't know what I'm doing.

"Go back to your friend."

That's it? Am I hired? I said nothing.

Maybe not. Great. I stripped in front of a stranger for nothing. I felt so violated.

I dressed and walked outside to find Yessenia puffing away at a cigarette. She hadn't smoked in a while and must have bummed one from the security guard.

"You two wait here." Hercules left us alone.

"Did you have to take off your clothes?" I asked.

"Yep." She took another drag.

"Why didn't you warn me? I was wearing granny panties."

She stopped to stare at me and laughed. I didn't think it was funny, but found myself laughing, too.

We were giggling like two little school girls when the security guard returned. "You two are hired. He said to come back tomorrow night and he'll get you on the schedule."

That was it. We were officially going to be dancers. A thrill shot through me. It was like sneaking out of the window as a teenager; I knew it was wrong, it felt wrong, but was exciting nonetheless. Being young and daring, I figured why not?

*   *   *

"Mommy, I wanna go to the park." Jacob stood in the bathroom doorway, holding his bicycle helmet.

It was a beautiful sunny day. I didn't have school and Yessenia and I didn't have to go to work until the evening. It was a rare opportunity to get outside and spend some time with my son.

"I said we would go," I said. "Give me and Yessenia a few minutes to get ready."

"I wanna go. I wanna ride my bike."

"I know, Jacob. Be patient."

"I wanna feed ducks and ride my bike."

I squatted down next to him. "Sweetie, mommy needs to get ready. Can I get a hug?"

"I wanna go to the park." He turned and sulked into our room.

Yessenia laughed. "Oh my God, I'm so glad I don't have kids. Nothing personal, but I don't know how you do it."

"Me neither."

Within a few minutes, we were both dressed in shorts, shirts, and sandals. I walked to my room to get Jacob. The bedroom was dark and silent.

"Jacob?" I opened the blinds. "Jacob? Come on, we're ready to go now."

He didn't answer.

"Don't you want to go to the park?"

Yessenia came into my room. "Is he playing hide-and-seek again?"

"Yeah, maybe," I said. "Can you check the living room? I'll look in here."

Yessenia agreed and left.

"Jacob? Come out now or we're not going to go feed the ducks. Don't you want to go ride your bike?" Silence. I bent down and lifted the bed skirt. Nothing but a few socks and papers. "Jacob, stop hiding and come here now." I opened my closet doors. My shoes were in rows on the carpet. I brushed aside my long dresses. Jacob wasn't there. My heart raced.

Stay calm. I'm sure he's here somewhere.

"Yessenia!" I yelled. "Did you find him?"

"No. He's not out here."

My stomach tightened. I jogged out to the front room. The baby gate was still in place, blocking off the staircase. There's no way Jacob could get around it. I scanned the kitchen, ducked under the dining room table and ran to the front door. The deadbolt was still locked.

"Oh, my God, Yessenia. He's not here."

"But where else would he be? Did you check under the bed?"

I nodded. "Can you check again?"

She ran to my room.

"Jacob!" I screamed. "Where are you? This isn't funny. Come out, honey. Jacob!"

Yessenia reappeared. "You're right. He's not in the room. Wait, didn't he get out onto the back porch last month? You said he opened the window and pushed out the screen, right?"

"Yeah, you're right. He's probably out there again. I need to childproof those windows." I rushed to the back door and unlocked it. Peering outside, I saw nothing. Only the back porch and a few toys. The six-foot-tall picket fence was locked. My chest heaved. "Jacob!" I screamed. "Jacob!"

"He's not there?" Yessenia asked.

I shook my head. Tears spilled down my face. "It's been fifteen minutes since we last saw him. Someone kidnapped him. Oh my God, Ricky took him."

"Check the front windows."

We both raced to the living room. At first glance, all of the windows and screens looked fine. A breeze picked up the broken corner of one screen.

"Yessenia, he went out the front. Oh my God. Oh my God. Oh my God. The street!" We lived around the corner from an eight-lane boulevard. The cars whipped down our road to and from the main street at all hours of the day. What if he'd been hit by a car? "I should call the police. Wait, first I'll check the street. You check the alley by the garages."

I ran two circles around our fourplex and one circle around the next set of apartments. Panting and delirious, I stood in the middle of the street and cried.

"You didn't find him?" Yessenia yelled. "I'll go back and check inside again."

I looked up and down the empty road. "Jacob!" I screamed.

From across the street, a teenage girl stared. Wearing jeans and a t-shirt, she approached me. "Are you looking for someone?"

I wiped my eyes on my sleeve. "Yes, my son's missing. I think he climbed out a window. I've looked everywhere. Have you seen him? He's about this tall." I held my hands above my knees. "He has brown hair and green eyes. I think someone kidnapped him. I need to call the police."

She shook her head and motioned with her hand. "I think I know where he is. What's his name?"

"Jacob." I followed her across the street to a small sedan. Jacob was sitting in the back seat. My eyes widened. He was alive. Tears streamed down my face.

"Mommy." He jumped out and wrapped his arms around my legs.

"Yeah, I found him," the girl said. "He was walking across the street and I worried a car might hit him or something. I came out here to look for his parents. I was about to call the cops."

"Oh, my God. Thank you so much." I hugged her.

She shrugged. "Glad I could help."

I scooped Jacob up into my arms and squeezed him. "Mommy was so scared."

Sobbing, I went back home and told Yessenia what happened.

After that, I was too shaken up to go to the park. I convinced Jacob to sit down to watch a Disney cartoon so I could hold him close. I never wanted to lose him again.

*   *   *

As evening approached, Yessenia and I prepared for our first night of dancing at the bikini bar. With my focus on taking care of Jacob and finishing college, I managed to ignore my insecurities. I was going to go in, dance for money, and get out.

I arranged for Jacob to stay overnight at the sitter's house and I'd pick him up in the morning.

Yessenia and I packed our stripper shoes, bikinis and the dresses we had bought from the trashy shops on Hollywood Boulevard. We crammed make-up, curling irons, perfume, mouthwash, and little purses into our duffel bags. Yessenia lent me foundation, powder, and a sponge to cover up my stretch marks. We had tried different colors and brands until we found one we thought would do the job.

With bags slung over our shoulders, we tried to sneak out but my mom appeared at the top of the staircase. "Where are you two going?"

"To work." I kept my head down.

"Where's Jacob?"

"At the sitter's."

"What's in the bags?"

"Just stuff."

She pointed to our sweatpants. "Why aren't you dressed for work?"

"We're going to change there."

She glared down at me. It was the same kind glare she gave me when, during my childhood, I talked back, or didn't clean my room, or was up late reading.

"Miranda—"

Too late, Mom; my mind was made up. I reached for the door. "Love you, Mom. Have a good night."

Yessenia and I headed out to her car.

Kevin, the manager, a clean-shaven dark-haired man in his forties, gave me and Yessenia a quick tour of the Tropicana. A few customers were scattered around the large dark room. There were two stages; the smaller circular one was not in use. The larger rectangular one had two brass poles on opposite ends. Dancers in bikinis rotated on stage. The club had recently lost their liquor license and the men looked disappointed when they realized they couldn't order a beer. Without a liquor license, it became a bikini juice bar.

While Kevin walked Yessenia and me around, I kept getting distracted by all the lights reflecting off shiny surfaces. Pounding bass made it hard to hear what the manager was saying. The chilly air carried the smell of dusty old wood. I had goosebumps.

Kevin led us up a stairway that had huge windows which allowed cars passing by to watch the dancers on their way to the dressing room. I didn't like that and hurried past the windows. I didn't want anyone to see me.

The dressing room was a wide open space. Individual dressing stations with mirrors, counters, and lockers lined both walls.

"I'm going to introduce you to the house mom," Kevin said.

"What's a house mom?" I asked.

"She helps the dancers out," he said. "You'll want to take care of her later." He rubbed his thumb against his fingers, to show he meant monetarily. "You can do that when you tip out the DJ and the club." He introduced us to an older woman. Wearing a matronly dress and with her salt-and-pepper hair pulled back into a tight bun, she looked more like a maid in a hotel, not a "house mom" in a strip club.

How she helped the dancers I couldn't understand, but didn't ask. In other words, we were supposed to give her cash for doing nothing. Why would I want to give anyone my money, if I was going to strip for it?

He pointed to two side-by-side empty stations. "Go ahead and change clothes. Meet me downstairs when you're ready."

Uncomfortable, I felt like I was back in my high school locker room where nobody wanted anybody else to see her body. With my t-shirt still on, I slipped my panties down and put my bikini bottoms on. I quickly changed from bra to bikini top.

Facing Yessenia who was taller, darker, and thinner, I saw my reflection in the mirror.

How could I, of all people, believe I was capable of stripping? I hated wearing bikinis without cover-ups. My friends had to do a fashion intervention when I was fifteen because I only wore baggy men's t-shirts over jeans, which often had holes in the knees from my tree-climbing. As a teenager, I didn't feel comfortable with my big hips and hid my curves. I had poor posture because I didn't want anyone to stare at my breasts; it disgusted me to have men look at me in a sexual way. I was always one of the smartest girls in my honors classes. Praised for my intellect—that's how I wanted to be judged. I was scared to be judged with no clothes to hide behind. I couldn't strip.

"I can't do this," I said.

"Why not?" Yessenia asked.

"My stretch marks. I can see them all over."

"That's in your head. I can hardly see anything." Yessenia patiently helped me apply cover-up and powder until it was caked on my stomach, thighs, and hips.

"I can still see them," I whined.

Another dancer, a petite Mexican girl, returned to her station directly to the right of ours. She watched our make-up application activity.

"Hey, I'm Marisol. You two new?"

We nodded.

"Shit, you guys worried about going down there?"

"Yeah," I said. "I can't cover up all of my stretch marks." I didn't admit I was terrified of becoming a sex object, practically naked, in a room full of strange men.

"Damn, girl. Don't be getting worried. Check out this." She barely lowered her bikini bottom, which revealed a scar. "That's from my C-section, from my baby girl. It's so dark down there nobody's going to see shit. Fucking creeps don't care, as long as you shake your ass." She laughed.

Yessenia raised an eyebrow and motioned for us to go. Downstairs, the manager pulled us into an office to sign papers and pose for Polaroid pictures. He pinned our photos up on a wall covered with hundreds of other women, dated only by their hairstyles.

We went to the "floor" where all the action was. The club didn't seem to have many dancers or customers.

Kevin brought us over to a dark corner.

"Neither of you have ever danced before?" he asked.

We shook our heads.

"There are rules. First of all, you can't touch the customers and they can't touch you." He stared at us for a moment and said, "I think you two should practice first."

"Practice what?" I asked.

"Table dances. You can practice here. Who's first?"

Soon Yessenia and I found ourselves slithering all over him. It felt gross.

"That's good," he said. "Go ahead. You can get a little closer. Move slower."

It wasn't too difficult. Move to every other beat and slink around him like a ferret.

"Why don't you turn around and shake your ass a little," he said.

Luckily the disc jockey, an obese Mexican man with a shaved head and a triple chin, chose this moment to approach us. "Hey, do you two want to go up on stage together?" His voice was deep but kind. "Sometimes it's easier when you're new to this."

"We can do that?" I asked.

He nodded. "Tell me when you're ready."

If it were up to me, that would be never.

"What music do you two want?" he asked.

"I don't know." I shrugged and looked at Yessenia.

She shrugged.

This went back and forth a few times before the DJ said, "I'll play some Enigma. It's slow and sexy. When you hear the song, it's your turn on stage. What are your names again?"

"Cassie," came out of my mouth before I could think otherwise. Best to stick to the same thing, I figured.

It wasn't long before we were called to the stage. Unfortunately, we both came down with a horrible case of stage fright and our song had to be restarted several times before we could be coaxed to ascend the high steps to the stage.

Dressed in string bikinis, Yessenia and I each rushed toward one of two poles at either end of the stage. The brass pole was my comfort blanket.

Men around the tip rail had glasses of sodas since they couldn't order beer. Quiet and sober, they seemed annoyed at having to wait so long for us. Some leaned back in chairs with arms crossed, others rested elbows on the rail. They stared.

Although we had studied the dancers' moves at the clubs we had visited, we now couldn't emulate their sexy moves. My mind went blank and I stood still.

"Do something," Yessenia whispered to me.

I grabbed the pole, which looked like it belonged in a fire station, and tried to swing around it, but had no clue how. I awkwardly slid down and stopped on the other side. The girls made it look so easy. It wasn't. My stomach cramped. Nauseated, I tried to focus on the music, but couldn't. It felt like I was going deaf. Enigma faded into the distance.

Not a single smile or sign of encouragement from any man. One picked up his drink and walked away.

Yessenia nearly tripped over in her heels, and now was crawling across the tip rail countertop. I thought "what a sexy move" until she knocked a man's drink over. I looked away.

I grabbed the pole with both hands and pumped my butt back and forth toward it, so that I looked much like a dog humping a man's leg. Yessenia gave me a glare to stop, so I instead slid up and down against the pole, wiggling around as I went. I forgot how to dance. Did I ever know how to dance? I wished I was at home, at college, at church, anywhere but there.

It was torture. When would it end?

At last the forty-minute (or so it felt) song faded out. We walked along the rail. Not a single fucking dollar. I held it together long enough to grasp Yessenia's hand and walk off the stage, one step at a time. I wanted to cry.

Before we could flee to the dressing room, an older dancer approached us. Maybe the other dancers couldn't bear the embarrassment of watching us and had sent her over. She was tall, thin, had fake breasts, sagging skin, and the face of someone who had stayed up all night for seven days in a row, covered up by a mask of makeup and a plastic grin.

"I've been around longer than any of the others here," she said. "I want to help you two."

Maybe the manager sent her.

I was wrong. Never had I been as humiliated as when this dancer informed us that the manager had taken us for a ride, a grinding ride. "He made you two give him lap dances?"

"Yeah, he trained us."

"Darling, he's a pig. Don't ever let that asshole touch you again, or he'll deal with me."

I changed the subject because I didn't want to think about how we had just been used by Kevin. "How do we make money?"

She pointed toward the dark center of the room. Men were seated on chairs and dancers were all over them. "Dollar dances."

"You do that for a dollar?" I asked. "That's all it costs?"

"Every girl charges different amounts. But to start off, they'll offer you a couple of bucks. They stick it in your bikini, but they can't touch you. You stop dancing for them after like fifteen seconds or so unless they keep feeding you money. Get it?"

Too stunned to ask any more questions, Yessenia and I split up and asked men for dances. We didn't understand how to get more than a couple dollars from each.

By the end of the night, I was exhausted and had only earned $68. After tipping out everyone, I walked away with $41. This paltry sum made me feel like I'd been tricked into taking off my clothes for free. Being an adult entertainer wasn't fun or thrilling. It was emotionally, physically, and spiritually draining.

I felt dirty. The first thing I did when I came home was to take a long, hot shower. I focused on the floral-scented shampoo and berry body wash. I massaged my scalp and lathered soap all over my skin.

After getting into my comfortable sweats and t-shirt, I crawled into bed and cried. I loved Jacob but wished I had never gotten pregnant. I had to support a child on my own, so I was doing something I swore I'd never do: selling my body.

Jacob stirred. I couldn't let him hear his mommy crying. With a sniffle, I wiped my eyes on my sheets and took a deep breath. I only had two years left in school. I needed to stop the tears and repress this disgust. To compartmentalize. To not think about it. Otherwise, dancing for money would be torture.

CHAPTER TEN
POLE WORK

THE EVENING AFTER OUR horrendous first night, Yessenia and I put on our bikinis and heels, and practiced dance moves in front of a mirror. Colors rotated around the room from my brother's cheap revolving disco light. Enigma's "Mea Culpa" and "Sadeness" played on the stereo.

"Okay, let's pretend this is the pole." I pointed to the corner edge of my mom's tall bookcase. "Let's try it out."

We took turns on the "pole." There was no way we ever wanted to repeat our embarrassing act on stage. Anytime either of us crossed the line from erotic and sensual to humiliating or disturbing, we cut the music.

Yessenia tried lifting her leg up and out to the side in the kickboxing-style stripper move. Not flexible enough, her leg couldn't reach her waist height. "You look like you're a dog peeing on a hydrant," I said.

"At least I'm not fucking the pole." She smirked.

"Don't be jealous. I know it looked sexy."

She grabbed the edge of the book case and started pumping her butt back and forth, humping the corner. "Look familiar?"

"I'm ignoring you." I stuck my tongue out. "Seriously, we need to practice."

Settling for only using the "pole" for support, we leaned against it while moving in slow motion to the Gregorian chants and intoxicating vocals.

"My muscles hurt. I can't move this slowly." Yessenia sat down on the floor.

"I'm out of shape. Dancers make this look so easy."

"Help." She lay down. "I've fallen and I can't get up."

"I'm tired, too."

"No, I mean I can't stand up in these damn heels. I'm gonna trip and kill myself."

"Sshhh. You're gonna wake up my mom."

She started laughing. Yessenia was entering the it's-so-damn-late-that-I'm-slap-happy mood, which had always infected me.

I fought it off. "Sshhh. If my mom or brother wake up and see us in these string bikinis and six-inch stripper stilettos, we are...so...dead."

She kept giggling. "I don't care. I can't get up. Help me." She reached her arms out to me, like a frustrated child who had fallen down in the roller skating rink.

Sometimes she pissed me off when she acted like that, but this time it was funny.

I kneeled down next to her. "Fine. Let's try the 'floor work' like the strippers do in the nude clubs."

Her laughter started sounding maniacal. "I can't do it. I can't do it." She started pounding her fists into the carpet in mock frustration.

I glared at her. "C'mon, be serious. I need help. I don't remember how they do that thing where they cross and uncross their legs."

On my back, I lifted my legs and opened them to a "v," following her lead. Or at least we tried to. Neither of us was flexible, so it looked horrible. Because our knees were bent, it looked more like a crooked "u."

"Now, open your legs and give the men a show. Or do that doggy-style thing." She bent down on her hands and knees and imitated the sexual act.

I copied her. "Okay, this is easy." I looked down. "I don't like how my boobs jiggle when I do this."

"It's like saying to the men, here kitty-kitty, you know you want some pussy."

"Kitty-kitty?" I couldn't contain my laughter any longer. Next thing we knew, we were both rolling around on the carpet, nearly hysterical.

The floorboards upstairs creaked. I reached over and cut the disco lights. Yessenia and I went silent and peeked around the corner of the bookcase.

Upstairs in her nightgown, my mom stood there looking half-asleep. "What are you girls doing down there?" She squinted.

Yay. She didn't have her contact lenses in.

"Sorry, Mom," I said. I was glad that she couldn't see me—her perfect daughter—for what I was: imperfect. When my mother thought of me, I wanted her to remember the daughter who was the Gifted-And-Talented-Education straight-A student, eighth grade salutatorian, winner of several community service and leadership-based scholarships, the one who passed her AP tests and graduated high school with honors; not the daughter who got pregnant at eighteen and was now stripping.

"You're making too much noise. I have to work in morning." She was a customer service rep at a call center. "What are you two doing up so late?"

"Just talking. Sorry. We'll go to bed. I love you." I winked at Yessenia.

"K, night." Mom shuffled back to her room.

"Let's turn off the music," I whispered. My arms and legs were already shaking from muscle fatigue. "We need to get more flexible so we can do the floor work."

Until then, I'd have to settle for a boring stage routine. I couldn't do pole work and I couldn't do floor work. The only option left was to hold on to the poles and squirm around.

Yessenia and I had better luck on Friday. We drove to Tropicana and pulled into the empty parking lot. Assuming we were employees, a security guard waved hello and a couple of men on the street whistled and eyed us. Now I felt it was official, because we were being looked at as dancers. I wasn't sure how I felt about that. On one hand, great, I was pretty enough. On the other hand, I felt like I did in high school when my brother's friend's creepy dad came over to pick up Kirk: while the dad waited for the boys in my living room, he tried to converse with me so that he could stare at my breasts, even though I crossed my arms to cover them up. That made me feel gross inside and now here I was seeking that same attention for money.

Inside the club, the older dancer we had met the night before approached us with some more tips and advice. "I'm Kelly by the way. Tonight, we're doing mud and oil wrestling."

No way. Give me baby steps, one at a time. "Do we have to?" I asked.

"No, you need to be auctioned off to do it. I gotta go. My customer's here."

"You wrestle guys or dancers?" I said. "I'm confused."

"Sometimes girl on girl, but guys can wrestle dancers too." I gave her a look of horror. "It's a way to make better money," she added.

"I might do it," Yessenia said.

Yessenia and I planted ourselves in one spot, observing our surroundings. Marisol, the short Mexican girl who introduced herself to us in the dressing room the other night, approached us.

"You two ain't gonna make money just standing there like that."

"We don't know what to do," I said.

"Watch the dancers," Marisol said. "Copy them. That's what I did."

While trying to "work the floor," Yessenia and I went our separate ways. Neither of us was making more than a few greenbacks, so we joined back together to study the other dancers, to try to learn what we were doing wrong. Intimidated by the groups of men, I hadn't approached anyone besides the singletons up until that point.

"I don't understand," I said. Across the room, two dancers were grinding away on men's laps. "I thought that we are supposed to keep our feet on the ground and that the men can't touch." The customers' hands brushed against dancers' thighs, hips, and waists. What happened to following the rules?

"To each her own." Yessenia walked away.

A tough-looking young Hispanic male came up to me. "'Scuse me. Ay, what's your name?"

"Cassie." I smiled.

"I want you to dance for my homie over there. He's all depressed because his ol' lady broke it off. How much?"

I didn't know what to say. "Ten dollars."

He pulled a five out. "How 'bout five? See if he likes it."

Copying what I saw the other dancers do, I held my bikini string out for him to tuck the money in. I followed him to a group of chairs where two other guys sat. One stood up and pointed to his lonely-looking friend. A few years older than me, the man had a shaved head, cratered face, and dark under-eye circles. His muscular frame lay hidden beneath a black hoodie and Dickies work pants.

I felt the pressure. His friends were watching me. The man I was supposed to dance for looked miserable and I had to make him happy? I almost wished I hadn't agreed.

I raised my arms to tousle my hair. I swirled my hips around from side to side.

The man looked up at me.

Okay, at least I got his attention. I pouted my lips, placed my hands on my hips, bent over and gave him a nice view of my ass.

His friends gave me an approving nod.

Feeling brave, I put my hands on my knees and pumped my hips back and forth, jiggling my butt.

Oh, yeah, I forgot—his friends were the ones paying. I winked at them seductively and licked my lips.

"Damn, girl," one of his friends called out. "Work that thing."

I grew bolder. I whipped my hair around and turned to face Mr. Miserable while I kept shaking my booty.

He grinned.

I felt his friend slip another five-dollar bill through my bikini string.

I glanced down to make sure that the cash was staying put. I figured out how the system worked: every so often I'd act like I was going to stop dancing and a few more dollars would appear in my bikini. Mr. Miserable didn't want me to leave so he pried open his own wallet.

"What's your name, sweetie?" I whispered in his ear, making sure he felt my warm breath along his neck.

"Mario," he said. "Stay here. Keep dancing." He held out a ten-dollar bill.

I wanted it.

He tucked it into my string bottom. I watched him do this and noticed my money was falling to the floor. I picked up the cash, shoved it into my small evening purse and put it under his chair.

My legs shook from exhaustion. I couldn't keep going, but I needed the money. If the other girls could bend the rules, I figured I could, so I said, "Can I get up on your lap?"

He smiled. "Hell yeah, baby. Come ride up here."

I held back from cringing. I straddled him then realized I couldn't dance in that position. Getting up on my knees, I grabbed onto the back of his chair for support. This allowed me to at least wiggle around and move my shoulders. I taunted him with my breasts close to his face.

Mario moaned.

Leaning forward, my hair formed a canopy around my face. I stared at his lips, pretending I might actually kiss him. My hair draped over his shoulders. That's when I noticed his sad look had returned.

"Want more or want me to stop?" I asked.

He shook his head. "Damn. You look like my ex." He sighed. "I mean you're fucking hot…just like my girl."

I stood back up, not sure what to do.

"Baby, I'm sorry," he said and took my hands into his. "Damn, girl. Don't get me wrong. You've got that shit going on, but you look like my ol' lady. I can't do this."

I shrugged at his friends and took off. I doubted I looked exactly like Mario's ex. After all, his breath smelled like beer. I headed to the restroom.

I opened my purse and shook out the cash. $158. I flipped through the bills again, putting them all in the same direction. $158.

The bathroom door swung open and Yessenia appeared.

"I see you did well tonight," she said.

"Not really, it's mostly ones." I shoved the money into my purse. "Some guy thought I looked like his ex-girlfriend."

"I didn't make shit." She threw her purse onto the counter. "Fuck this place. I don't want to come back."

I closed my purse.

Near the end of the night, Yessenia and I slumped into a couple of chairs at the other stage, which was dark and not in use. Business was dying down.

Marisol came up to us. "Ay you guys, want me to show you some pole work?"

"Absolutely." Yessenia perked up. She followed Marisol up onto the small circular stage that hadn't been in use the whole night.

I sat down and waited for my turn. I figured the other dancers decided to teach us to dance rather than watch us continually embarrass ourselves and bring shame to the entire dancing profession.

Marisol showed us her impressive acrobatics. She climbed the brass pole and once half-way up, she twisted and turned her body around and down the pole using such skill and speed that firemen would be jealous.

Upon her landing, her heels hit the ground with a loud thud. "Oh shit, we can't mess up the girl's set on the big stage." She kicked off her shoes and climbed back up.

She grabbed the pole with both hands and opened her legs into mid-air splits. Not done yet, she flipped upside down and spread her legs again. With amazing control and grace, she floated back to the stage floor with a triumphant smile.

Yessenia and I applauded.

"That'll take practice," Marisol said. "Don't expect me to teach you all that yet. First, here's how you turn around the pole. Use your wrists. Then, you gotta kinda hop a little and hook one leg around the pole. If you get going with speed, then you'll go around it. It's like swinging around in a circle. You land on your knees or the floor or whatever."

It sounded simple enough. Yessenia and I tried but couldn't do it.

"Can you show me how to climb the pole?" I asked.

"Okay. You do need a lot of muscle strength. You gotta use the top of your foot and this part, your ankle." Marisol pointed to my shoes. "You're gonna slip and fall with shoes. It's easier barefoot. Your skin grabs the pole that way, so you don't slide down."

I took my shoes off and grabbed the pole like she showed me. Yessenia sat and watched.

"So, it's not hard," she said. "Reach with each arm and pull yourself up. Wrap your legs around the pole and climb with the tops of your feet and your inner thighs."

It took a few tries, but I figured it out. On my third attempt, while suspended in mid-air around the pole, I called down to her. "Marisol, how did you do that leg thing?"

"I don't know if you should do it," she said. "You gotta have good arm muscles and hold on tight. Push your skin into the pole for support. Can't do it if the pole's slippery, either."

Stubborn as usual, I didn't heed her warnings. I climbed up as high as I could. Like she had done, I successfully turned myself upside down on the pole. My hair hung down.

"Wow, you did it," Marisol said.

"That looks really good," Yessenia said.

That should've been enough for me, but it wasn't. I had been the one who had climbed trees since I was little, had swung from the monkey bars in my backyard, and had once climbed up a flag pole on a dare from Kirk.

Still upside down, I gripped the pole with both hands. With my back leaned against the pole, I unwound my legs from the cold metal and spread my legs open.

I did it. It was perfect. And on my first try, too!

But something wasn't right. I knew it almost the second I unwound my legs. I hadn't paid careful enough attention to her hand placement during her pole stunts. My hands should've been above me, not underneath me. Unable to support my weight in such an awkward position, I fell.

So many thoughts flew by in those nanoseconds before impact.

Damage control. I'm going down fast. My head will hit first. Maybe my neck. I was up too high, probably over six feet in the air. The stage is hard. I might break my neck. This could be it. What about Jacob? Was it worth it? Of course not.

I remembered hearing that drunk drivers kill other people and yet they themselves live because the alcohol completely relaxes their bodies, minimizing their injuries from a crash.

I tried to relax.

Everything went silent. I didn't hear the music. I didn't scream. I did catch a glimpse of the horror on Yessenia's face. It was going to be pretty bad. I closed my eyes and focused on breathing. I hadn't prayed in a while, but I did then.

My body hit the floor with a thud. Yessenia and Marisol rushed to my side.

"Oh my God!"

"Can you hear me?"

"Oh shit!"

"What are we going to do?"

"Should I get someone?"

"Cassie, say something."

I didn't want to move because I was afraid of paralysis. I heard the girls around me. I took a deep breath and opened my eyes. I was still alive.

"Are you okay?" Marisol said. "I'll get some ice and ibuprofen." She took off running.

The initial shock wore off. Sharp pain settled in. My head, my neck, my back throbbed.

I imagined paramedics having to bring me out of the strip club on a stretcher. I thought of my mom seeing me in a string bikini at the hospital. Wonderful.

"Can you move?" Yessenia asked.

I wiggled my toes and my fingers. "I think so." I moved my right leg, then my left.

Okay, so I wasn't paralyzed. Yet.

I groaned. "Did the whole club see that?"

"No," Yessenia said. "The music was too loud and it's too dark over here."

She grabbed my arms and slowly I tried to sit up. It hurt a lot. But at least I could sit.

Yessenia leaned in close, lowered her voice, and said, "Since you're going to live I have to tell you that that was the fucking funniest shit I've ever seen."

"I could have died or become crippled."

"Hell yeah. That fall was horrible. I honestly wasn't sure if you were going to make it."

Marisol came back with ice packs. She helped me apply them to my neck and head. In her other hand, she held out some ibuprofen and water.

"Here, drink this," she said. "Oh my God Cassie, I'm so sorry. I shouldn't have let you."

I leaned into the ice.

CHAPTER ELEVEN
BACKSTAGE DRAMA

AUGUST 1998

AFTER I RESTED FOR a few days to heal my aching neck and back, I considered myself lucky to be alive.

"You want to dance again after all that?" Yessenia asked.

"I have to," I said. "I need money. I'll take it easy."

We tried one more shift at Tropicana. Yessenia and I exited the stage from another rather disappointing set—at least we made a couple of dollars each—to our familiar songs by Enigma.

The head dancer, Kelly, the tall, thin strawberry blonde, approached us after we exited the stage. She grinned, deepening her smile lines. I couldn't tell if the dark circles under her eyes and her sunken cheeks were the result of age or drugs, since I didn't consider myself an expert in either.

"I'm wrestling next," she said. "Come watch."

"Wrestling who?" I asked. I hadn't been to any wrestling events in person and could only picture the wild antics I'd seen on TV. I imagined Kelly being body-slammed against ropes and hitting another girl over the head with a chair.

"Wrestling whoever bids the most," she said.

"Are you wrestling a girl?" Yessenia asked.

"Not tonight, my regular's here."

"How do you know he's going to bid the most?" I said.

"Oh he will," she said. "He has money. I don't know what he does for work, but he's loaded. Always comes in a limo."

I couldn't picture anyone coming to this alcohol-free club in this seedy part of town in a limo. Then again, it was Hollyweird.

Because we were changing costumes, we missed seeing Kelly's auction, but made it down in time to see her match. The floor of the ring was covered by a blue tarp. The few customers had gathered around.

"Isn't there supposed to be mud?" I asked Yessenia.

"I don't know. Maybe they bring it out or something."

A bald man in his 60s with a beer belly walked to the center. He was wearing a t-shirt and shorts, courtesy of the Tropicana Club.

Oh yeah, I thought, he's exactly who I'd want to fondle me in the ring with people watching.

"Okay, remember the rules," the DJ said. "You can touch the dancer anywhere, except where you want to touch her." A handful of men chuckled. "Are you ready?" The DJ tried to pump up the sparse crowd's energy, no small feat in a "dry" club. "So, who do you think'll win this round? Is Kelly going to kick his ass, or what?"

The contestant grinned and leaned into the mic. "I sure hope so." More laughter.

I rolled my eyes. "This is lame. Seriously?"

Yessenia ignored me.

Kelly came down a flight of stairs in a string bikini. She entered the ring. A few floor guys held what looked to be plastic condiment bottles, the kind you see holding mustard and ketchup on dinner tables. The guys squirted shiny liquid on both contestants and drizzled more on the ground.

Inside the ring, Kelly lunged at the old man, who more than allowed her to tackle him to the ground where they slipped and slid around in the oil. On his stomach, the man attempted to get up, but fell back down. She straddled his back and acted like she was riding a rodeo horse, slapping him on the butt. The men in the audience loved this.

"Oh, are you going to take that, sir?" The DJ laughed.

"This looks so cliché," I whispered to Yessenia. "Does Kelly do this same act with him every week? That guy needs a better hobby."

When the man rose to his knees, Kelly slipped to the ground. Their skin shimmered under the lights. He reached for her and she allowed him to pin her to the ground. Before he could celebrate, his hands slipped off her wrists. She smirked, rolled out from under him, and shook his face into her voluptuous implants.

Awww, poor guy. I leaned close to Yessenia. "This is stupid."

She didn't say anything, but studied their moves.

It was cheesy, but I couldn't stop watching. There was nothing else to do, since they cut the music and nobody could do dances during the match. Eventually, Kelly was declared the victor. Big surprise.

"Next up, we'll be auctioning Marisol," the DJ said.

I was surprised to hear Marisol's name. I scanned the club, but didn't see her anywhere.

Bored, Yessenia and I headed upstairs to the dressing room. Upon entering the large room, we saw Marisol crying at her dressing station; a manager was yelling at her.

"You have a choice to make," the manager demanded. "Get down there now."

"I told you I ain't gonna wrestle no guy."

"Then pack your shit and leave!" He stomped away.

Yessenia and I moved to our station and pretended to fidget with our hair.

"Fuck you!" Marisol yelled. "I guess you want me to go back on fucking welfare! That's your fault. You fucking dick." He must have heard her, but left anyway, ignoring her insults. She wiped her eyes, began throwing her makeup in a bag, and acknowledged our presence. "This sucks. He's such an ass. I was all proud of myself getting off welfare and supporting my baby girl, but I guess I have no choice. Now, I gotta go back on it. Asshole."

"There're other clubs," Yessenia said.

"Yeah," I said. "Why don't you get hired at another place?" Having been in the same desperate situation, I couldn't help but think of Jacob. If I didn't start making more money soon, I would've had to go back on welfare, too. I remembered how shitty I felt on it and how good it felt to close that chapter in my life, albeit I had replaced one bad feeling with another. I hated to see Marisol have to resort to public assistance again.

She sniffled and paused a moment. "Maybe I will. I dunno."

Not wanting to be sucked into her drama, Yessenia and I went downstairs to make money. We didn't have any luck and sat down instead. There were more dancers than customers.

At the end of the night, after tipping out the "house mom" and the club itself, we realized how bad our shift had been—we barely had enough to cover the gas, food, and energy to get there—not more than $50 apiece. Two worthless shifts out of three wasn't a good sign.

Kelly approached us. "Can you two give me a lift? I'm not far from here."

On the way to her place, Kelly gave us some details about her life. "Yeah, so I'm the typical story: Small town girl, came to California to make it as an actress. Pretty stupid huh?"

"No, I don't think so," I lied. Since Kirk was acting and had some extra roles on television, I knew how hard it was to "make it" in Hollywood. Most wouldn't survive.

"Well, I still wanna act, but I'm dancing for now until it pans out."

Judging from her face and mannerisms, she had turned to drugs to ease her disappointment.

"You can slow down." She pointed to a run-down building that appeared to be a cross between a motel and apartment. "I'm up ahead, on the left." It was an extended stay place. At one time in its history, it might've been a nice hotel. Not anymore. Tattered curtains blew in the breeze from an open upstairs window. Shopping carts and trash lined the parking lot. Buildings on either side of hers had black metal bars across the windows, graffiti on the walls, and fencing around the front yards.

I couldn't imagine having to live there. Life wasn't so bad for me after all. At least my neighborhood was safe. I didn't want to end up like her and thought God sent her as a warning.

"Thanks for the ride. See you both next time." Kelly hopped out.

As it turned out, there wasn't a next time. Yessenia and I refused to drive all the way to Hollywood if we weren't even making close to what we had made at Club Flamingo. Plus, neither of us realized we'd be expected to be mud and oil wrestlers. Maybe we'd return once the place regained its liquor license. Until then, it was too dead to make money unless you were a major hustler. We weren't operating at that level yet.

*   *   *

Humiliated, we walked past the street beggars and ascended the creaky steps to Club Flamingo. If our noses weren't upturned before, they sure were now.

"Another ten free minutes special?" Staring at my reflection in the locker room mirror, I reapplied my lipstick and smacked my lips together.

"I'm going for a smoke." Yessenia led the way and I followed.

"Do you think the owners will notice we skip all the specials?" I asked.

"Don't care." She flicked open her lighter and lit a cigarette.

I sat down, leaned against the grimy wall and looked at the Los Angeles skyline. "This place grosses me out so much. At least at the Tropicana, we were in charge, not the men. Here, they keep grinding on me."

She took a long drag.

"Having to hold hands, dancing against them." My stomach hurt. I stared out the window. The sparkling lights seemed dimmer than before.

"I'm calling out sick tomorrow," she said.

"No, please don't," I said. "I hate coming here without you. My credit card's maxed and I have to buy milk and diapers for Jacob."

She didn't answer.

"I can't stand clocking in and out." I closed my eyes. "The whole thing makes me feel like the life is being sucked out of me." I blinked and let the colored lights fade into one another. My life felt like a suffocating trap: I would hostess for money, feel disgusted when someone grabs me, call in sick, need money more than ever, go back to the club and feel disgusted. It was as if every man who clocked me in polluted my soul a little bit more. And because neither Yessenia nor I liked to drive in alone, I was subject to her depression and whims and she was subject to mine.

*   *   *

We continued to see our clients outside of the club to make up the difference between our bills and our ability to pay our bills. I hated having to pass up seeing Jason or the other men I was interested in so I could arrange everything around Mark's availability and my shifts at Club Flamingo. Working nights wasn't as good as it first seemed.

The last weekend in August before the start of my first semester at the university, I had to buy a car, though I wasn't sure how I'd make the payments. Even with Mark's kind offer, I couldn't rely on him alone—I didn't know how long I could keep up the charade with him.

I researched autos through *Consumer Reports* and found that the Honda Accord had the highest safety rating and the best resale value. I felt that all decisions should be logical, practical ones, of course. After haggling for hours, I drove home in my new sedan. My contract noted my down payment would be paid the next day via cashier's check, which would replace my dummy check that I had given them.

At home, I opened my briefcase one last time, counted out exactly $5000, placed it into an envelope and slid it into my purse.

At the bank, I rested my hands on the counter. "I'd like to get a cashier's check."

The young, good-looking teller smiled. "Okay, miss. Write down the amount and the payee here for me."

I did and slid the paper back to him.

"And how would you like to pay for that?"

I looked around, lowered my voice, and said, "Cash. I have it all here in cash."

He raised an eyebrow. We both knew I quite frequently purchased money orders with an awfully large number of small bills. This was a record amount.

"Would you like to have a seat?" he said. "It's going to take me a few minutes to count and verify this." In his two hands, he took the fat stack of money back to his manager.

"No problem," I said. "Take your time."

Bet you wish you knew how I acquired all that cash, I thought. And you'll never guess, either.

I kept him and the other tellers curious. It was my dirty little secret. And I acted increasingly proud of that, even though I felt empty inside.

"It's ready." He handed me the check.

I glanced around, folded the check in half and put it securely into the bottom of my purse. No way was I going to lose that check.

*   *   *

With a new car, it became easier for me to go to more nightclubs and parties than before—distractions from my reality. It didn't matter that Yessenia and I weren't yet of legal drinking age; we were friends with club promoters, which assured us easy entry.

We both knew the value of short skirts, tall heels, and girly giggles. We never owned fake IDs; we didn't need to. As long as we dressed cute and flirted freely, we were welcome to walk past the hours-long lines, past the VIP line, and right onto the red carpets. Our club promoter friends quickly ushered us past security. I felt like a celebrity. Although we gained entrance into the 21-and-over venues, we opted not to drink alcohol in them. No sense in getting busted for doing something stupid.

Men bought us sodas and waters and slipped us their numbers. We didn't need to bring money for drinks, all it took was some suggestive dancing on the dance floor and we could be assured we wouldn't go thirsty. To fend off the more aggressive men, Yessenia and I did the "lesbian act" (dancing with each other to prove we weren't interested in men) and pushed away anyone who tried to get too close.

*   *   *

In addition to Jason, still my favorite, and the other miscellaneous men I met off the Internet, I began dating a police officer named Robert.

Robert bought booze for me and Yessenia—he was probably trying to get me in bed, but never succeeded. Through Robert, Yessenia and I gained easy access to feed our increasing at-home alcohol consumption. At 6'-4" with a blonde buzz cut and blue eyes, he wasn't my typical dark-haired type, but I was an equal-opportunity dater and didn't discriminate.

"When are you going to wear your cop uniform for me?" I asked him after a make-out session on my couch. Since he was a foot taller than me, it was awkward to kiss unless we were sitting down. I ended up straddling him like a booster seat.

"I don't know. There's something I want to talk to you about." Robert brushed his fingers along my cheek. "Are you still dating other people?"

I gave him a sideways glance. "Yeah." I changed the subject. I sensed he wanted to express emotions I wasn't ready to hear about.

The next weekend, Robert came over late in the evening after his shift to pick me up for a date.

"Where are we going?" I asked.

"To the beach." He took my hand and led me to his car.

"But isn't it going to be closed?" The beach curfew was 10 PM; it was well after 9.

"We'll see." He opened my car door. We sat in his Jeep and drove off. The wind whipped my hair around.

"How's work?" I asked. Before Robert, I never personally knew any police officers and since he wasn't much of a talker, it was still so new to me.

"I had to stay late to fill out a report. We all hate it when anything happens at the end of a shift. I don't like the paperwork."

"Any word yet about them letting you get a motorcycle?"

"Nope. I'm still waiting." He pulled into the beach parking lot. "But if they don't let me soon, I might find a job in another city."

I looked at the clock. "It's after ten. They already locked up the gates on the pier."

"Come on." He grinned.

Uncertain, I held his hand and followed him along the fence. Robert looked both ways. He grabbed hold of the chain link fence, climbed over it, and hopped down on the other side. This was an interesting sight. Here was a tall, muscular cop "breaking in" to the beach. I climbed over the fence after him. Within minutes, we were laying on the sand kissing to the sound of the waves crashing. It took me two days to get the sand out of places it didn't belong.

My nights felt like life in the fast lane.

One of my friends—never dated him—borrowed his dad's Porsche to impress me. I sat down inside the soft leather bucket seat and hardly noticed at all when the car smoothly accelerated to three digits on the freeway, whisking us away to a dance club.

I felt invincible.

While I continued studying and taking care of Jacob during the day, I met other people off the Internet and Yessenia and I partied more during evenings we weren't working.

One night, I couldn't decide whether to go out with Robert the cop or another guy, James, a nice Jewish man whom I had started dating. Dark-haired and handsome, James had a prior history of athletic steroid abuse. He confided in me that the steroids shrank his penis. I didn't know how to respond to that and actually kept my mouth shut for once. He worked in a successful family business, and was sweet, to the point of being more a friend than a date.

Being indecisive as usual, I accepted both invitations. I made another terrible lapse in judgment and allowed Robert to take me and my son to the movies. I introduced him to Jacob as "my friend" and Robert and I maintained the friendly façade around my son. If I could go back in time that would've been one of the many decisions I might have changed; I wouldn't have exposed Jacob to any man I wasn't exclusively dating.

Robert couldn't understand why I rushed him home afterward. I used the excuse that Jacob needed to go to bed, which he did. After Robert left, I went to dinner with James in the later evening. Robert did not know about my double-booking; James did but didn't care.

I figured my behavior was what college partying was all about.

A couple months after Robert and I had started dating, he came to my house to pick me up for dinner.

When I answered the door, I found Robert holding a large bouquet of colorful flowers. He smiled, handed them to me, and we hugged.

To get eye-level with me, he took steps down and held my hand. With a serious expression, he opened his mouth to speak then paused.

I tilted my head. "Yes?"

"Miranda." He took a deep breath. "I love you."

My jaw dropped. I couldn't help it. I didn't see it coming. I was speechless.

He searched my eyes, waiting for my response.

Robert was such a sweet guy. I couldn't mislead him. "Thank you." I embraced him to avoid his stare. It would've been easier to return the words then make some excuse and blow him off the next day.

He pulled back. "That's it? That's how you feel?" He shook his head and closed his eyes. "Are you still dating other men?"

"Yes. I told you I was."

"That was months ago. I'm not dating anyone else." He let go of my hand. "Miranda, I can't do this anymore." He backed up. "I'm going to go now."

That was it. I stood there on my doorstep and watched Robert walk away. I never meant to hurt him and I felt terrible about that. But beyond that, I was irritated that he didn't heed my request at the beginning about not falling for me.

*   *   *

Growing up, my friends used to tell me that I was book smart but had no common-sense.

I felt fearless until I met the handsome young Italian, Giovanni. He was another random Internet date. I made a stupid decision and, without knowing him, agreed to have him pick me up from my place. We drove toward the Pacific Coast Highway. With the window down, I let my hair whip in my face. Eventually my cheeks felt as cold as ice and I put the window back up.

No other cars were near us on this late night. Giovanni stared at me, looked back at the road, and back at me.

"Do you trust me?" he asked abruptly.

"What?" I said.

I must have heard incorrectly. I realized I had no idea where we were going, nobody knew who I was with, and I had never asked him for his last name.

"I said, 'Do you trust me?'" His voice deepened and took on a menacing tone.

The hairs on the back of my neck bristled and my stomach jumped into my throat. I could see the headlines: "Unidentified female, age 20, discovered in the fields. Cause of death: asphyxiation." I realized I might have to jump out of that moving vehicle.

I turned toward him and said, "I don't know. Do you trust me?"

He chuckled like a maniacal villain in a horror flick. "You don't know me."

I wanted to go home. "You don't know me, either." I had no better strategy than to mirror his threatening attitude.

Fortunately, he stopped the nonsense, took me to shoot some pool as we had planned, and returned me home. I promised myself never to go out with Giovanni again.

But did I learn my lesson? No. All I knew was that I was having fun. The dates had nothing to do with money, unlike my work and my clients, so they felt like an escape.

Because of Giovanni, I arranged to meet my next blind date at a public location, a coffeehouse. While I stood in line to order, a man approached me and flirted. I assumed it was my date Antonio.

I was wrong.

When the stranger picked up his coffee, he said, "I don't think I'm who you think I am."

Unsure at first whether it was Antonio who was messing with me or a stranger, I laughed it off. The man realized I was there to meet someone else and excused himself.

I took my hot chocolate outside, where I ran into anther good-looking imposter. Flabbergasted with two false alarms, I sat down by myself at a small table.

Two men approached me. "Hey, mind if we join you?" one asked.

"Sure." I shrugged. "Why not?" Everyone else and their brother were hitting on me.

"Are you waiting for someone?" asked the second one.

"Yes." I relayed my two mishaps.

"Are you all by yourself?" the first one asked.

"Yes."

"That's not safe," he said. "I know we don't know you, but I'm uncomfortable seeing a pretty girl like you waiting for some stranger late at night out here alone."

"Want us to wait with you?" his buddy asked.

I assured them I was fine.

"We're going to catch a movie over there in a few minutes," the first one said. "Would you mind if I gave you my phone number? If this guy you're waiting for turns out to be a creep, call us. We can be back real quick."

I agreed. That should have been an omen. But I wasn't superstitious.

Soon after the pair left for the theater, Antonio arrived. He was as he described himself: about 5'-8", a muscular Italian with brown hair and intense brown eyes.

"Would you like to go for gelato?" Antonio said. "I know a great place down the coast."

My spidey sense wasn't tingling, so I agreed to hop into his convertible classic sports car.

When we drove past the last signs of civilization nearby without stopping, I became uncomfortable.

"Where are we going?" I said.

"I want to show you something."

"What?" I hoped it wasn't a part of him I didn't want to see.

"We're almost there." He turned off of the main road and ascended a deserted hillside street. The car pulled into an empty lot.

I thought, he is going to kill me. Why do I keep doing this to myself? Am I a thrill-seeker or something? Should I call those guys? Wait, I don't have access to a phone. I don't know where I am or this guy's license plate.

"Come here," he said as he turned off the ignition. "Follow me."

Where else could I go? I stared up at the moonlit sky. Nobody would hear me scream from up there. He led me toward a cliff.

"Look." Antonio tried to reach for my hand, but I pretended not to notice. He pointed to a large abandoned white tent—its sides were flapping in the wind—a perfect place for a crime. "They've cleared these fields to build houses and a golf course. All this beauty will be gone." He motioned toward the coast.

Beyond the cliff, the black ocean stretched as far as the eye could see. It was beautiful, but I couldn't shake my discomfort, the feeling I wasn't safe.

He seemed to notice my lack of interest. "C'mon, let's go get the best gelato around."

Grateful to be back in the car, I remained silent.

After a chilly dessert, on the way back to the coffeehouse, he said, "Why did you get in the car with me?"

Here we go again with the "do you trust me?" bit.

I shrugged. "I don't know." Because I'm a freaking idiot, I thought.

"Did you get in because I asked you to? You don't know me. I could be some dangerous guy."

"But you're not," I said, hoping I was right.

"But I could be. You need to be more careful about who you get in the car with. It's not safe to be out here by yourself."

Well, I thought, why did you invite me? I let the rest of his lecture fly out the window with the wind. But I knew he was right. Along with the Giovanni incident, that night was too weird to be passed off as a series of unrelated incidents.

I repositioned my head on my pillow and the reality of my stupid behavior hit me.

Jacob. What would have happened to him if I had been killed?

* * *

Looking back on the many mistakes I've made in my life, I realize my younger self didn't understand how extreme my situation and behavior were.

I had avoided dealing with the twisted reality of my job, the burden of single motherhood, and the fear of being alone the way my mother was by seeking attention from men.

After I entered my thirties and had another child, I also realized how much of a kid I was when I had Jacob. Jacob was especially difficult because he had special needs which weren't identified until he was older. As a small boy, he had been exhibiting what I now understand to be ADHD and Asperger's symptoms: speech delays, inability to relate socially to others or to read nonverbal cues or to maintain eye contact, inattention, lack of self-control, emotional outbursts, and constant neediness which no amount of affection could quell.

All this, along with the financial burden hanging overhead, overwhelmed me to the point that I sliced my life into many roles: mother, student, single woman, hostess, and now dancer. The problem was that they couldn't be in the same room together. And, for self-preservation, I wouldn't let them.

Chapter Twelve
WALK OF SHAME

SEPTEMBER 1998

WHEN I BECAME AN upperclassman at the university, I became so busy with school that I didn't have time to think about relationships and dating.

With a schedule that alternated between late night shifts at Club Flamingo, client dates, and daytime classes, I hardly had time for Jacob, much less myself. Friday mornings consisted of a three-hour long accounting lecture by a professor from India with a heavy accent.

It was all I could do to stay awake. The only lesson I remembered from that class was that bottled water was a stupid idea, a waste of money, and a detriment to your health.

* * *

I became friends with Wesley, another business major. He had warm brown eyes and wavy brown hair. He reminded me of a surfer.

"Hey." Wesley nudged me while we stood outside economics class waiting for the professor to show up. "Mr. Jones is giving us a boring lecture today. Let's ditch."

"What?" I said. "What will we miss?"

He shrugged. "I'll get the notes from my roommate. C'mon, let's get out of here."

"And go where?"

"Shoot pool."

I shifted the weight of my backpack onto my other shoulder. "I have another class in two hours. I don't think I have time to leave campus and get back. It takes me forever to find parking."

He laughed. "No, you goof. I meant at the student center."

"The student center?"

"I can't believe you've never gone there. Follow me."

That was the start of our pool playing and hanging out. We never dated, but I enjoyed our platonic friendship.

∗   ∗   ∗

I continued to see Mark outside of the club. Since upping the ante by offering to pay my $400 car payment each month, he carved out a bigger portion of my life for himself. Worried about becoming too reliant on his money, I accepted my other regular Hiroki's request for a "date."

While I had become accustomed to feeling like Mark's paid girl-friend during our casual meetings at the track and restaurants, it was different with Hiroki. Hiroki didn't know my address and still believed my name was "Cassie," or at least that I preferred to be called Cassie.

"Since you live over an hour away," Hiroki said, "why don't we meet at the Hilton, at the halfway point? I'd like us to go to dinner to discuss our expectations and come to agreement." Being the bank president he was, Hiroki approached everything as a business deal. "At 7:00 on Friday night, meet me in the lobby."

"Which restaurant are we going to? I'm not sure what I should wear."

"I prefer if you dress as you usually do—skirt, dressy blouse, and heels."

I expected him to tell me to dress casual, formal, or semi-formal. I wasn't used to being told exactly what to wear. This was an early in-dicator of what escorting would be like with Hiroki.

The following Friday, I walked into the hotel lobby promptly at 7 PM. Hiroki wasn't there. My heels tapped on the marble floor echoing against the cathedral ceiling. I settled into an overstuffed chair in front of a tall column facing the entryway and waited. What if Hiroki doesn't show, I worried.

An older couple took notice of me on their way to the front desk. I realized that with my legs crossed, the slit along the side of my lace-trimmed mini had ridden up. I pulled it down.

My watch said 7:05 PM—no sign of Hiroki.

The concierge, a woman about twenty years my senior, glanced at me and exchanged smirks with a male employee. I'd been leaning forward on my elbows, which caused my shimmery top to reveal a fair amount of cleavage. I sat up and shifted.

I shouldn't care what they think, I argued to myself. I was sure plenty of people waited for each other in hotel lobbies. It was none of their business. I draped my hair in front of my shoulders.

At 7:10 PM, I debated whether or not to drive home empty-handed. Give him five more minutes. That's it. I fumbled in my purse for my lipstick and compact mirror to give myself something to do.

"Cassie?" A familiar voice called out.

"Hiroki." I plastered on a fake smile and greeted him. He looked about ten years older under hotel lights than he did under club lighting. The chandeliers reflected off his glasses. I stood and politely hugged him hello.

When I noticed curious looks upon the faces of a couple of children and horrified glares from their parents, I saw what they were seeing: a wealthy Japanese man in a business suit and a young Caucasian girl in club attire, hugging in a hotel lobby—I looked like a hooker.

Hiroki put a hand behind my shoulder and led me outside.

"Did you valet your car as I instructed?"

I sure hoped he was going to pay for that. "Yes."

"Good. Let's take my car."

I sat across from him alongside a window in a restaurant high in the hills above Los Angeles. I picked at my salad. Normally I had no problem eating in front of dates, but client dates made me nervous. Being so focused on acting the part of an interested companion, I usually lost my appetite anyway.

"How much do you charge and for what?" he asked.

I almost spit out my iced tea at his bluntness. "I don't know," I said. "It depends." One of my business professors had told our class that when asked a difficult question during a meeting, answering with "it depends" was always a safe bet: it sounds intelligent, is usually acceptable, and delays the conversation long enough to give you time to think. See, college *did* pay off.

"I'm sure it depends on the amount of time you spend. What do you normally charge?"

At least he was talking time spent, not bases covered. What a relief. "It's negotiable." Good save. Another bullshit word. "My other client pays me about $400 per date. What were you thinking?"

Hiroki's eyes widened. "I was thinking closer to $200 for a couple of hours. How does that sound to you?"

I took another sip of tea. Damn, he probably thinks I'm doing "extras" for that $400, which couldn't be further from the truth. Although disappointed, I needed the money. I justified the price cut by considering the extra phone time Mark required that Hiroki would not. I sighed. "I suppose I could do that."

Hiroki relaxed back into his seat. "Great. I'm glad we settled that. I have a restaurant I'd like to take you to next week. How about Saturday night?"

I had already scheduled a date with Mark. "Saturday doesn't work for me. Can we make it Friday?"

"That's fine. Do you have any business suits? I'd prefer if you dressed in a skirt suit or slacks."

The hotel lobby scene had irked him. I knew this man had an image to uphold. I thought of my closet full of short skirts, tank tops, jeans and t-shirts.

"I have a pair of lilac slacks with matching jacket."

"Purple? Does it look professional?"

"I've worn it to job interviews." I couldn't imagine having to purchase an expensive outfit for one date; the suit would probably cost more than I'd make. Still new at this escorting thing, I didn't know who should be expected to pay for clothing requests. I didn't want to look naïve by asking. I still had a lot to learn about the business.

He agreed and drove me back to my car where he paid the valet and casually slipped me $200 as we hugged goodbye.

Over the next couple of weeks, I enjoyed panoramic views from the revolving lounge on the 34th Floor of the Bonaventure Hotel, as well as fine cuisine at the Biltmore Hotel in Pershing Square in Downtown Los Angeles. The best part: unlike Mark, Hiroki didn't want to openly hold hands unless we were in his car. The worst thing I had to deal with was an occasional hand on my thigh during the drive. I thought I could get used to escorting, so long as it didn't go any further than that.

"I have two tickets to *The Phantom of the Opera* at the Pantages Theater in Hollywood," Hiroki said. "I want you to accompany me."

I'd wanted to see that show but couldn't afford it.

"That's sounds fun. What would you like me to wear?" I had become accustomed to asking him.

"Do you own an evening gown?"

*   *   *

Whenever I went to Hollywood, I ignored the theaters and other venues that were way beyond my financial means.

While Hiroki and I stood in line at the Pantages, he explained, "When this place opened in 1930, it cost $1.25 million dollars, and that was during the Great Depression. They held the Academy Awards here for over a decade."

I was impressed even though the outside of this Hollywood landmark was a bit disappointing. The elaborate interior, however, was amazing. Holding onto Hiroki's arm, I felt as though I had gone back in time as we walked through the extravagant lobby.

We had great seats in the orchestra section. At that moment, it became my most enjoyable paid "date" yet. The singing was phenomenal and the lighting, music, and dramatic acting breathtaking.

During intermission, I excused myself to the ladies' room. Of course there was a wait. I stood patiently and admired the expensive-looking evening gowns on the women surrounding me. I admired their sparkling jewels and meticulously-applied makeup and hairstyles. My hair hung down; my make-up was simple. I compared their classy attire to my black spaghetti-strapped full-length dress with a sheer lace midsection. I had bought it on clearance at the mall. I held my head high; they looked rich, but I looked hot.

Still, I felt inadequate, like a fraud. But Hiroki was paying for confidence and I was going to deliver.

After leaving the restroom, I heard a female voice call out, "Miranda?"

Hiroki didn't know my real name and I didn't want him to. I turned my head, scanning the many faces.

"Miranda, I thought it was you."

Visions of laughter and juicy gossip flashed through my mind. Standing before me was Julie with her mousy blonde hair, green eyes, acne, and imperfect teeth. Her boyfriend Aaron had been my manager at the restaurant I worked at during high school. I remembered civics class, my senior year in high school. Julie and Yessenia kept talking and giggling, and I couldn't hear the teacher's lecture. I tried to hush them, but they made fun of me for being a goody-two-shoes.

"Julie, oh my gosh," I said. "It's been years. How are you?"

"Great. Shit, I can't believe how fast the time's gone."

My stomach sank. What if she found out who I came with? She could tell my other friends.

I took an offensive approach. "I'm here with a guy from work, a networking thing." I acted nonchalant and changed the topic. "You know, I'm studying for my bachelor's degree. What about you?"

"Right on. I'm not in college, but I'm still dating Aaron. He surprised me with this." She spread her arms up toward the ceiling. "We got seats up on the Mezzanine. Isn't it awesome here? Where are you sitting?"

Out of the corner of my eye, I saw Hiroki coming toward me. I had to get rid of her. "Down in the main section. I have to go, but it was great seeing you again."

The lights started to dim, signaling the end of intermission. "Can we meet up later?" she asked.

Yeah, much later. "That'd be cool." I hugged her good-bye, wove my way through the crowd and hurried Hiroki back inside for fear that Julie might see him.

During the second half of the play, I slouched into my seat and pulled my hair alongside my face. I kept feeling like Julie was up on the Mezzanine, looking down at me. To keep my mind off of her and the embarrassment of being Hiroki's escort, I studied the faces of the lead characters Christine and the Phantom as they became caught up in their doomed attraction for each other. I wanted to be Christine, to have a man fall so desperately in love with me that he'd do anything to rescue me from my life.

* * *

Although our rendezvous were usually during daytime, Mark sprung a night date on me. "I thought you'd enjoy taking a stroll along Universal Citywalk, near Hollywood."

Oh, great—tons of college kids my age. "Sounds good."

I had had fun people-watching with my friends there. I didn't want to be one of the people being watched, which is exactly how I felt as Mark insisted on holding my hand in public.

The eyes of passersby lingered a little too long in our direction. Holding hands with a man nearly three times my age who was not my father made my stomach churn.

They seated us at a table in middle of the restaurant.

Mark studied my face. "Mia, is something wrong?"

"No, why?"

"You don't seem yourself today."

Funny comment, I thought, since you don't know who I am, only who I pretend to be. "Why do you say that?"

"It seems like you don't want to be here."

"No, it's not that."

"What is it?"

"You want to know?" *I wish I could tell you the fucking truth: you're older than my dad, I'm ashamed to be with you, and even though I'm not selling my body for sex, I feel like a whore.*

"Yes," he said.

"I have bad cramps. My stomach hurts."

Mark laughed.

How insensitive, I thought. "Why are you laughing?"

"I thought you were embarrassed to be here with me."

Damn, you're smarter than you seem. "Do you have any Tylenol?"

"No, but I can buy you some."

"Do you mind if we cut our evening short? This hurts so badly that I want to cry."

He reached across the table for my hands. "Mia, why didn't you say something? Of course."

His fingers rubbed mine. It made me feel gross. I fought back tears. I needed the money.

He took me home. When he embraced me, I stiffened. When he kissed me on the cheek, I cringed. He handed me cash and said goodbye, but only for another week. I forced myself to feel nothing.

After he left, I remained standing on my doorstep. Cold air numbed my face. Only a few more years of college, I reminded myself—hang in there.

∗   ∗   ∗

I knew what it meant to hang in there.

For my sixteenth birthday, much to my disappointment, my first boyfriend Henry had bought me lingerie. I had wanted a teddy bear.

Even though I objected and it made me feel uncomfortable, Henry pressured me to watch pornography. I liked Disney movies.

He tried to convince me to do a threesome. I wanted to play Monopoly.

When I finally tried to break up with him, he raped me.

Good-bye childhood.

I hated myself for not fighting back. I hated myself for hanging in there. Afterward, he said, "I guess I raped you." Between my sniffles, I nodded, wanting to throw up.

*   *   *

Years had passed and I wasn't helpless anymore. I couldn't be, with Jacob to support. On the other hand, I wasn't in control, either. At Club Flamingo, the men checked us in and out like library books. It was upsetting.

The more upset work made us, the wilder Yessenia and I acted in the real world. As she drove us home from the beach one afternoon, Yessenia pulled two bananas out of a bag and gave me one.

"Did I say I was hungry?" I said. "We just ate."

She peeled her banana and wrapped her mouth around it, without biting the end off. She looked toward the driver to our left. The man's eyes widened and he failed to notice that the light turned green.

"Are you crazy?" I said.

"Your turn." She took a nibble and accelerated.

"Oh yeah?" I was game. I peeled mine and waited for the next light. Once a car pulled up alongside, I copied her performance. The guy didn't notice. More dramatically than before, I opened my mouth and slowly guided the banana in and out of my mouth. Somehow, that did the trick. He did a double-take. I saw the glare of a woman in the passenger seat. I tried not to choke on the banana when I burst out in laughter.

Yessenia and I found we had more power than we knew. We didn't need to be at the mercy of men at work.

We could be the ones in control.

*   *   *

"So you stopped seeing Robert, the cop, because he said he loved you?" Jason asked.

"Basically, yes," I said, "I don't need that stress."

"And you're irritated that your sugar daddy called you on the phone yesterday?"

"He's my client, not a sugar daddy. And if he wants my time, he should compensate me for that."

"Doesn't he make your car payments and give you cash each time he sees you?"

"Yes, but that's the agreement we have."

Jason brushed my hair from my bare shoulders. "I told you that this job was going to change you."

"What are you talking about? I'm the same person you met."

"True, you're still not having sex with me, but otherwise you're different." Jason lay down in his bed next to me and kissed my hand. "You used to trust people more and not view men like this. You were a little more naïve and innocent."

"I haven't had sex with anyone for two years, not just you."

"Why is that?"

"I told you. After getting pregnant with Jacob—even though we used protection—I'm terrified of another accident. And after Ricky and his abuse, I'm not ready to be that close to anyone."

"Close emotionally, maybe." Jason laughed. "But you're ready to take off your clothes for strangers."

"I'm still wearing a bikini. It's not any worse than going to the beach."

"I have nothing against dancers. I'm friends with more than a few. But dancing for men is not the same as hanging out at the beach."

I gave him a dirty look.

"Miranda, don't you see the difference? Besides, you say you hate hostessing."

"Yes, I do. That's why I'd rather dance. Dancers are more in control than hostesses. Besides, there's nothing wrong with me doing whatever I feel like doing."

"That's true, but you're changing. Things that you would have never done are now okay for you to do. You conveniently change what you're willing to do when money is the goal, even if it involves taking off your clothes."

"For Jacob, I'll do what I have to." I smiled. "Anyway, my clothes are off right now. You don't have a problem with that, do you?"

"Of course I don't." He caressed my shoulder. "Why aren't we together?"

"We are together right now." I squirmed closer to him.

"Yes, I love being with you right now. But tomorrow, are you going to be with someone else?"

"Let's focus on right now." I wrapped my arms around him. "This is fun. Besides you're dating other people, too."

"I don't like hearing about you putting yourself in danger with strangers. Now you're meeting men in hotels for money—"

"Wait a minute. I didn't go inside his hotel room. Dancing and hostessing are only jobs. I would never sleep with men for money."

"How far would you go for money?"

"That's not fair."

"I don't want you to get hurt, or hear about you on the evening news." He faced me. He had a sad look in his eyes.

"I have a kid. I can take care of myself."

He squeezed my hand and kissed my cheek.

My heart fluttered. I closed my eyes. "Life will be different soon," I assured him.

"I'm sure it will be." He grabbed his pack of cigarettes and lighter. "I'm going to have a smoke."

I watched him leave the room, wanting to stop him, but not knowing why.

CHAPTER THIRTEEN
CHAOS

October 1998

MOM WAS UTTERLY FRUSTRATED with my stonewalling.

"How on Earth did you buy such an expensive car?" she asked.

Since when was a Honda Accord considered "expensive"?

My parents had been divorced for years and didn't communicate often. "Dad cosigned for me, so I was able to get a low interest rate, and a long loan term." In truth, I wouldn't let them extend me beyond a forty-eight month contract, which I fully intended to pay back in two or three years. I didn't want to graduate college with a lot of debt.

"You and Yessenia have been buying a lot of new clothes lately."

"Not really. It was all on sale."

"And you and Yessenia have been going out to eat a lot."

"I wouldn't consider the cheap corner diner as eating out. And we don't go out that often."

Mom pursed her lips together; her eyes burned into me.

* * *

I made my car payments with Mark's help and paid my rent and other bills by working a few shifts at Club Flamingo each week. Yessenia and I still wanted to quit, but we couldn't get hired at a topless club until we were twenty-one, which wouldn't be for three more months. Nude clubs hired at eighteen, since they didn't serve alcohol, but we hadn't worked up the nerve to audition at a nude club, especially since we didn't do so well at Tropicana, with bikinis on.

*   *   *

My younger brother Kirk and I had grown up together at our mom's house, spending the weekends at our dad's. Our half-sister Amber was six-and-a-half years older than me, but lived solely with our dad. A few years after she graduated college, she met a man at work, and a couple of after that, he proposed. She asked me to be her maid-of-honor.

As Amber's October wedding approached, my semester grades were looking good so far and I focused for the time being upon my duties as maid-of-honor. I threw her a bridal shower and endured her bachelorette party, where I viewed the male stripper more as a colleague than as thrilling entertainment. Like everyone in my family besides Kirk, Amber had no idea what I was doing for a living and had never heard of hostess clubs. For their sake, I continued to play the part of the smart little honors student who made a mistake by getting pregnant, but otherwise led a respectable life.

My mother booked a hotel room—no small task since nearly every hotel on Hospitality Lane in San Diego was filled to capacity for some unknown reason. I made arrangements for Jacob to stay with a babysitter for the weekend. The plan was that I would meet Kirk and our mother back at the hotel room late Saturday night, after the reception was over.

*   *   *

Jason took me out to dinner the weekend before the wedding. Knowing he was a massage therapist at peace with little, I knew he didn't have much money. Therefore, I wasn't expecting anything fancy. With anyone else I would have, but Jason was different.

"Where are we going?" I sat in the passenger seat of his car, wondering why he wanted me to dress up. Usually with him I wore jeans and a t-shirt.

"It's a surprise." He smiled and squeezed my hand.

I liked his touch.

He pulled the car into a parking lot in front of a bead store. Inside, the owner recognized him and gave him a warm welcome. Jason introduced me.

Jason asked, "Would you like me to make you a necklace?" Jewelry-making was one of his hobbies.

"I'd love that, but isn't it a lot of work?"

"You're worth it." He pointed to cases of sparkling colors. "I was thinking a Y-shaped necklace would look nice on you. You can pick out what colors you like."

"Aren't they expensive?"

"Don't worry about it." He led me to a display in the corner where he picked up a tear drop-style necklace and put it around my neck. "What do you think?"

I smiled. Although men had given me gemstones, gold, and diamond necklaces, not one had ever offered to make me one. Warmth rose to my cheeks.

After leaving the store with a beautiful silver chain and pretty purple beads, we continued our date and ended up at a parking structure near a hotel.

"Do you mind walking?" he asked. "I'd rather spend money on you than a valet."

"Of course, I don't mind."

He came around to open my door, held out his arm, and led me into the hotel, through the lobby, to their signature restaurant. Soon we stood, hand-in-hand, at the host desk.

"We have reservations," Jason said.

The maître d' led us to a comfortable corner booth.

Different servers filled our water glasses, brought us bread, and took our order.

I marveled at how no other date—besides clients—had taken me to a place so nice. Jason had dressed up for me. He was clean shaven, his long hair pulled back. That's when I noticed Jason's shoes. Why didn't I see that before? Was it because he looked more dressed up once he put on his suit jacket after we exited his car? Below his slacks, Jason sported tennis shoes. I was mortified. This was why I never dated college guys, because they didn't have money and didn't know how to behave.

I concentrated on cutting my steak, trying to ignore his shoes and the fact that he wouldn't valet. I remembered the necklace and tried to focus on that. I smiled and stared into his eyes.

"Your sister's wedding is next weekend, right?" he said. "I'm going to miss you."

"Yeah. It's going to be hectic between the wedding and the pictures at the beach and the reception. I'm not even bringing Jacob." And even if it wasn't going to be hectic, I thought, I would not bring a man in tennis shoes.

* * *

The next week flew by. The wedding was a lovely outdoor ceremony with a rose-petal lined path, a harpist, and a violinist. I fixed my sister's wedding gown train when she stopped at the altar to say her vows.

Before I knew it, I found myself on a sandy beach in a dark green full-length bridesmaid dress, along with my sister in her extravagant wedding dress, three other bridesmaids, my new brother-in-law, his best man, and three other groomsmen. The photographer snapped pictures, trying to catch it all before the sun completely set. The limo driver waited in the car up on the street.

"Now that we did all the serious pictures," my sister said, "let's do some silly ones."

I blinked away the oncoming effects of the limo champagne and watched the guys goofing off for the camera. Then it was the ladies' turn. None of the women could agree on a pose and kept laughing, probably from intoxication.

Mostly quiet up until this point, I spoke up. "Why don't we do a sexy pose?" With my sister in the middle, adorned by two bridesmaids on either side, we pulled up our gowns, lifted one leg and pointed our toes down into the sand, in a can-can style pose. I gave my most seductive grin. After the camera flashes died down, my vision focused on the best man who was staring intently at me.

He winked and approached.

Dark and handsome, the best man was an old high school buddy of my new brother-in-law's. He was charming, worked as a waiter, and was going nowhere in life. I later discovered he had no aspirations to do much else than chase every short skirt that crossed his sight, but I wasn't making my wedding plans.

Mr. Best Man suggested that we ask the limo driver to take us to a nearby liquor store to buy additional booze for the group, since we had depleted our supply.

What a great idea that was.

"C'mon out," my sister said. "Everyone's waiting upstairs at the reception hall for us."

In the limo, I couldn't see the door. Everything was jumping in circles around me, the people, the hotel entrance, the world. I felt sick to my stomach. The best man grabbed my hand and pulled me out-side.

"Here's another toast to the new couple." The room of nearly two hundred raised their practically empty champagne glasses. I lost count of how many toasts there were. Maybe it was the champagne, or maybe the tequila shots being passed to me from under the head table by the best man.

I'm sure I slurred through my speech. I danced the night away and was disappointed when midnight arrived.

"I'll walk you to your car," the best man offered. He slipped his hand around my waist to support my wobbly frame.

"I can't drive like this." I giggled.

"We don't have to drive anywhere." He squeezed me closer.

Somewhere along the walk, I explained my current views on sex-free relationships and said I wasn't going to change my mind.

He assured me of his honorable intentions.

I ended up making out in my car in the parking garage with the best man. It felt good, I was drunk, and so I went with it. He thrust his tongue into my mouth and I played with it.

I pulled back and wiped my lips. "My hair hurts."

"If you take your hair down, it will help." He reached over and pulled about thirty bobby pins from my hair. His fingers massaged my scalp and I moaned with pleasure. White baby's breath flowers scat-tered over us. I leaned on his shoulder.

Not long after, I found myself in the passenger seat of my sedan with the best man crouched on the floor in front of me underneath my dress.

"Are you hot down there?" I stopped him.

He peeked out from underneath my gown and wiped sweat from his brow. "No, I'm fine. Does it feel good or do you want me to stop?"

"No, I like what you're doing."

He grinned and went back under. I jumped as he nibbled and kissed the insides of my thighs. I pushed the seat back as far as it would go.

Heat rose to my cheeks and my toes tingled.

Before we got any further, he said, "Let's go back to my hotel."

I agreed, called my mom, told her I'd been drinking so I couldn't drive and was staying with one of the bridesmaids.

Bridesmaids? Bridesgrooms? What was the difference?

We went back to his hotel room, where I promptly fell into a drunken slumber.

*   *   *

"Miranda, I can't believe you!" Jason exclaimed. A few days had passed and I was back at home, spending my evening on the phone with him, as usual.

"What do you mean?" I asked. "You know I date a lot of different guys."

"But you made out with the best man. He was fifteen years older than you, and you didn't even know him."

"I was drunk." At that moment, I realized that telling Jason about my weekend escapade was going to do no good for anyone, but it was too late to shut my big mouth. I had become too accustomed to telling him everything without filter.

"When I said have a good time," Jason said, "I didn't mean to have *that* good of a time."

"I didn't have sex with him."

"He went down on you."

"But that's not sex. I'm still holding to my promise to myself. Since I'm not ready for a serious relationship, I'm not going to have sex. Besides kissing and touching, I didn't do anything for him. Oral sex isn't sex." Was I convincing myself or him? I felt I was copping out like President Clinton did about smoking marijuana, when he claimed he never inhaled.

"Yes, it is sex." Jason was quiet for a while. "Fine."

"Fine what?"

"That means we can do that too."

I laughed. Is that what his argument was about?

Not long after, I realized what I had been missing out on. Jason had talents that I soon discovered. Being a masseuse, he was good with his hands and he knew the human body well, but that I never imagined over so well to his tongue.

I had never been so glad to have taken that step with a man before.

*   *   *

A few weeks later, during one of my lackadaisical make-out sessions with Shane, a hot blonde-haired frat boy I had met fourteen days prior, I succumbed to temptation. I figured if guys could be all about sex, so could I.

Looking back now, I recognize that my first boyfriend Henry was not characteristic of the average male, but at that point, I based my opinions of men on him.

Shane opened the door, but I hardly entered his apartment before he pinned me against the doorframe. With an intense hunger, he kissed me all over. We made out in the doorway for all to see. He ravished my body, tore off my sweater and warmed my skin.

I nibbled on his ears. He licked my neck, stretching my dress down lower and lower and lifted my hemline up with his other hand until my bra and panties made me look like I was dressed for a dip in the pool.

Finally aware of a horrified glance from his neighbor, he pulled me inside the apartment—our bodies sandwiched together in a slippery dance. He kicked the door shut.

I tore at his shirt, he unclasped my bra. We littered the hallway with our clothes.

Soft like dough, his lips kneaded a trail down my neck, across my breasts. His cologne and pheromones blended into a drug and I was getting high.

Keys turned in the front door, reminding us that he had roommates.

He grabbed my hand and thrust me into his bedroom. He locked the door and pressed me up against the wall. Sweat from my back met the hard coldness of the wall. Two twisted branches, our bodies wound together.

His hands wrapped around me and lifted me up. I locked my legs around his waist, his face at level with my breasts.

I cried out for him to stop. Tossing aside my born-again virginity hurt.

He stopped. He wasn't angry.

I apologized, went to the bathroom, and got dressed. When I came out, he had his clothes on, too. He offered me water and we sat down next to each other on his couch. I awkwardly explained it had been awhile since I had sex, which was why it hurt.

I stared out the window while we tried to make small talk.

Less than ten minutes passed before I came to the conclusion that there wasn't much substance in him, and that we had nothing beyond attraction in common.

I politely excused myself and went home. We never spoke again.

* * *

It was about that time that an old friend of mine, Dan, came back into my life.

In high school, I didn't even know what I wanted from a boy-friend. My views were warped and my growing up skewed thanks to Henry. I didn't fully comprehend until much later in life how abnormal my teen years were.

I wanted to experience romantic love. At the time I thought Henry was the best thing that ever came along in my life, but in reality he was the worst. After he exited my life, rather than dealing with the hurt and the pain, I sought to fill the void.

During my senior year in high school, when I was drowning in tears, alcohol, and self-degradation, I met a man off the Internet who renewed my faith in humanity. A couple years older than me, Dan differed from Henry in more ways than one. Henry was Hispanic and came from a family that immersed their early adolescent boys in a world of pornography and machismo; Dan was Asian and came from a family that encouraged traditional values and respect. Henry was in his fifth year of high school; Dan was in college. Henry pretended to be a nice guy; Dan was a nice guy and he became my second boy-friend.

Dan lived a couple of hours away and comforted me on the phone while I was going through counseling for what Henry had done. It was only after our friendship developed that Dan and I briefly dated. When we met in person, his 5'9" frame and kind smile didn't intimidate me, but melted the frost. Articulate, refined, and sensitive to my needs, Dan was into art, music, and computers.

But we didn't last more than a month before I flitted to the next good-looking guy who paid me any attention. Ricky was tall, dark, and handsome, and he flattered me. He was confident and took the lead. While Dan was gentle with me, Ricky was assertive and I let him be. Ricky—another terrible mistake.

Within weeks, I was pregnant by Ricky who turned out to be physically, emotionally, and mentally abusive. If I had known, I would've never gone out with him in the first place, of course.

A counselor I convinced Ricky to see questioned whether or not his blackouts were from drug use or psychosis. The cause was neither here nor there. Within a year after Jacob's birth, after Ricky held me hostage with a butcher knife for a couple hours, I called the police who finally removed Ricky from my life.

By then I was a single mother. I was hypersensitive about being hurt by another man, yet I desired love and acceptance. This meant I sought out attention from men but kept them at an emotional distance, which only deepened my loneliness.

After our brief relationship, Dan went off and dated another woman. He also ended up with an unintended pregnancy and a failed relationship.

Dan and I started talking again and soon returned to that safe haven we found in each other's arms.

This didn't mean I forgot about Jason, however. It meant I wanted them both.

One evening, Dan came over to watch a movie with me. Wide-eyed, he stared as I tossed a vase of roses out to make room for the bouquet of flowers Dan had brought for me.

"Dating a lot of other men?" He looked hurt.

"Well, yes and no. Those roses were from a client."

"Client?" He raised an eyebrow.

"If I tell you, please don't look at me differently."

"You know I won't."

"Have you heard of hostess clubs?"

He shook his head.

I told him about Club Flamingo and about my clients. Like Jason, Dan withheld judgment.

After the movie, we reminisced about the first time we met.

"My brother, who I dragged along, thought I was nuts for driving two hours up there to see you," he said. "On the way, he kept making bets that you'd be missing limbs or be a man or something worse."

I laughed. That was before the era of electronic pictures. "So what did you think of me when you saw me the first time?"

He grinned. "You were sweet and pretty, and I loved your cat eyes."

"Cat eyes?"

"They change colors. There's a line through them, like a cat's." He faced me and took a deep breath. "Miranda, there's something I never told you."

"What's that?"

"Did you know I loved you?"

My cheeks blushed. "No," I said. "I didn't know, but we weren't serious. We only dated a couple of months."

"You were my first love. I never told you that."

Searching into his almond brown eyes, my stomach fluttered. I reached for his hand. Our fingers perfectly intertwined. His hands were smooth and soft, his touch gentle.

"You were always so good to me," I said, remembering how he never pressured me, never expected anything from me, and was always there for me when I allowed him to be.

"That's because I cared about you so much." He smiled. "I still do."

A week later, I had sex with Dan for the first time. It was sweet because it was evident we both cared for each other. Unlike with "frat boy," sex with Dan was not painful but enjoyable.

Then I thought of Jason.

So what did I do? Same thing I usually did when I became confused—phoned Jason and told him what I'd been doing.

Silence on the other end of the line.

"Jason, are you there?" I asked.

"You're fucking unbelievable, you know that?"

It was a mistake to have run to Jason this time to solve my inner problems, especially since my feelings for him were part of the problem.

"I'm not trying to torture you. I swear I'm not." Unfortunately, although I knew how I felt about him, I was incapable of telling him.

"Hold on a sec. I need a smoke."

While I waited, I tried to sort it all out, but couldn't. What was my problem?

Jason came back to the phone. "I don't know what to say, hon."

"I'm sorry."

He took a drag off his cigarette. "No, you're not."

He was probably right.

"Damn it, Miranda, you caught me off guard. You said you weren't going to have sex and I respected that. So you turn around and make out with the best man and have sex with two different men within a couple of weeks? How do you think it makes me feel?"

"I don't know what I'm doing."

"Yeah, I figured as much. I mean, when you decide to do something, you go for it, don't you? You could've at least told me 'Hey, Jason, I'm going to sleep with a bunch of guys because I can't handle the emotional intensity we share.'"

I didn't see the truth until he said it. "I don't want to hurt you." I didn't know how he understood me better than I did.

"It's a little late to say that, Miranda. You say guys are jerks. Stop and look at what you're doing."

*   *   *

I vowed to quit the Internet dating and sort out my feelings for Dan and Jason. I continued dating Dan and Jason and grew closer to them both, which only further complicated my feelings.

Neither was happy with the situation but both appreciated my candor.

*   *   *

While I had thought clubbing, dancing and gallivanting around town in the evenings would relieve my stress from hostessing, studying, and single-parenting, it had only caused more fatigue and stress.

This couldn't have been more apparent than the day I woke up late in morning and panicked when I didn't immediately see Jacob, again. After the last missing child incident, I locked him in our room every morning to keep him out of trouble until I could manage to pry my eyes open.

I found Jacob quietly sitting on the floor playing with my stereo. The remains of his breakfast—a bowl of dry Cheerios, and a sippy cup of milk—lay on his makeshift table (a milk crate). His chair, a plastic bin in which I stored papers, was overturned. Jacob looked up me and smiled. He had a big milk mustache and soggy Cheerios stuck to the front of his white footed pajamas.

"Poor Jacob." I dragged myself out of bed.

He turned away from me and rolled the dial on my stereo, flipping through the fuzzy radio stations.

I wiped his mouth clean and swore to try to take better care of him. "I promise I will get my degree and give you a better life."

Jacob stopped playing with my radio and stared up at me. His diaper was sagging. I shook my head and reached for a clean diaper and wipes. Jacob needed me and somehow I knew I needed him.

CHAPTER FOURTEEN

WAKE UP CALL

NOVEMBER 1998

NOW THAT I HAD a car, Yessenia and I took turns driving to work. Coming home late at night, after two in the morning, we talked to each other to stay awake.

One night, the conversation abruptly changed direction.

"Miranda," Yessenia said, "I'm getting pulled over by the cops."

"Shit. Are you serious?"

"Yes, but listen to me," she said. I was surprised at how calm she remained. "You need to pick up my purse. I have some pot in there, and if I get my ID card out, the cop's gonna see it."

"You have pot in here? Oh, my God. We're so dead."

"No, we're not. Roll down your window." She slowly rolled down hers as we exited the freeway, which happened to be our normal exit. "Now find the bag and hide it somewhere."

Great. Now I'm an accessory to a crime. I panicked. "Where should I put it?"

"Hide it under the seat or something."

"They'll find it there!"

"I need to pull over now, so put it somewhere. In the center console."

"Fine."

A highway patrolman approached the driver's window. "You were going pretty fast there." When he caught sight of Yessenia's model good looks, his demeanor changed. She gave him a demure smile and batted her eyelashes.

He let us go with only a warning.

"I can't believe he didn't give you a ticket," I marveled.

She shrugged. "That's probably been the twentieth time I've been pulled over and I haven't been given a ticket yet."

Not more than a few days later, we were pulled over again. This time it was by the city cops. Again, no ticket.

But when we were pulled over for the third time within a couple of weeks by the same city cops, we suspected harassment.

"Rabbit, is it?" Yessenia already knew the cop's nickname. "Are we done?" She leaned against the hood of her car.

Rabbit and his partner laughed. "So, where do you two go so late every night to be all dressed up?"

"I don't think it's any of your business. Look, I'm tired. Can we go home now?"

Reluctantly, Rabbit sent us on our way. Paranoid that he would follow us, we took a different way home. The cops didn't know where we lived. Yessenia had never changed her address with the DMV after moving out of her parents' house the year before.

*　　*　　*

During one of my scheduled "dates" with my client Hiroki, I discovered a new side to him. Up until that point, I was more comfortable with the strictly-business relationship we shared, as opposed to the one I had with Mark, who was delving into the gray area between client and boyfriend.

"I paged you and you didn't call me back last week," Hiroki complained.

"That's because I couldn't keep paying for my pager and canceled it." This was true. No need to have a cell phone and a pager anymore.

"Why don't you buy a cell phone?"

I did, I thought, but I'm not about to give you my number. It was bad enough that Mark had the number. "Because they're too expensive."

"I will buy you one."

Oh, I wasn't going to fall for that—an electronic leash. Besides, I'd be the one stuck in the contract should anything go wrong.

"I don't want a cell phone." I had only recently bought one. They were relatively new; I remembered the chunky "car phone" my friend had—it looked like the communication radios the Army used during the Vietnam War. Cell phones, although smaller, were still too bulky to fit into a sexy little purse, so I didn't always keep it with me.

"I'll buy you another pager," he said.

"I don't know. You don't need to buy anything for me. I'm okay without it."

"I cannot get a hold of you, so it makes it more difficult for me. If we are going to continue this, I need to be able to contact you."

What did I have to lose? I agreed.

We walked into the wireless store together. If it weren't for him being Japanese, I would've pretended to be his daughter. Instead, I became absorbed by the display models to create space between me and him.

A salesman came over to assist. "Sir, have you been helped yet?"

"She needs a new a pager," Hiroki said.

Damn. He's bringing me into this conversation.

"Sure I can help you with that. Which model do you have in mind?" The salesman looked curiously around for Hiroki's other half.

Hiroki motioned me over. Reluctantly, I came.

"Cassie, what would you like?"

The handsome college-aged associate couldn't hide his surprise and confusion. His eyes moved back and forth from the old man in a business suit to me, a young woman in a short skirt, tight top, and tall heels. Oh, how I wanted to melt into the ground under his accusing stare.

I faked a grin back, on Hiroki's behalf. "I don't know. Whichever one is the cheapest."

That answer apparently worked to exit me from the conversation again. Hiroki haggled with the associate for a while before I was summoned over to sign the contract.

"What will be my monthly payment?" I asked before giving my John Hancock.

"Absolutely nothing," the cutie replied. Not sure of how to address Hiroki, the sales associate pointed to him and continued his explanation. "He's prepaid a year, including activation and equipment fee. After that, this will turn into a month-to-month contract."

Back in the car before turning on the ignition, Hiroki clearly wanted to tell me something, but he acted like an awkward high school boy, dodging around his question. "Cassie, we have known each other for several months now."

"Yes," I said. My stomach dropped. I had accepted a paid pager, never stopping to consider how much that would cost. I had become so used to receiving gifts that I expected to be showered with them at no price to me. Now, Hiroki wanted to collect payment.

"I bought something for you to wear."

"Oh? That's sweet of you." Play dumb. Play dumb. Maybe he'll change topics.

"You'll look beautiful in it. I want to see you try it on."

"Do you want me to wear it next time?" Innocent eyes and blank stare. I lowered my IQ a few notches.

"That's not what I meant. I was thinking that we could go get a hotel room and you could try it on there." He squirmed a bit in the driver's seat.

"Why a hotel? I can wear it the next time we go out." If he wants to be a pervert, I get to be a bimbo.

"Cassie," Hiroki was holding back his irritation. "It's lingerie."

I didn't see that coming. I felt like a mouse cornered by the cat. Here I was, sitting in his car in a dark parking lot an hour away from home. Again, nobody knew where I was.

I pasted a blank expression on my face. I tilted my head and giggled. "That's silly. Why would I wear lingerie out?"

Hiroki took a long breath. "Look, we don't need to do it tonight. I think you understand what I'm saying. Think about it. I know you will like what I bought. It's in my trunk right now."

Fuck you. Say something. I want to go home alive without being raped. "Okay, let's talk next time." I smiled. "Thank you for the pager."

I leaned over and gave him a tight hug. He held it a bit longer than I was comfortable with before kissing me on the cheek. Please God, I thought, don't let Hiroki force me to do anything I don't want to do.

He didn't let go. He embraced me tighter and rubbed my back.

I have a little boy who's depending on me, I thought. Maybe I can jump out of the car, scream, and run back to the store.

In Hiroki's ear, I whispered, "I'm tired. Can we head back now?" No money was worth this danger.

"I don't want to." He breathed deeply and pulled back, a hungry look in his eyes. "Fine. Next weekend?"

I nodded and forced a smile. He drove me back to my car. After another long hug goodbye, I hurried into my car, locked my doors, and swore never to speak to him again. All it took was a call to my wireless provider to change my pager number.

That's when I knew that my days at Club Flamingo and escorting were numbered. I cut off all contact with Hiroki.

*   *   *

Thanksgiving approached, although we didn't have money for a bountiful feast. Because Yessenia and I hardly showed up for work at Club Flamingo anymore, we relied too heavily on our clients for financial survival. My mom didn't have any cash to contribute. My brother only made enough to pay for his car. So when the festive week came, the best we could afford was a rather small frozen turkey, a few cans of cranberry sauce, yams and green beans, and some rolls.

That was until our computer phone rang. We had two phone lines in the house: a house phone and a second line dedicated to our dial-up Internet. Whenever Yessenia or I needed to give our phone number out—be it to a guy we met online or to a client—we gave the computer number out, knowing that there was no answering machine and that we rarely turned on the volume.

The ringer was on tonight. It kept ringing. To shut it up, I answered.

"Mia?" a male voice asked.

Only one man called me that name. "Hi, Mark," I said.

"Happy Thanksgiving. Have you eaten dinner yet?"

"No. Unfortunately, since I've never cooked Thanksgiving dinner by myself before, I didn't realize that the turkey needed to defrost so many days in advance."

"What's your family going to eat?"

"I don't know. Macaroni and cheese?"

"Mia, Mia, Mia." I wondered why he frequently liked to say my name in three's. "I cannot believe that. Why didn't you tell me you needed money for dinner?"

I sighed. "I didn't want to ask you for anything else. You've already helped me out a lot."

After a moment of silence, Mark said, "Let me call you right back. Promise you'll answer the phone? Because many times you don't."

"I'm not home often. When I am, I'm with Jacob."

When Mark phoned back, he told me to go pick up food he ordered for us. He was upset the restaurant refused to take his credit card unless he would sign in person. Therefore, he coaxed me into charging it to my VISA with the promise that he'd mail me a check for $200 to cover the food and a little extra.

At dinner time, we gathered around the table to give thanks.

Mom's eyes widened at the sight of the sumptuous feast spread out over the table. "Miranda, how did you afford all of this?"

"It didn't cost that much. It was on sale, like a last-minute deal thing. Let's have a toast."

Mom had us join hands and bow our heads. "Bless us O Lord, and these thy gifts, which we are about to receive, from thy bounty, through Christ, our Lord. Amen."

"A-men." Thankful I was—thankful that Hiroki didn't know where I lived and thankful that I hadn't been raped, maimed, or murdered. And now that my eyes were open to the dangers of my job, I felt trapped in a dark pit. I realized that clients cost far more than they provide and that it was only a matter of time before Mark changed like Hiroki did. Worse yet, Mark knew my address.

"By the way," Mom said, shaking me from my thoughts. "I'm thinking about moving."

I nearly choked. "What? Where?"

"To New York in a few months, where your grandma and aunt live."

"Are you kidding me?" That would mean a spike in my rent. I looked from my brother's blank stare to Yessenia's—both continued to eat. Did nobody else care? What the hell's wrong with everyone? We're all going to be homeless. I'll have to quit school. And what about Jacob?

Mom stared at me for a moment before retracting her statement. "I don't know yet. It's something I've been thinking about. But...I am going to go to Vegas next week to try skydiving. Isn't that neat?" She grinned.

My eyes bulged. Was this a midlife crisis, or was mom's bipolar disorder out of control?

"That's cool," Yessenia said before taking another sip of her egg-nog.

I felt the room shrink and the oxygen get thinner. I needed to reconsider my options. This was a twisted wake-up call. I needed to find a steadier source of income, to get my own place, and to find a way to get rid of Mark.

But how?

CHAPTER FIFTEEN

THE AUDITION

DECEMBER 1998

JASON KISSED MY SHOULDER. "You're pretty much depending on this client."

"Yeah, that's why I need to do something else. I can try dancing again." I leaned unto his bare chest. His bedroom walls and ceiling appeared blue from the color-changing night light over his vanity. The snake's terrarium on the long dresser at the foot of Jason's queen-sized bed glowed red to green.

"Go for it." He stroked my hair. "What's stopping you?"

Not having the guts to strip naked in front of a bunch of strangers, I thought. "I don't know how to dance."

"Hon, I've seen you dance. I've dated other dancers and am friends with quite a few. Trust me, you can dance."

"I don't know." I cringed at the thought of him dating strippers. I didn't think of myself as a mere stripper. Even though I had tried exotic dancing, I was a single mom putting myself through college and felt my pure intentions placed me on the upper echelon of adult entertainers. I judged other dancers without knowing their situations.

"Would you like me to show you how to do lap dances?" he asked.

That was a funny visual. Jason lap dancing me?

"I'm serious. Come here." He stood up and brought a dining room chair into a corner of his bedroom. With a few buttons on the remote control, his stereo switched from the mellow new age music to a faster rock beat.

This should be interesting. Wearing only a bra and some sweat pants, I walked to the chair, sat down, and stared expectantly up at him.

"I was going to sit there," he said. He kneeled down in front of me and kissed me passionately. When he pulled back, I sat there in a daze from his touch. "C'mon, get up." He reached for my arms and lifted me from the seat. He settled in. With a big grin on his face, he said, "Go ahead. Dance for me. I'll give you pointers."

"Okay." I tousled my hair and swayed my hips in front of him.

"That's sexy. Come closer now."

"Like how?" I asked.

With an arm around my waist, Jason pulled me in. Next thing I knew, I was straddling him.

"Hold on. Not yet. You need to tease men. We like that. Take your time. Do this without touching me, even though I wouldn't mind." He flashed his eyebrows.

I tried again. This time I grabbed the chair corners behind his shoulders and leaned in.

"Grab my shoulders for support."

"I don't want to hurt you."

"You're not going to hurt me."

I did as he instructed. Pushing off of his shoulders, I slinked up and down and side-to-side, inches from his body.

"There you go. Like that. Why don't you turn around and shake your butt a little?"

I did this for a few minutes. My thighs began to tremble and I ended up pressed against his chest.

"Nice. Do you remember me saying how much I loved the small of your back?"

"Yes." I remembered that strange compliment.

"Your lower back is sexy in the way it curves. You should try to arch your back more when you're in that position, almost like you're sitting up on an imaginary chair, but sticking your butt out. You can rub a little against my lap."

It hurt a bit to stretch my back in this way, but I figured, like my legs, my flexibility would develop over time. I grabbed his knees and pumped my hips back and forth, lightly brushing against his shorts. He was getting hard. Jason turned me around, grabbed my face and pressed his lips hard against mine. He leaned me back onto the bed.

I guess my lessons were over for the evening.

*   *   *

Yessenia and I avoided "lingerie" night at Club Flamingo by simply refusing to work those shifts. The owners became more creative: "lingerie contest" night was now followed by "wet t-shirt contest" night.

Yessenia and I exchanged looks of disgust as we watched a couple of girls get drenched with water until their white cotton t-shirts hid nothing from sight. My customer was quite turned on by this and asked why I didn't participate. When the contest was over, he tried to drag me to grinder's corner. Life was pretty much sucking for me at that point.

In the locker room, Yessenia debated with a couple of hostesses.

"Why not strip if you're willing to dance around in lingerie or wet t-shirts?" Yessenia said.

The girls scrunched their noses and rolled their eyes. "Gross. Those girls take off all of their clothes for money."

"What's the difference?" Yessenia said. "At least strippers don't have to sit around on red couches and wait for men to control their night. They ask the men, not the other way around."

"You do it if you want to," another girl said. "I'm not going to strip for money. Even if I wanted to, I couldn't get the nerve to do it."

Yessenia and I gave up on them. Was it easier to have strangers grind against you in a dark corner? Or feeling you up in the TV room? Or waiting around for the "ten free minutes"? We came to the conclusion that either the girls were too ugly to be strippers or didn't have the balls to do it.

When Yessenia and I exited the hell hole, aka Club Flamingo, we were accosted by a street bum wearing a mound of dirty rags, the same bum who stood there every night.

"Got a couple a bucks?" he asked. Same question as every other night.

"No." Sometimes we answered him; sometimes we ignored him.

"That ain't true. You just got outta there. C'mon, gimme some change."

"We work hard for our money," I said.

"C'mon, you can gimme a couple a bucks."

Yessenia and I had our arms locked together as we always did while walking to and from the parking lot. It felt more secure and we could avoid stepping on needles or condoms.

I stopped and turned us around to face him.

"Get a job, asshole," I said.

"Fuck you, you fucking whores!" he yelled.

"Fuck you," I said. "At least we have a job. That's more than I can say for you."

He growled and stared daggers at us.

Yessenia and I hurried back to the car. She locked the doors, turned the ignition, and gunned the engine. Her tires screeched.

Oh, this was a new low in my life—having a yelling match with a street bum. Yet, I wasn't far off from being homeless myself. I didn't want to make the connection.

While Yessenia drove away from Club Flamingo, I dumped my paltry sum of money onto my lap. Not even enough to buy food for the week. Could it get any worse?

I knew it was time. I was desperate enough to strip off my clothes.

*   *   *

Yessenia persuaded her client Gary to take us to a strip club in L.A. The purple neon-lit club was small, the mood festive, and the stage a short runway with seating all around. Some dancers did acrobatic moves on the poles that seemed more likely to be seen in the Olympics than in a strip club.

Yessenia poked me. "Miranda, go up to the lap dance area. Girls are waiting for us up there, but we have to hurry up before the song starts. Gary's paying for dances."

"What? Where?" I followed her to the club's elevated private dance corner.

"Sit there." Yessenia rushed away.

The cushy chair I sat in was semi-enclosed by partitions on both sides with a mirrored wall behind. I blinked and there appeared a bikini-clad black-haired dancer in front of me. She leaned her bronzed arms on my thighs and my shoulders, all the while rotating her hips and twisting her hour-glass waist.

I couldn't breathe. What was happening to me? I felt warm hard flesh, bathed in a light floral scent, pressed against my cheeks.

When she pulled back, I realized she had squished my face between her hard boobs. *Those should be soft, not stiff,* I thought. That was the first time I had been so close to breast implants. I wasn't at all impressed.

The dancer disappeared as soon as the three-minute song ended.

Yessenia returned. "I don't know if I can get him to buy another one."

I laughed. "That's okay. She wasn't my type." Did I even have a type?

*   *   *

I wrote out a budget to get myself ready for the big day when I'd finally do it:

$60 spandex boy short underwear—the law required dancers to wear lap dance shorts while performing lap dances.

$100 wigs—I could disguise myself so no one would ever know.

$40 nails and pedicure—fake French tips were a must.

$50 tanning salon—this would ease my discomfort.

Yessenia and I took out our VISA cards and charged our way to a new career, or at least to a new source of income that didn't come with strings attached, as our hostessing clients did.

In the meantime, I saw Mark a few times a month to collect my car payment and rent money. The end was near. He, on the other hand, had no clue our escorting relationship was almost over.

In fact, he became bolder. Whenever we sat in his car, he felt the need to squeeze my hands and kiss me on the cheek. I held my breath and zoned out when he did this. I tried to pretend his skin wasn't coming into contact with mine. He reached for my lips. I squirmed in my seat and turned my head at the last moment to avoid his pass. I closed my eyes and tried not to cry. My stomach churned. Struggling to paint a partial smile on my face, I hid my repulsion. I didn't think any amount of sanitizer could wash away my feelings of disgust.

I hoped dancing would work out.

*   *   *

"I've looked up all the clubs in LA. I think I found the one where we should audition." Yessenia pointed to the listings on our computer monitor.

We had become frequent web visitors to Zbone.com (Z Bone) and The Ultimate Strip Club List (TUSCL.net) websites.

"Didn't you search to see what the dancers said about it and found out that the place is dead?" I asked. I didn't want to repeat the

Tropicana mistake.

"Yeah, but girls say Lacy Street Cabaret will hire almost anyone. They're not picky, so it wouldn't be stressful like a real audition. It's only to get used to it. After that, we can try to get hired at a better place."

"What do we have to do for the audition?"

Nothing more than to strip off my clothes and expose my naked body to the world, I thought. Without fabric to hide behind, I would need to find a way to conceal myself beneath my skin, to pull myself deeper inside, to separate my physical body from who I felt I was as a person. It was like acting. *What you see will not be what I am. I'll hide behind the veil of a smile.*

*   *   *

On Thursday, December 10, 1998, Yessenia and I drove to Los Angeles to audition. I couldn't believe I was actually going to get naked for strangers. On the drive up we had to pull off the freeway several times, because Yessenia had to run to the bathroom, sick to her stomach from nervousness.

I was about to find out whether or not I could take it all off.

Inside, the club had an industrial feel. There was blue and purple neon lighting, and everything was painted and designed to mimic steel. The large stage was like a long runway ending at a circular platform with a pole in the middle. The air was cold and gave me goose bumps. I began to wonder why the strip clubs were always so cold.

The daytime manager, a thirty-something clean-cut, well-shaven blonde looked more at home in a bank than a strip club. He greeted us with a smile. "Let me give you two a tour of the club." He led us behind the stage. "Here's where you change your clothes."

When we entered the dressing room—much smaller than the one at Tropicana—we confirmed the club's liberal hiring policy. Apparently, if you could strip it all off and weren't 200 pounds, you could work here. These girls weren't lookers. Several were slightly pudgy with plain faces.

Yessenia and I searched for a spot to put our bags. The dancers glared distrustfully at us. I wanted to tell them not to worry, that we weren't going to compete with them, and that we were using this club as a way to overcome our inhibitions.

Yessenia mad-dogged them back. She threw her bag down, raised her eyebrows, and glared at the others much like a wild animal would do to assert its dominance over the pack. Everyone needed to know their pecking order, and she instinctually knew we had to at least convey the desire to end up on top.

I set my bag on the floor and took my time. I shuffled my clothes around, trying to stall. Deep breath. *I can do this,* I thought. *It's like walking around in a bikini at Tropicana. Except that I need to take everything off. Damn it, why does the lighting have to be so bright? Maybe it isn't.* I peeked back to see that Yessenia already had on her thong and a short sheer black lace camisole negligee. She was applying more mascara—or were those fake eyelashes?—and curling her hair. She looked hot.

Dancers came in and out of the dressing room, but nobody spoke a word to either of us. I reached into the bottom of my bag and reluctantly grabbed hold of my outfit: a baby doll dress with a shiny silver bodice that reflected rainbow sparkles in the light. Below the empire waistline, the dress became black, sheer, and free-flowing. This see-through portion ended below my butt. It came with a matching black thong—size: way too small—which I couldn't fit into without it digging sharply into my hips. I opted for another thong, one that fit more naturally. Ironic, yes, I know (no thong fits "naturally").

Yessenia finished her makeup, or gave up on trying. "Are you ready?" she asked.

I grimaced. "This makes me look fat."

"No, it doesn't. You're not fat. Let's go."

I sighed. It's a funny thing how your mind can exaggerate and distort perception to the point that you don't see what everyone else sees. I leaned against Yessenia while I wiggled my feet into the glass slippers. She left her tall platform stilettos at home and resorted to a much shorter pair of black strappy heels because they were easier for her to balance in. I didn't wear anything that had ankle straps, knowing that they make legs look shorter. With Yessenia's long, slender legs, it didn't make much difference. She went to the restroom and returned to coax me out of the dressing room.

Finally, we went out to the main dance area to find the manager.

"How are we supposed to do this?" I asked him.

He had to know we were green. "You'll be on stage for two songs. For the first song, you need to strip off either your bottoms or your top. You need to get completely nude for your second song. Who's going first?"

"Give us a second," I said.

"No problem. Let me know when you're ready." He was patient

with us. Without many customers in the club, he didn't have much to do but stand around and chat with the bartender—provider of over-priced sodas and juices. Like all nude clubs in California, they couldn't serve any liquor. It was probably safer for nude dancers to deal with sober customers.

Yessenia and I went to the edge of the bar to check out the scene.

"There're only two customers in this whole place," I said.

Yessenia shrugged. "It's the day shift, but it doesn't matter. We're not staying here."

"I don't know if I can do it. My stomach hurts so badly." It was more than butterflies. I wanted to throw up. I couldn't go through with it. But what other option did I have? Grinder's corner, where I'd have to relinquish control? Mark's girlfriend, where I'd have to date a man more than twice my age? Oil wrestling, where I'd have to allow grungy men to grope me in front of others for thirty or forty bucks a pop? Quit school?

"Yeah, well I just had diarrhea," she said, "so don't talk to me about your stomach hurting."

"That sucks." I wasn't surprised. Her diarrhea was proof that our work was detrimental. "I'm afraid I'm going to fall up there."

"You're not the one who can't walk in heels."

"Which are you going to take off first? Your dress or your panties?"

She shrugged and didn't answer.

I took a deep breath. "Let's watch a few girls go up first."

"Why? We've seen plenty of strippers at clubs."

I fidgeted with the hem of my dress, trying to make it longer. "Who's going up first?"

"I went first the last time."

"C'mon, that didn't count. This is fully nude."

"Go ahead." Yessenia sat down on a stool and crossed her legs.

Grumbling, I approached the manager who signaled to the DJ.

My heart pounded. I was going to go up there and have a fucking heart attack. Or freeze in place. What if I forgot to take my clothes off? What if I couldn't work up the nerve? I wouldn't get hired.

What happened next was a blur to me. I know there was one man on stage and that Yessenia ended up sitting next to him and talking to him during my set. Petrified, I stayed far away from them, at the back of the stage. I paced slowly, attempting to dance. My clammy hands and cramping stomach distracted me from the thudding in my chest.

Go for it, I thought. Get it over with. It'll be done in six minutes.

Without thinking too much about it, I pulled my black thong down and kicked it across the stage with my clear platform stiletto. There I stood, shaking, feeling horribly exposed even though I was still hidden beneath my dress.

I could see the manager across the room watching me. Sigh. I walked down the runway toward the circular platform with the fire pole—not danced, but walked over there. I grabbed onto the pole. It became my security blanket. *Don't let go.* I swung around it like Marisol at Tropicana showed us. It worked, except that I didn't land in front of the customer as I had intended, so I crawled toward him. Sitting up and leaning against the pole, I opened my legs in front of him. He put a couple of dollars up, but seemed more interested in his conversation with Yessenia, than with me.

Instead of feeling relieved to be by myself, so to speak, I scowled at Yessenia. If I was going to have to take off my clothes, I at least wanted to be noticed, not completely ignored. I needed validation that I was pretty enough to do it, and somebody to show appreciation for the effort I was putting in.

Was it my imagination? I could've sworn that over the blaring music, I heard the man say to Yessenia, "You're prettier."

Screw you both.

When my second song started, I hurried back toward the curtains. I hesitated until I saw the manager's eyes on me.

I pulled my dress up over my head. It wasn't in a sexy, watch-me-strip kind of way, but more of a bland I'm-changing-clothes kind of way. Fortunately, the back stage was darker than the front. I noticed another pole nearby and grabbed it. Holding on to it, I danced, and avoided humping the pole like before.

My song faded. I grabbed my clothes, slipped my dress back on over my head and marched to the end to pick up my tips. That's when I realized a few more customers had entered the club or returned from the lap dance area.

"Woohoo! Ow!" Yessenia cheered. I heard her coaxing the men near her. "It's her first time on stage." She put $1 up and in return, they put more dollars up. Maybe I didn't hate her after all.

I did it. I had the guts to bare my body for complete strangers. I didn't feel proud, but relieved—relieved that I could put my needs and those of my son ahead of my insecurities. So long as no one outside of Yessenia knew about the dancing, I could go on being a mom and student with a bright future. I could pretend that stripping was something another girl named Cassie did.

We decided to leave after we did a second set. Besides our stage shows, we didn't perform any lap dances. I changed back into my street clothes and stared at the twelve dollars on the counter in front of me. I thought strippers were supposed to make good money. This made Tropicana's $68 earnings look like gold. This better not keep up, I thought. There's no way in hell I could continue taking off my clothes on stage for mere pocket change.

"Don't worry about tipping out the house fees today," the manager said. "Give the DJ a couple of dollars. Next time, you two should pay the stage fee and tip the bar out. Do you know which day or night shifts you two want to work?"

How about none?

Yessenia said, "We'll talk about it and call you to let you know, okay?"

"Sure." He left.

Tip the DJ out? With what?

In the end, I donated five dollars to the DJ fund and exited the club with seven dollars in my purse, a measly seven dollars.

Chapter Sixteen
Going all the Way

December 1998

I NEEDED SOME COMFORTING, but didn't know who to call, Dan or Jason. Both were so sweet, caring, and affectionate—I couldn't decide.

Jason wasn't home, so I phoned Dan and told him about my first terrifying experience stripping off everything.

He was silent.

"Dan," I said. "Are you still there?"

"Yes." Another long pause. "Miranda, this is difficult for me."

"What is?"

"Hearing that the woman I love has to strip, knowing I can't do anything about it. You know how I feel about strip clubs."

Those softly spoken words were like a stiff punch to the gut. He said what I felt but refused to say: that exotic dancing was a last resort which most could not or would not do, but which I felt forced to do.

Dan had been vocal about his opposition to my dancing, not that he approved of hostessing, either. I knew he cared and this comforted me. But talking about the dancing and defending it somehow made it more real and more upsetting.

I phoned Jason later that night. He was almost too accommodating. "That's wonderful that you were able to do it. See, it wasn't too bad, right?"

Talking to Jason made me feel both better and worse. I felt better hearing how supportive he was. I felt worse because if he really cared about me like Dan did, would he be okay with me dancing for other men? Did he feel the same way as Dan, but wasn't being honest with me for fear of losing me?

*　　*　　*

After extensive research, Yessenia phoned a club called Century Lounge in Los Angeles and made arrangements for us to audition. We packed our bags, summoned our courage, and drove up the congested eight-lane-wide 405 freeway. Next stop: Century Boulevard. Rather than head to the Los Angeles International Airport (LAX) like most of the cars exiting the freeway with us, we looked for a nude strip club.

"What's the address?" Yessenia asked.

The midday sun shone brightly through the car window. I held the directions in my hands, which were starting to break out in a cold sweat. "We're almost there. Drive by it first, so we can check it out."

We approached a street light. I pointed. "It should be up ahead, past that light. After we go under that overpass, it should be on our right-hand side."

"Oh…my…God, Miranda. What the hell is that?"

We both saw it at the same time. The huge, gaudy sign. The type of tacky sign with large black removable letters that you'd expect to see on a marquee at a drive-in movie theater. But this sign didn't advertise the latest blockbuster. No, it read, in giant red and orange psychedelic letters: "LIVE NUDE NUDES." No one could accuse the club of false advertising.

"Wow, what genius thought that one up?" I said.

Yessenia made a U-turn at the first opportunity. She pulled into a fast food lot a few blocks away and parked the car.

"My stomach hurts," she said. "I need to go to the bathroom. I'll be back." She slammed her car door shut. It was awhile before she returned.

"Are you okay?" I asked.

"Not really. Diarrhea again. I want to go home. Let's do this another day."

I thought of Jacob. "Come on, let's do it. We've come this far."

"I can't do this." Yessenia started hyperventilating. "I can't do it."

I spent the next half-hour calming her down and coaxing her to go through with it. At last, she agreed.

"Are you sure you don't want to come back?" she asked. "Or go to another club?"

"We drove a long time. This one's near the airport. You said they supposedly get a lot of business." I grinned. "C'mon, it's funny. We can say we're working at the 'Nude Nudes' club."

"Don't get too excited," she said. "We don't know if they'll hire us."

Those were the magic sobering words. Yessenia turned on the car and we were on our way. Once in the parking lot, she maneuvered around the pot holes and pulled up next to a security guard who stood watch over the mostly empty lot.

She rolled down her window. "We're here to audition."

A middle-aged man in a security jacket peered in at us. "OK, you girls will need to park up in front. This side lot and back lot here are for customers." He pointed to a red Ford Mustang. "Pull on up around over there."

I leaned over. "Where do we go?"

"Come on back up here. That there's the front entrance."

Yessenia put the car in reverse. That's when we saw the next big surprise. Out of all of the Los Angeles, Hollywood, West L.A., and Orange County strip clubs we had visited in the past couple of months, this was definitely a first: a sex shop was attached to the front of the stand-alone building.

"Are you kidding me?" I said.

Yessenia shrugged.

I toyed with my hair in the rear-view mirror. "How do I look?" I needed some validation to boost my confidence.

"Fine."

That would have to do.

The security guard opened the front door and announced to the man at the register behind the glass partition that we were here to audition. The entryway was not like the other strip clubs. Although it was dark, there weren't any neon lights. The wood paneling gave the impression of a country saloon, not a strip club. I tried to peer around the corner, but couldn't see inside. Music blared out of speakers. There was bass, but the sounds were distorted by too much midrange, thus producing a tinny sound where there should have been ground-thumping bass.

We giggled, twirled our hair, and played the part of stripper bimbos until the day shift manager came to let us in. I stared at the short man with thick round glasses and thin brown hair, combed over. All he needed was a pocket protector. He didn't look as if he belonged here anymore than I felt like I did.

Bob introduced himself and motioned for me and Yessenia to follow him along a winding corridor, which ended in an abandoned commercial-sized kitchen. We didn't pass by any dancers. We didn't pass by any stage. There wasn't a dressing room in sight. I had fallen into the wrong side of the looking glass, and Bob was my tour guide.

Bob talked to us, but I couldn't hear him over the thoughts that rushed through my mind. What am I doing here? It's not too late to turn back now. Yessenia was right.

"Any questions?" he asked.

I looked at Yessenia and we both shook our heads.

"Follow me." He led us through another winding hallway.

As we approached the wooden door at the end of the linoleum floor, the music boomed louder. So did my heartbeat. He pulled the handle, revealing a new world. Red lights tinted the nude dancer on the large stage to our right. A few men, hunkered down underneath their coats, sat around the stage. The red patterned carpet held rows of tables, bolted to the ground, lined with barstools waiting to be occupied. Throughout the room, recessed lights were randomly scattered. I made a mental note to avoid these harsh spotlights by walking around their bright beams so as to not be recognized.

We reached for a brass handle and stepped two stairs up to an upper level. The edge of this level was lined with a long counter and more stools, for a slightly higher view of the main stage. The club felt homey, like the set for the TV show "Cheers," but with nude dancers.

I paused to stare at the dancer on stage. The irregular-shaped stage had a long mirrored wall with a red curtained door in the middle, presumably leading backstage, and two brass fire poles on either end. Alternating purple and red lights encircled the stage, illuminating the dancer's nude skin in a rosy pink.

Bob motioned to the bartender, a woman with long blonde hair tied back in a tight ponytail without so much as a single strand out of place. Her skin looked as tight as her hair. She wasn't particularly skinny, but had an average frame and didn't look much older than us. She scowled at us as she reached under the counter.

"Darling needs to buzz you in," Bob said as he motioned toward a thin wooden door hidden in a dark corner at the far end of the building.

Darling? The bartender went by the name Darling? Where was Bob taking us? Were we going to have to strip nude for the manager in a back room, like at Tropicana?

I hadn't even noticed the oval auxiliary stage on the lower level, and would have never guessed that there was another room tucked away behind this dark little stage, since it was camouflaged so well with its wooden paneled wall. Who built this place?

Buzzing resonated from within the wall. Bob yanked open the narrow door and the buzzing subsided. He led us into a tiny dressing room, which consisted of stacked lockers, a small carpeted floor, and a few steps that led down to a curtain—the only separation between the dressing room and the small satellite stage.

"Let me know when you're changed," he said. "You two will take turns auditioning on stage. You each get one song to take off all your clothes. Another girl will be on the main stage, so you'll go up to her second song. Any questions?"

Yessenia and I shrugged. He turned and left us alone. At the end of this room, a square window had been a boarded up. I put my ear to it and decided that the club entryway was on the other side of the wall's boarded window. It was as if the old Winchester Rifle Widow herself designed this club, which I would later discover had once served as a bowling alley in its pre-strip club life.

We dropped our bags to the floor. I sat beside mine and ruffled through the scant contents. Since I didn't have more than two dresses—ones which I wore out on the weekends—and a couple of bikinis in my bag, it wasn't as if I needed time to decide what to wear.

"Who's going up first?" I wanted her to offer.

"Whoever's ready first," she said.

She took her makeup bag out, walked over to the single counter and mirror, and took a seat on the only chair in the room.

She was ready before me. My stalling tactics had worked.

"Are you going out there now?" I asked.

She ignored me.

I watched in strange fascination as Yessenia parted the curtains and disappeared. No sooner had they swung close than she came back in.

"Fuck…this," she said. "It's too fucking bright out there."

Bob came knocking on the door and entered.

"What's wrong?" he said.

"Can't you turn that spotlight off?" she asked.

He sighed. Yessenia and I followed him out. That's when I saw it. Who the hell could possibly look sexy under a blinding white beacon of light?

"Is this better?" Bob twisted a dial and the light dimmed a bit. "I can't turn it off, so are you two going to audition, or not?"

We returned to the room, not much bigger than a walk-in pantry.

"Here goes nothing," Yessenia said as she disappeared through the curtain.

My heart pounded in my chest. I hopped over to the mirror to take another look at myself. I had on a red dress with spaghetti straps, a black lace bra, a black lace thong, and clear six-inch stilettos. I looked like I was dressing up like a slut for Halloween. My stomach tightened and I swallowed back the nausea. I put on more mascara to make my lashes appear more voluminous and applied another coat of lipstick. I stood up, stared at my profile, and sighed. I couldn't even look my reflection in the eyes.

The song faded. Yessenia appeared. She only had on her thong. She held her black lace dress up to her chest, which covered her bare breasts. I saw a few dollar bills crinkled in one of her hands. She panted.

"Oh my God, so what happened? How was it? Did you do okay?" I fired the questions at her, my own anxiety building to an uncomfortable peak.

She wouldn't speak. Bob called out to me from the other side. "Next up now."

That was me. Shit. I descended the stairs and parted the curtain. I stared down at my feet so as to not trip on the shiny black waxed linoleum floor. I looked up to see a few men seated around the stage. Bob stood a few feet back.

Another dancer was on the main stage and didn't seem too happy to be sharing the limelight, since these men would've been at her tip rail. I couldn't hear the music over the thumping of my pulse. Everything went silent and noisy at the same time, depending on whether I retreated into my head, or allowed my senses to become overwhelmed.

I grabbed the pole and wriggled around in front of it. But this time, I moved slowly. I dropped to my knees and sensually crawled toward the men. *Think sexy. Be sexy.* I saw a few greenbacks hanging on the tip rail.

I stood back up and sashayed my hips, while I slid one shoulder strap down at a time. Reaching behind my back, I unsnapped my bra and tossed it down.

The hungry look in the customers' eyes encouraged me. I fed off their energy and became what they desired. When I stared into their eyes, I no longer remembered that my breasts were exposed. It was my eyes locked on theirs. Whenever one pair of eyes moved down, I locked onto the next pair of eyes. It was as if from my neck down, there was a different girl in my place.

I squatted down and leaned against the pole for support. I slid my panties down and stepped out of them, kicking them back near the curtain. For the first time, many men—strangers—were staring at my whole glory. I should've been revolted at their fascination, but instead I was too stunned to feel anything. I danced. *This is what they came to see. This is why they're here.* I kept my dress around my waist, which made me feel more comfortable.

The end of the song approached. I glanced up to see Bob motion for me to take off my dress. *Damn it.* I stepped back, away from the light and pulled it off. Now there was nothing between me and these men, except my stilettos. Now I felt my nakedness. Now I was on the verge of losing my nerve. Now it was too late to cry.

Fortunately the song cut off at its three-minute mark. I quickly threw my dress on, and grabbed my panties and bra. I picked up the few dollars and thanked each man.

Men had paid to see me nude. This realization was numbing; I could not believe that people were paying to see me nude. I wasn't making sandwiches, ringing up a cash register, or sweeping a floor. I was being paid to simply take off my clothes. Amazing.

The spotlight went dark. It was over. I was relieved to be back inside the tiny dressing room. I put my dress back on and flopped onto the ground, out of breath.

I saw that a young green-eyed blonde had arrived during my audition. She stuffed her belongings into a locker.

"I'm so glad that's over," I said to Yessenia. "Do you think they'll hire us?"

"I don't know," Yessenia said. "I guess we'll see,"

"Hi," the dancer smiled. "Have you two ever danced before?"

"No," I said. "We just auditioned."

"Oh, okay. I'm Dee. I've only been dancing for a few months. I know it's like totally sucky at first, but it gets so much better. You'll see. You two will do good. Trust me, it totally gets easier. A lot of the girls are super nice. That's what was important to me."

I was blown away by her welcoming kindness—quite different from the cold reactions we received from the dancers at the last club.

Bob reappeared in the doorway. His jerky mannerisms made him appear nervous. His blue eyes bulged through his thick glasses. "Yessenia," he stared at her. "You're hired." He cast his eyes downward. "Miranda, you're a cute girl, but I'm sorry, we can't hire both of you."

My jaw dropped. The air vacuumed out of me.

Yessenia demanded, "Why not?"

Did I want to know the answer?

"Howard, the owner, would say Miranda needs to lose some weight."

No, I didn't need to hear that. Even though I was a healthy weight, I guess size seven was too big for his liking. I fought back the tears. In addition to the obvious insult about my body, I felt I had bared everything for nothing. How would I pay my bills? Stay with my clients? I couldn't imagine returning to Flamingo's. I was too stunned to say anything.

"She had a baby a few months ago," Yessenia stretched the truth by a year. "She can lose the weight. We're going to the gym. I'll help her."

"Yeah, I'm working on it," I said. "It won't be a problem." Please God, don't let it end up like this.

The other dancer came to my defense. "Y'know the best exercise is dancing. That's how I lost weight from my baby."

Given her petite frame, I was surprised to hear that she had a child. I stared down.

"I...I don't know what the owner Howard will say," Bob stammered. He seemed like a nice guy who didn't like being put in a difficult situation. "I think you're a pretty girl, but Howard is picky. It's not me."

"Well," Yessenia said, "if Miranda can't work here, neither will I. It's both of us or neither. She can lose the weight in a few weeks."

A few weeks? Probably not. Well, thank God Yessenia's defending me, rather than accepting the job without me, I thought.

"I've already lost a lot of weight," I said. "I know it won't be a problem. I'm on a diet and with the dancing...."

Bob sighed. After a long pause and a hard look at me, he said, "I suppose we can take you, too. But if Howard says something, it's out of my hands, you know."

Yessenia and I jumped to our feet and gave him a big hug.

He smiled sheepishly. "I like you girls. But, I hope you do get in shape before Howard sees you, or he'll chew me out."

Ironically, this would be the start of one of the best employee-manager relationships I'd ever have.

"Alright, you two," Bob backed up, his cheeks slightly pink. "Come see me when you change, so we can figure out your schedules." He retreated. The door swung shut behind him.

What happened? He hired me? But he almost didn't. I guessed I was officially a stripper.

I turned back to Dee who was curling her hair at the counter. "Thank you."

"No problem," she said. "I've been there." She looked at us. "Don't even worry about Bob. He's a sweetie. Howard's a little loony. He's old and senile. I'm sure you'll be okay."

I wish I could say that I felt the same. Unfortunately, what pride I had had crumbled. If I hoped to make any money, I needed to quickly pick up the pieces. And get in shape.

* * *

Since I was on winter break from college, I took whatever shifts Bob wanted me to work without complaint. My first day, Tuesday December 15, 1998, was not encouraging: I felt sick to my stomach and only took home $31. However I learned a lot about the lap dance booths, the private nude table dance partitioned area, the stage, the rules, the dancers, the club, the customers, and the fees.

On Wednesday, December 16, I used $34 of my earnings to purchase used costumes from Dee, but I still walked home with $191. This looked more promising.

On Thursday, December 17, Yessenia and I parked in the dancer lot and were escorted in through the back door—the stripper entrance—by a security guard. That day I had to fork over $10 for a CD magazine which would hold six of my CDs at a time. The DJ handed me a slip of paper; I had to select which track from which CD number I wanted him to play for the first and second song of each set I'd get on stage.

Still, after tipping out the DJ, the house, and the bar, I left the building with $294. I counted a second time to be sure. Yessenia's experience mirrored mine. Everything was going to be all right. Rent? Daycare? Food? Gas? School? Hope was restored.

It was time to cut ties with my client.

I picked up my new cell phone—that was the first purchase I

made with my increased income—and dialed Mark's number. Without the caller ID block set up yet, my cell phone number was visible to whomever I called. I made a mental note to have the cell phone company fix that soon.

When he answered, I broke the news.

Mark stayed silent on the other end of the phone before he said, "Mia, Mia, Mia." Another sigh. "Why?"

I grinned. "Because I need to support my son and I'm tired of Club Flamingo." *And I'm tired of you,* I thought.

More silence. "I could help you. You know how I feel about those kinds of places."

Now, he sounded more like a father than a client. Does he actually think hostess clubs and escorting are somehow better than strip clubs?

"I want to do this," I said. "They hired me." *My God, that felt good to say. It's final. No turning back now.*

I heard a gasp and disapproving tongue clicking. "Oh, my. Mia... why?"

Because I need to take control of my life again, I thought. "My son's my priority. I appreciate everything you've done for me. You've helped me out a lot. But now, you don't have to worry about me. I can focus on college. I only have two years left." I attempted to change the conversation.

He let out a deep sigh before he said, "Oh, Mia. You know how I feel about this. If you've made up your mind, that's it. I won't be a part of this. This is the end of it. You won't hear from me again."

I thanked him again for all his financial help and ended the call. When I hung up, a heavy weight lifted from my shoulders, one which I hadn't even realized had been there.

I slept well that night and felt more at peace with myself than I had been in a long time. Ironically, dancing—the profession I initially judged with such scorn—is what gave me back my freedom, the freedom to continue my education. I no longer needed to rely on one customer. I could regain my independence. I had never realized how far clients had encroached on my normal life and contributed toward my unhappiness, until that moment.

*   *   *

Dan and I took Jacob to the park.

I handed Jacob a bunch of bread crusts. "Here, sweetie. There are some ducks over here."

Dan and I walked on either side of Jacob, so he couldn't fall into the lake. The sky was a pale blue, a few white clouds floated by in the crisp breeze.

Jacob threw his handful of bread into the dark water. The ducks swam to us, quacking and dipping their beaks. Their tails wagged as they paddled, making ripples.

"More." Jacob held out his open palms.

"This is the last of it." I tipped the bag upside down and shook the final crumbs into his hands. I ruffled his hair, which I noticed had been darkening over the last several months.

His big green puppy dog eyes looked up at me. "More bread?"

Dan reached his arm into a tote bag. "Here, Jake. I brought a few pieces."

Jacob jumped up and down, dropping a piece of crust on the ground. A brave pigeon swiped it before he could retrieve it. Jacob threw the rest at the mallards in the lake.

"I wanna swing. Please can I swing?" He skipped in circles around me.

"Give mommy a kiss." I bent down. He kissed my cheek. "And a hug." He squeezed my neck. "All right." Before I had finished the last word, he took off running. Dan and I chased him up the hill, through the trees, and down to the sandy playground.

By the time we caught up, Jacob had changed his mind and was going down a slide.

Dan reached for my hand. Our fingers intertwined. We sat on a nearby bench and watched Jacob play.

"This is nice." I smiled.

With a big grin that lit up his almond eyes, he planted a kiss on my hand. "Yes, it is."

* * *

Finally free from my client's grasp, I saw my earnings rise. Work stayed at work. I no longer had to go on dates for money. No one from work would know my real name, address, or phone number.

I went to Jason's house the next Saturday and told him how well work was going for me at Century Lounge.

"I'm happy for you," he said. "I know it's what you wanted."

"Well, not exactly," I said. "But it will help me get through school. Guess what?"

"What?" Jason lay down on his pillow and smiled up at me.

"My fall semester report card came in the mail. I earned two As, two Bs, and passed my writing proficiency test. Now my overall GPA is 3.5 and I'm on the honor roll. I know it's not as good as high school, but with Jacob and working and everything, I think it's not bad."

"That's great. I know you're a smart girl."

"See dancing is totally going to help me out."

"Yes, but you need to understand that dancing is going to change the way you view men. Trust me: I know a lot of dancers."

"Come on, it's a hell of a lot better than hostess dancing and dating clients."

Jason was quiet for a moment. "Yes, I agree. I just hope you make it out okay. I care about you."

I wished he had said more than that he "cared" about me, because I more than cared for him.

"In less than two years," I said. "I'm going have my college degree and I'll have a respectable job. You'll see."

"I know." He sat up, swept the hair from my face, and kissed me on the neck.

* * *

No one warned me that I'd have to take on a double identity to forge distance between stripping and schooling. It became necessary to create a bubbly flirty persona to make money at the strip club and a conservative one to hide my dancing job from my peers. To protect my future career and my son, stripping had to be kept secret. Because my college connections might have become long-term, none of my classmates or professors could ever find out.

In a strange way, I initially felt that stripping would help me to return to who I was, a way to recover my independence and the life force that had been drained through months of hostess dancing and escorting. I thought of exotic dancing as the means to an end.

I didn't know how wrong I was.

PART TWO
EXOTIC DANCER

Chapter Seventeen
Music

I LOVE MUSIC. I love the sounds of piano concertos, violin lullabies, and guitar solos. I'm not particularly good at playing the piano, which I taught myself to play at the age of twelve simply because we had one in the living room collecting dust. After I took a couple of college music courses—where I was able to perform a recital on a grand piano—I stopped practicing. Another box checked off on my life to-do list.

I don't sing well. I sing in the car with the radio blaring out of speakers. When I was young, I sang in my church choir, often comprised of a woman with a tambourine, a man with a guitar, and me. I didn't stand too close to the microphone for fear of hearing myself sing off-key.

So when I say that music surrounds my life, I don't mean it by any talent of my own.

Many people hear an old tune and fondly reminisce. For me, music doesn't bring back memories; it causes me to relive them. Some listeners avoid certain melodies because of the feelings they evoke. I, on the other hand, relish the experience. I flip a remote control of memories with every twist of the radio dial. One song conjures childhood memories of jumping on beds with friends and singing into hairbrushes. Another puts me back into a doomed relationship.

Many times, music puts me in front of a stage, where I watch a woman disrobe and tauntingly strut across the floor. It could be a thin blonde, or a tattooed brunette, or a bodacious redhead with her dark roots showing. I can actually see the fling of her hair, her legs spread open before me, the curves of her breasts.

On occasion, I see my own reflection in a mirror, dancing on the stage.

Music brings me to life and makes me smile. When other people fantasize naughty little dreams, I recall a memory. This is what causes me to smile.

Smiles are funny. They can get you in trouble or get you out of trouble. To strangers, I smile. To my friends, I smile. What I hide behind my smile might not be innocent, but smug. I know what others don't know—what others couldn't possibly know—about my past.

I am the ambitious student, the sweet girl-next-door, the friendly coworker. I am a mother, a daughter, a friend. I love to chat and I'd tell you anything and yet, you still wouldn't know what lay beneath my smile.

I hide behind smiles, sticking out my tongue at the world.

Take the song "Red House" by Jimi Hendrix or Paula Cole's "Feelin' Love," for instance—I love those songs.

I tap my foot to the beat, my mind hits play and there I am again—on stage.

CHAPTER EIGHTEEN
STAGE SHOW

JANUARY 1999

MY HANDS PARTED THE thick red velvet curtain. I deliberately placed one platform stiletto in front of the other.

Don't trip.

I slid along the mirrored wall and zoned out to the bass and guitar from Jimi Hendrix's "Red House." With my mascara-laden lashes, I scanned the tip rail to count the customers. One... two... three... four... five... oh yay—Zach, my regular, was there. Establishing eye contact, I acknowledged his presence with a smile. At least this set would mean a few bucks for me.

"There's a red house over yonder!" Hendrix wailed out as I turned around and leaned against the wall. I played with the silky red shoulder straps of my dress and sauntered over to the brass pole furthest from Zach. I felt his eyes on me, but ignored him for the time being. With a twist of my wrist I twirled around the pole.

Ewww. A wet spot. Goddammit.

I tried to hide my disgust and casually wiped my hand on my dress and inched it up a bit to show off the thigh-highs clipped into my garter belt.

Which nasty bitch was on stage before me?

Two guys from the second row back grabbed their drinks and headed up to the tip rail.

Okay, good sign, I'm feeling the music. Move slowly.

I lowered my gaze as I headed toward the other end of the stage. When I reached for the second brass pole, my shoe slipped on a wet spot. I flung myself into a swing around the pole, landing gently on

175

my knees on the black stage floor.

Nice save.

Avoiding the lotion or other mysterious crap on the stage, I sat up and crawled over to the edge. Once there, I bounced up and down simulating a sexual act, but it was more of a routine habit than anything else at that point. The song was halfway over.

Time to take something off. Top or bottom first?

Top, I decided and playfully slipped one arm at a time out of my dress straps. I folded the top half of my dress down, revealing my lacy bra.

I bet they weren't expecting another layer.

I giggled and crawled across the stage in front of a few men to tantalize them. I rolled over, leaned back onto my elbows, tilted my head, and arched my back. With finesse, I twirled and kicked each leg out, opening them wide to tease the men with the sight of my sheer lacy panties.

I stood up and swayed over to the other end. It looked like a couple of gardeners were on break. They had two dollars up between the three of them.

Oh, hell no. They aren't going to get away with being cheap. Everyone knows that you're supposed to tip at least a dollar per song if you sit at the tip rail.

Rather than ignore them, I decided to beat them at their game. One hand grabbed hold of a vertical pole, one heel stepped over the tip rail. I squatted down and parted my legs, but pushed my dress down to block any view they might steal of my racing stripe. I pulled at my silky black garter belt straps and let them snap against my legs.

Staring down at their measly two dollars, I raised my eyebrows. With my manicured nails, I stroked my inner thighs. They knew what I wanted and I knew what they desired. But they weren't holding up their end of the bargain. I whisked my leg back and stood up, pouted, bit the corner of my sparkly pink lips, and turned away.

I grabbed hold of the pole next to me and bent over in front of these dirty, smelly men. Peeking at them through my legs, I reached my arm back in between my legs and caressed myself. I made sure that my dress was down far enough so that their imagination would have to unravel the rest.

The men understood and a five-dollar bill went up.

But I pretended not to know that these were the scummy types— the ones who would take their money back after I went behind the curtain in between my set. I knew the trick; I wasn't stupid. So as I kicked my right leg up over their heads, I purposely brushed their cash onto the stage. To be sure, I crawled in front of them, nonchalantly pushing the dollar bills out of their reach.

"That's where my baby stays," Hendrix moaned.

Oh, damn. Forgot to take off my bra.

I giggled and stood up in the middle of the stage. With my back to the men, I peered over my shoulder and unstrapped my bra. I flung it near the curtains. A few more bucks hung over the rail. Zach had two five-dollar bills in front of him.

This was the moment they've all been waiting for. I twirled around. The customers who hoped to catch a glimpse of my creamy white breasts were disappointed again because I cupped them and hid my nipples from view.

Haha. I am such a flirt.

Finally, I raised my arms up to tousle my long brown hair, and from the looks on their faces I could see they all got their money's worth. The song ended.

I exited through the velvet curtains. "Destiny"—the stage name Yessenia now preferred to be called at work—was primping in front of the mirror backstage. She would go up after me. I walked to the sink and washed my hands with soap and water.

"Oh…my…God…Destiny." I slipped my panties off to prepare for my second song but kept my red dress on, still folded at the waist.

"What?" Destiny flipped her long wavy hair over her shoulder. Both of us had added blonde highlights, but hers were more radiant.

"There's some slippery crap on stage. I touched some of it on the pole, too," I said. In front of the mirror, I bent over to perform a close inspection. Even the smallest piece of fuzz or toilet paper glowed under the black lights on stage. No need for embarrassment. Satisfied, I stood up.

"Gross," she said. "Tell them to clean it up."

Paula Cole's "Feelin' Love" blasted out of the club's speakers.

"It's all right," I said. "I'm not going to touch the poles right now."

"Ewww. I don't want to get some nasty girl's juice on my hands."

"I think it's actually lotion. Who was on stage before me?"

"Peaches." Destiny scowled. "She needs to quit using lotion before her set. It's dangerous."

"Yeah, and have you seen the way she rubs her ass against the poles?" I stuck my tongue out. "I'm so disgusted."

The DJ restarted my song and announced, "Let's all welcome back, Sexy Serenity." I thought it was clever for Yessenia and I to go by Destiny and Serenity.

I cautiously stepped up the two wooden stairs and reached for the curtains. The platform beneath my feet wobbled. Everything in that damn joint seemed to have been nailed together as an afterthought.

"Don't touch the poles," Destiny said. "I'm going to go find Popcorn and tell him clean up the stage before I go up."

"Popcorn" was the nickname of one of the floor guys who also doubled as a janitor. The other floor guys acted as security and counted our lap and table dances to make sure that the club received their "fair" cut of our money.

"Okay, I'm leaving my dress on so I don't have to touch the stage during my floor work." I disappeared between the red velvet curtains.

During my second song, I mentally checked out. *Do I have a research paper to write tonight, or is it due next week?*

I smiled at my reg while I spread my thighs to expose myself to him from underneath my dress.

I hope Jacob sleeps better tonight. It's hard to get up in the morning after dealing with his night awakenings. I dislike having to use so much under-eye cream to hide the sleep deprivation.

I mouthed hello to Zach, who grinned. I crawled over to lather some attention on my other customers at both ends of the stage.

I'll call out sick on Saturday—that is if Dan spends the night. Jason never stays over at my place, he prefers for me to go to his apartment.

I bounced up and down in front of two entranced men.

It's probably better not to bring Jason over since it's hard enough to sneak Dan out in the early morning hours. Thankfully, I'd been able to clean up before Jacob could start asking questions. I wished I'd been married before I had a baby, so life wouldn't be like this.

On all fours, I slowly dove down onto my arms, waving my butt in the air for a nice view.

I need to quit stringing Dan and Jason along. I know it's not fair to either, but if only I could piece their best qualities into one man, I'd be the happiest girl. Dan's coolheaded, intelligent, romantic, and humorous; Jason's passionate, fun, adventurous, yet peaceful; both are sweet.

My song faded out. The men clapped while I slipped back into my dress and collected my tips.

That's funny that they clap. It proves this is like any other performance—it's only an act.

CHAPTER NINETEEN
PRINCESS DRESSING ROOM

WINTER 1999

AFTER THE TREK DOWN the long linoleum pathway to the "princess" dressing room, I kicked off my heels and tossed my bra onto my duffel bag. I unsnapped my garter belt and slipped off my stockings—quality stockings, not the cheap kind that they sell in regular stores, but handmade ones with dark seams up the back reminiscent of stockings from the 1940s.

Wearing only my thong, I sat down on an outdated orange swivel stool and opened up a handheld blue metallic lock box which I called a purse. Dollar bills dumped out onto the chipped tile counter. I separated the cash into piles, taking care to turn them all into the same direction—as the bank tellers preferred—before counting out twenty-six dollars. Not too shabby. Not excellent, but not bad for my second stage set of a dayshift on a Tuesday.

Sometimes it could be bad—like less than five dollars bad—when the place was empty and the only fun on stage was to make silly faces at the bartender, waitress, and other dancers.

The real money was in the lap and table dances. I counted the bills in rapid succession a second time to be sure, neatly folded the stack in half and tucked it back into my purse.

Each station in this dressing room had its own mirror framed by round light bulbs, half of which were usually out. On the day shift there were only about eight to ten girls on average, split between three dressing and locker rooms: the little one—not so cool to be assigned to that one, the middle one—great place to get weed, and the princess one—better get permission to move into there unless you want to get your ass kicked.

New girls were assigned to the crappy little dressing room, on the other end of the club near the satellite stage where Yessenia and I had auditioned. It sucked for them to have to walk all the way across the club to get to the main stage. Been there, done that.

Thank God Yessenia was able to get us moved to the princess dressing room soon after we started work at Century Lounge. The girls there didn't mess with other girls' stuff. We were all on relatively friendly terms—not what's-your-real-name-and-address type of friendly, but more of the small-talk-and-I'm-not-going-to-burn-cigarette-holes-in-your-outfit kind of close relationship.

Without any real need to use the lockers on the day shift, the few of us in this dressing room used the extra stations of the U-shaped counter to sprawl our curling irons and outfit changes across.

At the other end of the counter, brown-eyed, black-haired Blanca, sat nude, spaced-out and drunk. She reached up, grabbed her thick black curls and twisted them around her dark tanned fingers. She stared at her reflection in the mirror and mumbled to herself.

Destiny wasn't back yet from her set. Nicole, a thin strung-out blonde, and Sara, a voluptuous blonde from Texas, hadn't shown up for work in several days, which left me alone in the dressing room more or less.

I glanced at my reflection in the mirror. Surrounded by glitter, my eyes looked dead. Not dead tired—I had under-eye cream to fix that. This was a more of a metaphysical deadness, one caused by spending eight-hour shifts in a loud club, changing outfits in 30-second increments, hustling men for dances, stripping my clothes off and putting them back on every hour, crawling across the stage, holding my body weight up in the lap dance booths to avoid full lap contact, keeping my balance in platform stilettos while maintaining my role as Serenity-the-actress, keeping my stories straight, plastering on a smile or seductive grin or teasing pout, entertaining men with my body, my words, and my guises, leaving work with a ringing in my ear, throbbing feet, swollen knees, and a mental and emotional exhaustion caused by the physical and psychological demands of the job.

I blinked and found myself staring at my reflection in the dressing room mirror. Remembering the mystery lotion or whatever it was from the stage, I rushed over to one of the two sinks to scrub my hands again. I grabbed a baby wipe to rub my butt and thighs to be sure, because one could never be too careful.

All the dancers—whether or not they had children—kept a steady supply of baby wipes. Working at a nude club meant guys could see *everything* and also meant that we could be exposed to anything.

I knew my reg Zach, a middle-aged unhappily-married man, was out on the floor, but I also knew he'd wait for me. I stared into the mirror. Who is that stranger with the tan lines around her breasts? Is that me?

I recalled the advice Blanca gave Yessenia and I on our first day in this dressing room. Upon learning that "Destiny" came down with a bout of nervous diarrhea before her stage performance, Blanca shared her dancing wisdom: "Are you sure you wanna do this? It's not too late to turn back now."

Yessenia and I had empty bank account balances and images of potential eviction notices in our minds as we nodded.

"Well," Blanca said, "let me give you three reasons why you need to get up and leave right now." She held up one finger. "First of all, this job is a money trap. There's no other job that's going to give you this much immediate cash. You can't quit when you say you will." She held up another finger. "Secondly, this'll change your views of men. You won't be able to look at them the same—all of them—from the leaf blower to the dentist or lawyer." Swaying a little from one too many beers, Blanca opened her ring finger. "Thirdly, you'll eventually succumb to a vice if you keep doing this. It might be drinking or it might be drugs."

Yessenia and I stared at Blanca through the mirror—that's how we always communicated, through the mirrors. We almost never actually turned to face one another when speaking. Reflections only. Yessenia and I remained silent.

Upon noticing that we had no intention of turning back, Blanca continued, "You better have a strict timeframe on when you're gonna get out of this job or you'll never leave it. Do you understand?"

Yessenia took a hit off her cigarette; I stared off and acted blasé about the whole thing. I didn't feel that I had any other option at the time than to dance.

"Blanca's coming up next," blared out of the loudspeaker. Blanca crushed her beer can and tossed it in the trash can on her way out. I listened to her heels clicking down the hallway.

Yessenia mumbled, "That old bitch doesn't want us to take a piece of the pie."

So, how long had it been already? A month? But, this job was better than my last. I knew that for a fact, but what about before that? Before my twentieth birthday? Back when we were both eighteen-year-old seniors in high school. It seemed so long ago when I gave Yessenia a hard time about wanting to be a cocktail waitress.

"It's not all about money," I had said. "Some things are just wrong. I wouldn't do anything immoral for money. Have more respect for yourself."

"Miranda, never say never," she had responded. "You don't know what you'd do. Don't be so judgmental."

I glared back at her. *How dare she tell me that? If you want something badly enough, you can achieve anything.* Besides, I told myself that I'd never do anything that could ruin my chances at politics later on in life.

I glanced back at my glittery green eyes in the mirror: I was officially a hypocrite.

Then I hostess danced, escorted, and now I'm doing this until I graduate. Stripping is only a temporary solution; after I graduate college, I'll pretend it never happened. Only two years to go.

Now, Yessenia went by the name Destiny and I was known as Serenity. Oh yay, life was looking better already. So what if I had to bare everything for a couple of bucks on stage and do lap dances for perverts? Now I could pay the rent and put food on the table.

I regretted that Jacob had spent so much time at the sitter's house. She was a great lady, but I felt as though I was paying her to raise my son. I loved Jacob more than he'd ever know—he'd never understand to what extent I had been willing to go for him. I had tossed aside my upbringing, my morals, my pride for him.

I sighed. No sense in thinking anymore about that which I couldn't change.

Speaking of change, I decided to change my thong.

I pulled my lip gloss out of my purse and slathered it on. After puckering my lips, I pulled my satin lap dance shorts on over my thong. After throwing on a short shiny silver dress decorated with planets, I reached into my bag, found a body spray and doused myself in floral splash. I slipped my aching feet into my clear glassy slip-on platform stilettos and headed out the door and realized that I smelled cheap.

Perfect.

CHAPTER TWENTY
TIP-OUTS

WINTER 1999

I STOOD ON THE sidewalk in front of the movie theaters under the bright Southern California sun, waiting for Wesley, my surfer college buddy. Unlike most of the other men in my life, Wesley was one I never dated. Rather than shoot pool between classes at college like we usually did, he suggested we go see a movie. I looked at my watch. He was late.

"Miranda." Wesley came from behind me and punched me in the arm playfully. He seemed to think of me as another one of the guys. "So what do you want to see?" He pushed his wavy brown hair from his eyes. Today he had dressed up, rather than a t-shirt, he wore a shirt with a collar.

"I don't know." I pointed to the long line snaking around the building. "Not the new release. That line's crazy."

"Follow me. I know someone here." He led me around the crowd and into a side door to the theatre. "Shh, hang out here for a moment." He disappeared down a corridor.

I tapped my foot and stared at the red carpet. Within minutes, Wesley reappeared.

"K, come with me." He motioned with his hand.

The next thing I knew we were in a theater. I sat down next to him.

"How much do I owe you?" I reached for my purse.

He chuckled.

"What's so funny?" I asked.

"We snuck in."

My cheeks reddened. "Are you kidding me?" I lowered my voice. "Aren't we going to get in trouble?"

"Nah, I do it all the time. Sometimes it works, sometimes it doesn't."

"Oh, my God. I've never done that. I can't believe you didn't tell me."

"If I told you, would you have done it?"

"No."

He laughed and slouched down into the seat. "Exactly."

Hanging out with Wesley was fun for me because I didn't have to worry about him trying to kiss me or pay me to date him. I could relax and enjoy innocent fun with a friend.

* * *

"Serenity, do you want another cranberry juice?" Charlene yelled rather than asked. She tilted her head and raised her eyes expectantly down at me. Her long, poufy red spiral curls framed her sour face. Usually, she was the only daytime waitress at the nude club. From South Africa, Charlene had a cute accent, but since she was a bitch, it never sounded as adorable as it could have. Being an alcohol-free joint—as were all nude clubs in California—the club, the bartender, and the waitresses made their money off overpriced sodas and watered-down juices, and our tip-outs.

Zach, my regular customer who visited weekly, glanced at me.

"No, thanks," I answered. I smiled and slurped the last remaining drops through my straw. *His money is mine, not yours.*

Charlene threw me a dirty look before storming off to hound the rest of the customers, especially the ones with dancers at their sides. I heard her repeating over and over, "Buy the lady a drink?"

Dancers usually felt obligated to take any drinks offered to them. In fact, many clubs required the girls to sell a certain number of drinks a night—to convince the customers to buy them drinks. Otherwise, the dancers had to pay out the difference at the end of their shifts.

That wasn't the policy at this nude strip club. I knew about how much money Zach spent each time he came, and I wanted his money spent on me, as did he.

"So how have you been doing?" Zach asked.

I turned my attention away from Blanca who was doing a headstand on stage and bicycling her feet. "I have a couple of big assignments due next week that I've been working on. How about you? How's the job?" Zach seemed to make a decent living with his pool maintenance business. I knew he was married, but he was a nice guy—not a pervert like most of the other men—so I avoided asking him about his family. I didn't even know if he had children.

He shrugged. "The usual." He glanced at the stage and his eyes widened. Blanca, her black hair spread out on the ground, was moving her arms and legs in no particular direction while keeping balanced on her head. "Wow. She's pretty strong."

"Yeah." I didn't find her acrobatics sexy. Most men seemed to stare in amazement rather than lust at her muscular nude body.

"Should we do a dance?" Zach asked. This was his code for "I understand you need to make money, so let's go to a lap dance booth and make it look like you're working."

I laughed. "Okay. Sounds fun." I led him to a corner private booth. "Here you go." I pointed at the red leather loveseat.

He sat down and patted the cushion next to him. "Have a seat. You don't need to dance. Let's talk."

"Are you sure?"

"You know I'm more comfortable talking with you than ogling at you. Not that you're not beautiful—you are."

"I can dance part of it and we can sit for the rest."

"If you want to. I know you need to do dances. Didn't you say the club keeps a record of how many dances you do?"

"Yeah, but only so they can take our money." The house collected a couple dollars per dance in the form of coins we were mandated to purchase to turn on the coin-operated red lights in the booths. The machines automatically turned the lights off at the end of each three minute song.

The song started and I slipped a coin in the meter. Red light shone down on Zach and me. I tousled my hair, struck a pose for him, and danced. I twirled around, paused to pose again and look at him over my shoulder. These playful moves reminded me of how I used to dance when I was younger in front of mirrors.

Zach laughed. "You're so cute." He tapped the couch. "Come on, relax and have a seat, unless you're having too much fun."

I sat on my knees next to him. "So what's up, Zach?" I grinned.

He shook his head. "You're funny. I know you've told me you have to buy those tokens. Besides that, does the club take a lot of money from you?"

"The bartender—I use that term loosely—she's the one who sells us the coins, she keeps track of how many coins we buy so she can make sure we tip her ten percent at the end of our shift."

"For what? Does she deserve that?"

This is why I liked Zach. He understood. "No, of course not, but I don't have a choice. On top of that, we're supposed to tip out ten percent to the DJ."

"Okay, I can understand paying the DJ, I guess. What happens if you don't?"

"He could quote 'light me up like a Christmas tree,' as one DJ once told me, or screw with the line-up—the order of who goes up on stage."

"I see." He shook his head. "So that's a lot of your money that other people get."

"Wait…that's not all. The floor guys get a couple of dollars."

"Who?"

"The ones down there with the clipboards who count our dances."

"Isn't that what the coins are for?"

"Well, kinda. The guys tally lap and table dances for the manager's info, but unfortunately the idiots don't always know how to count."

Zach scrunched his forehead. "So why tip them? What do they do to deserve it?"

Good point. "Who knows? Supposedly that's how I can assure my protection should I need it. The nasty dancers probably give them extra so they can pretend not to notice the nasty dancers' 'accidental' rule-breaking, like grinding or touching."

"Wow."

"Oh, and I can't forget to give the outdoor security guard a few bucks on the way in and the way out for carrying my bags—they won't take no for an answer—or, they might sell my license plate number to a customer for $20—as was done to a friend of mine."

"You've got to be kidding."

"I wish I was. We also have to pay a stage fee." *When all's done and said, it's easy to go home feeling like you've been pimped out like a whore.*

"They're making enough money from those overpriced sodas and juices," he said. "Why don't we cheat the system? We can sit and talk at a table and drink juice and I'll hand you money and they don't need to know."

"That's nice of you, and I wish I could. Unfortunately, I need to do dances."

"We can do a couple of dances then I can tip you the rest, since the club doesn't know what you've been tipped, do they?"

"No."

"The reason I come here is for you. I enjoy spending time with you and I want to help you out. What happens if you don't do enough dances?"

"Let's say it isn't good to have consistently bad shifts; the manager can give us a crappy schedule, switch around our days, and not let us have the days off we ask for, which would affect my school." *If you don't like it, they'd say, 'tough shit.' Then you'd have to try the club down the street with the skanks.* I kept that part to myself.

After three dances, Zach slipped me a fat tip and gave me a hug goodbye. "I know you need to go make your money. I'll see you next week." He smiled.

Zach left happier than he came. Poor guy must have had a depressing home life. After his departure, I wasn't in the mood to fake flirt with customers to get them to buy a dance. Instead, I went back to the dressing room for a break.

I looked forward to the days Zach came. He put me in a better mood. It was like spending time with a friend who gave me cash every week. He was an easy paycheck, a nice way to pass the time, and nothing more.

I opened my purse to search for my cell phone. I had missed a call from one of my Internet friends. Not wanting to deal with the embarrassment from the New Year's Eve party Yessenia and I had hosted a few weeks earlier which was when I last spoke with this friend, I decided not to return the call.

The phone call reminded me that although Yessenia and I occasionally drank, I had cut back on the alcohol consumption since our last few get-togethers.

On the previous New Year's Eve, Yessenia had a yelling matching with her boyfriend Joe over the phone. She slammed the phone onto the cradle, stormed into the kitchen, and picked up one of the bottles of rum that we had convinced some strangers to buy us even though we were underage.

"What are you doing?" I asked.

She twisted open the cap, brought the bottle to her lips, and gulped mouthfuls of the amber liquid.

I threw my hands up. "That's for our party tonight."

She shrugged. "Buy another one." She guzzled the rum like a baby with a bottle. "Leave me alone."

I tried to wrestle the bottle from her hands. The alcohol splashed out onto my shirt and the carpet. She pulled it away. Tears rushed down her cheeks. "It's over."

"What's over?"

"We broke up." She took the rum and locked herself in the bathroom. "After two fucking years, it's fucking over!" she screamed through the door.

I tried to comfort her, but she ignored me. When she finally staggered out of the bathroom, she set the half-empty bottle down and grabbed her purse and car keys.

"Oh, hell no," I said. "Where are you going?"

"To Joe's."

"You can't drive like that."

"Try to fucking stop me." She intertwined the keys between her fingers and headed towards the front door.

I tackled her and wrestled her to the ground. Being six inches shorter than her, it wasn't easy except that she was sloppy drunk. She grabbed my hair. I yanked the keys from her hand and threw them across the room. They landed behind the china cabinet.

"Fuck you!" she yelled. "Why the fuck did you do that? I hate you. I fucking hate you." She jumped up, ran to the bathroom, and slammed the door shut.

I sulked into a chair. The half-empty bottle of rum on the table mocked me. I could hear Yessenia sobbing and screaming. Without a second thought, I grabbed the bottle, slumped down on the floor and rested my back against the wall. My lips wrapped around the dark, cold glass opening and I let the rum burn its way down my throat. Holding back the urge to gag, I drank more until numbness kicked in.

The empty bottle rolled across the carpet.

A couple hours later, I was still drunk and our party was about to start. The alcohol had hit me hard. Our first guests arrived. Yessenia and I had advertised the party to all of our online buddies, who must have forwarded the invite because there were people pouring in that we didn't know.

With a packed living room and pounding bass, I could barely hear the doorbell. I stumbled to the front door. Standing on my doorstep were two men with square chiseled jaws and sculpted muscles who looked like they'd graduated from college a dozen years ago.

"Do I know you?" I leaned against the wall to stop the room from rocking.

"No." They flashed me gorgeous smiles. One held out a bottle of champagne. "Will this get us in?"

I laughed. "All right, cuties. Come on in." I hugged them both as if we'd been long-time friends.

Inebriated, I didn't recognize half the people, including some who hadn't paid the liquid entrance fee. I didn't care. I danced by myself for an hour before passing out on the couch.

John—a six-foot-four-inch, blonde-haired surfer and an online friend of mine—rocked me, waking me up.

"What, John?" I saw two of him.

He shook his head. "Let me fix you." He adjusted my mini skirt to cover me up. "There, that's better. Some guys here were getting a great view."

"Did I miss the ball drop?" My eyes couldn't focus on the TV.

"Yeah," he said. "But you look like you've had a good time."

"Did I kiss anyone when the ball dropped?" Before I could hear his answer, I passed out and didn't wake up until the morning.

Although we continued to party after that night, Yessenia and I implemented a buddy system to ensure our safety. We alternated who could drink and who would drive home, which also entailed babysitting the drinker. At a hotel party a few days later, it had been my turn to drink, and drink I did. But because some part of me didn't have faith in Yessenia's self-control, I only started off with one beer. Good thing too, since her impulsiveness took over.

"Your friend's in the bathroom and won't come out," the host told me. "Other people need to use it, too."

Grinding my teeth, I walked to the bathroom and knocked lightly. I leaned into the door and whispered, "Yessenia, it's me, Miranda. Let me in."

"What?" she yelled back.

Since the music was pretty loud, I knocked again and raised my voice. "Yessenia, open the door. It's me. Let me in." This caught the attention of a few party-goers who threw me strange glances.

After I coaxed her more, she relented. Once I entered, she slammed the door shut again and locked it. She dropped to the floor, giggling.

"Stop it, Yessenia. It's not funny. It was my turn to drink. How much did you have?"

She held up her hand with one, then two, then three fingers open. She laughed.

"Let's go home," I said.

"No." She rolled on the floor.

"Get up!" I yelled.

"Make me." She stuck out her tongue.

In no mood to party anymore, I grabbed her by the arm and tried to lift her up.

Without warning, she started to scream, "Rape! Help! She's trying to rape me!" She crumpled back down and laughed so hard tears appeared. She continued to shriek, "Rape! Help!"

I pounced on her and covered her mouth with my hands, getting tangled in her sweaty hair. "Stop saying that shit."

She fought me back until someone pounded on the door and yelled, "Open the fucking door before I kick it down!"

I jumped up, unlatched the door, and tried to explain my way out of that embarrassing mess. *Note to self: don't drink at all outside of my house, since Yessenia can't refrain.*

I realized I had been staring at my reflection in the mirror for quite a while. I changed clothes and headed back out to the club floor. Leaning against a railing, I watched the dancer on stage; it was Sara, the voluptuous blonde with long, thick eyelashes from Texas who reminded me of Anna Nicole Smith.

Sara was beautiful and had a sweet southern hospitality about her. Her body was different from many of the other stick-skinny tanned blondes. Sara was softer, curvier, and had a very fair complexion, much like mine.

The longer I stripped, the more I noticed the diversity of women's bodies and the more intrigued I became. I realized the curve of a woman's body and the softness of her skin was nothing like the straight form and hardness of a man.

When Sara's first song ended, I looked around the club and spotted a man showing interest in my direction. With a smile and a wink, I sauntered over to him.

Time to make money.

After introductions, I sat down next to him. He bought me a cranberry juice and we turned our attention back to the dancer on stage. Since the song had already started and guys felt ripped off if you tried to start a dance half-way through a shortened song, I decided to wait another minute before offering him a dance.

I prepared to ask him for a dance when—to my shock—skinny-ass tweeker Emerald pranced by us and slipped a folded paper into the man's shirt pocket. He smiled and started a conversation with her.

I glared at her. She stood there, twirled her shoulder-length mousy brown curls and giggled at him. In disgust, I excused myself to avoid making a scene, exited the floor and headed to the middle dressing room where a few dancers were hanging out.

"That fucking bitch!" I yelled.

Tyger, our self-declared "house-mom"—experienced dancer who takes watch over the newer ones—turned to me. "What happened, Serenity?"

"Emerald. I was sitting next to a customer when she comes over and slips her number or something into the guy's pocket."

"No way." Gaunt and bony like Emerald, Tyger was older, louder, and more aggressive. She stood up. With her overly processed or-angey-blonde hair, intense brown eyes, and pale skin, she looked sickly like usual. "Seriously? I'm a take care of that little speed-addict right now."

The storm was brewing. Tyger, seemingly mentally unstable and at times delusional, could get out of control if we let her. She fiercely protected those she liked, and was territorial over music she felt she owned. Pity the girl who ever tried to play Stabbing Westward's "What Do I Have to Do?" since Tyger bragged that the lead singer wrote that song specifically for her—she did attend many of their concerts, still, her reasoning seemed suspect. Who would dare tell her that it wasn't true? Especially since Autumn, an exotic dark-haired beauty, claimed to have had a brief fling with Chris Isaak—they both played guitar. She claimed to have the photo to prove it, and she actually did. Never could tell with strippers out in Los Angeles. Anything was possible and I'd heard wilder stories than theirs.

Anyway, back to the crisis at hand. Destiny came down the hall-way from the princess dressing room in time to overhear the unfolding drama. Nobody liked Emerald anyway. She had come over from another club a few days prior, and we all shared more than a few suspicions about her and her after-work life.

Truth was that the majority of us on the dayshift were about as honest as it got for strippers. Besides that, I chose to work day shifts for a number of other reasons: less dancers, hence less competition; tamer private dances than the night shift girls as far as the nasty factor went; and easier to fit the days into my already-packed schedule of college and caring for Jacob. If I stripped on nightshifts, I didn't think I'd be able to live with myself.

Whenever a bad apple joined the dayshift, it threatened our livelihood even though management—profiting more money from the whore's many dances—often looked the other way. We had to take care of shit ourselves for self-preservation. It went without saying.

Destiny and I followed Tyger through the doors to the club floor. Emerald glowed red from the lap dance lighting in a booth around the corner. We watched her reflection in a convex mirror on the wall and scowled as she rubbed herself over this man.

"Come on, Serenity," Destiny said. "Let's wait by the bar."

I nodded. We hopped up onto a couple of bar stools.

The song ended and a giggling Emerald stepped down the stairs by the lap dance area. She gave the man a hug—as was customary after a customer gave a dancer a decent tip. When Emerald turned around, Tyger appeared in her face.

Destiny and I couldn't hear too much over the music, but we watched in amusement as Tyger flailed her arms dramatically and Emerald stormed off to the dressing room. We figured maybe Emerald was going to get high and would be too distracted to come back out for a few hours. I could only hope.

Tyger approached us. "Emerald said she didn't realize she did anything wrong, but I told her she better not interrupt a dancer next time."

"Thanks, Tyger." I embraced her for a moment.

She petted my hair. "Don't worry about it sweetheart. We watch out for each other here."

It was a fragile solidarity that we dancers shared.

Chapter Twenty-One
COSTUMES

WINTER 1999

AMY, ONE OF THE dancers who'd been absent for a while, reappeared one day with breast implants.

"Wow, they look so real," Yessenia said. "Did you get them under the muscle?"

"Yeah," Amy said. "Plus I already had breasts anyway. I wanted to lift them and go bigger."

"They did a good job." Yessenia nodded. "If I get them, I'd go under the muscle, too."

"They totally look natural," I said. "Not like Deb's," I whispered. "Hers look like two tennis balls taped to her chest." Deb, one of the night shift girls, had a bad boob job, of which there were many.

"Her doctor did hers too far apart," Amy said. "Plus Deb had nothing to begin with so implants stretched her skin out too much— that's why they look like that." She puffed her out chest. "Do you want to feel them?"

"You don't mind?" I asked.

"Of course not. Squeeze them." Amy came closer. Her tiny bikini top barely covered much, showcasing her overflowing cleavage.

Destiny touched and admired them first. Then it was my turn.

"Yours are soft." I cupped her breasts and gently squeezed. "I can't feel the bags." I rotated my hands all the way around for a fair test. "Blanca's are way harder than yours. I got grossed out when I squeezed hers because the implants moved."

We continued chit-chatting until we all decided it was time to get back to work. It was amusing how commonplace touching each other seemed to be. Gentle teasing or poking was fine so long as it was dancers, not customers, doing it to other dancers.

We didn't take offense to the touching but did learn to be careful whose butts we slapped. It was hard to tell who was straight, bisexual, or lesbian. Some dancers took a little touching as the green light to get more intimate. I actually wasn't doing too much of the touching, but I was getting touched.

Perhaps this was increasing my sexual interest. I hadn't gone there yet with another woman but was considering it more and more. I didn't know whether it was a natural progression of being surrounded by beautiful naked women whose bodies looked like works of art, a pre-existing tendency I had suppressed because of my Christian upbringing, or normal female curiosity.

After the years I would spend in the adult entertainment industry, I underwent a gradual change in sexual preferences to the point where I no longer considered gender as a hard-and-fast requirement for determining whom I could love: women and men had become equal opportunities in my mind. However, women seemed much more alluring, soft, and gorgeous. I don't remember when or how my viewpoint morphed from a "traditional" heterosexual one to that of bi-curious.

At any rate, I realized it was only a matter of time before I got to move from thinking about touching another woman to doing it.

Although we were comfortable with one another, most of us dancers didn't borrow clothes. We wore a handful of outfits over and over again on a regular basis. Customers recognized dancers by music and costumes since they weren't really looking at our faces most of the time.

I remembered how during my first week dancing, I had bought a couple of used bikinis, a black Lycra miniskirt, and a neon glow-in-the-dark yellow stretchy top and matching miniskirt—the 80s at their finest—from eighteen-year-old Kimmy for $20.

Relatively new to the dancing profession, I had little more than a couple of pairs of six-inch platform stilettos and some gallon-size plastic Ziploc bags of clothes stuffed in my duffle bag.

The Ziploc bags were a great idea that I learned from the more seasoned professionals. One bag held lacy thongs, one held silky lap dance shorts, and the others each held separate outfits. This kept everything fresh. Otherwise fabric seemed to absorb the stale scent of cheap berry fragrance or floral splash, and the smell of old, sweaty footwear.

Partly because I didn't want to waste money on this temporary dancing job and partly out of financial necessity, my money went to rent, daycare, college supplies, and food—I didn't spend much on dancer attire. That was until my coworker Heidi made me aware of my costume inadequacies.

"Serenity, that's a cute dress for going out partying," Heidi said. "Now—don't take this the wrong way—but you shouldn't wear that on stage. It's not flattering." Heidi, a bony Hungarian woman, brushed her short brown hair from her forehead.

I gazed down at my little blue flowered spring dress with a peek-a-boo opening at the chest. "I don't have many other outfits. What about the red dress I wear? Do you think that one looks bad, too?"

"No, that one's sexy. This one doesn't look good under the lighting. You're so pale that it washes you out." She flashed a sweet smile at me that assured me she intended no malice with her words. "I hope you don't mind me saying something."

"Not at all. I appreciate your honesty."

I sulked back to the princess dressing room and stayed there for the next half-hour before I ventured out to the floor to sell dances. I knew I needed new costumes but couldn't do anything about it at that moment.

Besides my wardrobe, my music repertoire was also limited. Although CDs lay stacked in piles at my home, I didn't know which ones constituted good "stripper songs." I used songs by Enigma, George Michael, Aerosmith, Massive Attack, Duran Duran, and many others, including "Last Dance with Mary Jane" by Tom Petty and the Heartbreakers.

Of course, I had to be careful not to add another song to my list without first confirming no other dancer had laid claim to it; that was one sure way to piss off dancers and it wasn't good to have enemies.

One day I tried a couple of new songs, one by Melissa Etheridge, and "Constant Craving" by k.d. lang. Josephine, an older—meaning in her late thirties—tall, curvy dark-haired beauty, came up to me after my set. She had a classy 1930s starlet look about her.

"You're into k.d. lang and Melissa Etheridge?" Josephine asked.

"Yeah, I like them," I said as I slipped my dress back on.

She smirked and waltzed away.

On my next shift, I was backstage getting dressed when Josephine approached me, her dark brown curls cascading down the back of her pink silk robe. With a sweeping gesture and a warm smile she showed me a brand new CD, one by k.d. lang.

"For you," she announced.

"Oh, that's so sweet. Thanks." I took the CD, even though in all honesty, I only liked a few k.d. lang songs.

"You and Destiny should come over to dinner at my house this Saturday." She raised her eyebrows. "What do you think?"

"I'll talk to her, and let you know," I said. "Thanks for the offer." I figured she was just being friendly.

"Great. I'd love for you to come over." She winked before she disappeared down the hallway into the middle dressing room.

Heidi had been backstage too, since she was onstage after me. While I slipped my lap dance shorts on over my thong, she whispered, "Be careful, Serenity. Josephine and her husband are swingers. She probably wants you to come over with that intention."

"I didn't even know she was married." I laughed. "Why would she think I'm into that?"

Heidi laughed. "You've been playing a lot of songs by lesbians lately."

If what Heidi said was true, I was quite flattered by Josephine's offer and even began to consider it.

Destiny wasn't having any of it. Although she and I had both been discussing our desires to explore bisexuality, she was neither attracted to Josephine nor interested in any group event.

"That's okay." Josephine pursed her lips together after I declined her invitation. "But how about if you and I go shopping for costumes? You need something better than those old dresses you keep wearing. Sexy lingerie will get you better customers."

A few days later, I found myself seated on an old burgundy velvet couch in Josephine's living room, watching her stoned mother pace the hallway. Josephine owned a quaint three-bedroom bungalow in the South Bay. Her house was in an older neighborhood, off of a busy street. Her eclectic furniture matched her airy style.

"Don't mind her," Josephine said as she handed her mom a bag of pot. "She smokes marijuana to calm down." I stood up and followed Josephine outside. "She used to dance, too." She laughed. "Runs in the family."

I withheld my surprised reaction. Runs in the family? My dad worked with computers and my mom handled customer phone calls. Her mom was a stripper. Our parents probably wouldn't have much in common.

While we traveled from the South Bay to Hollywood, I couldn't help but notice how thin Josephine's thighs were. Over ten years older than I, she still had better legs. What was her secret?

"We are exotic dancers, not strippers," Josephine lectured me. "The difference is in how you dress, how you carry yourself, and even what music you play. I think you should use the older classic rock like I do and you should wear a classy corset and garter belt. You'll immediately see the difference. Older men have the money. That's who you should be working."

To a certain extent, I already understood this. While some dancers chased after the young and handsome, they were missing the steady income of the middle-aged and older clientele.

Josephine and I stepped inside the small pink square building called Trashy Lingerie, a members-only store. I filled out an application, paid a membership fee, and was granted access to beautiful hand-crafted lingerie. There were cherry-patterned bikinis on racks, lacy negligee along the walls, stockings on the shelves. This store was an exotic dancer's heaven.

"They've supplied lingerie to Hollywood," Josephine said. "Julia Roberts had something made here for one of her movies."

I quickly realized this was no twenty-dollar-apiece bargain store. Many items had price tags that extended into the triple digits. I groaned. I was barely able to pay bills with my three or four shifts per week.

"This is a classy place," she said. "Hold on a moment. I'm going to get someone to take your measurements." She noted my hesitation. "Don't worry about the cost. You will more than make up for it in tips. Go ahead; choose something." She pointed to a wall of corsets made with satin and lace. "Take a look at those themed costumes on the racks over there." She winked and left. She had taken control and I had let her. She had become a friend and a mentor.

I brushed my fingers along the different colors and styles of corsets until my eyes caught sight of the pink one. It was exquisite. I'd never owned anything so nice. I ran my hands along the silky bodice and realized this handmade garment was of better quality than anything in my closet.

Before I could blink, I had signed the credit card slip and ordered a handmade pink floral corset with a matching garter belt, two pairs of old-fashioned stockings with actual seams up the back, and an authentic policewoman costume, complete with an official but illicit LAPD badge.

During the drive to Hollywood Boulevard, Josephine and I brain-stormed which songs were most appropriate for my new cop costume and we settled on "Bad Boys" by Inner Circle, which was heavy on the bass.

Once we arrived in Hollywood, I remembered when Yessenia and I had been propositioned for sex and ended up in a transvestite shoe store. Well, Josephine and I had a completely different experience.

Inside another lingerie store, I bought more corsets—one black and one white—and matching garter belts, three pairs of satin gloves that went up past my elbows and another pair of platform stilettos. I couldn't bear to look at the receipts I shoved into my purse.

I hoped Josephine was right, that the costumes would increase my tips.

* * *

The next weekend, Yessenia was back together with her on-again off-again boyfriend Joe for what would end up being the last month they would ever see each other. The three of us—I figured there was safe-ty in numbers—drove to a house party being thrown by our Internet friends.

We hadn't been there long before the party was cut short because the host's mom—who owned the house and knew nothing about the party—was unexpectedly on her way home. We wanted to leave be-fore his mom could see the piles of soap bubbles oozing out of her swimming pool—we had nothing to do with that but it was hilarious.

"Hey, we're getting together at someone else's house. Want to come?" asked John—the same friend of mine who several months earlier had protected me at my New Year's Eve party by fixing my skirt down to cover my ass. John and two of his buddies were in his car, ready to go. They had a couple of twelve-packs of beer in the trunk.

I looked at Yessenia and her boyfriend, who both nodded. "All right," I said. "We'll follow you."

After we found parking in the sprawling apartment complex, Joe, Yessenia, and I ascended stairs to the party apartment where John and his friends were already. I didn't know most of the people there. The music was loud, the room was smoke-filled, and there was alcohol of all sorts on every table and counter.

A man in his late twenties with curly black hair and a goofy smile approached me. "Hi, remember me?"

I could hardly hear him over the laughter and bass. Raising my eyebrows, I skimmed through my backlog of party memories and shook my head.

"I'm Frank." He grabbed a couple of beers from a cooler on the kitchen counter. "This is my apartment."

I blushed, supposing I should know that. "Cool party." I turned around to check out the place and realized Yessenia and her boyfriend had disappeared into another room.

Frank opened the two beer bottles and handed one to me. "You're Miranda, right?"

I nodded. Normally, I didn't care too much for beer, but I took a big swig to be polite. "Thanks." I wiped my mouth.

He pointed to his ear to indicate he couldn't hear me. Then he motioned for me to follow him outside to the patio.

Once in the cool breezy night, he closed the sliding door, took a deep breath and stepped closer to me. "We met before."

"When?" I drank some more. The bitter liquid rushed down my throat. I smiled, pretending that I didn't almost gag on the horrid taste.

I don't remember you at all. How do you know my name?

He stared intently into my eyes. "Didn't you have a New Year's Eve party at your place a couple weeks ago?" The corners of his lips upturned in a flirty smile and he winked at me before guzzling nearly half his bottle of beer.

Ha! I was so drunk I wouldn't remember if you were wearing a pink bunny suit and doing cartwheels. "You were there?" I said. "Sorry, there were a lot of people."

"Yeah." He chuckled. "You were pretty wild."

"I was?" Panic filled my mind. "What do you mean?" I hoped I didn't do anything too risky. *Oh, shit. Did I strip? Please tell me I didn't.*

He laughed and placed a warm hand on my bare arm. "I meant you were having a good time dancing before you passed out."

"Oh." I didn't know what else to say. I stared out at the trees. The leaves were blowing in the wind. I forced more beer down my throat, hoping to soon feel a buzz.

He finished his bottle and set it down. "Miranda," he said, "Has anyone told you how pretty you are?"

Yes, all the time at work. It's a nice but typical pick-up line. "Thank you."

However, his attraction toward me wasn't mutual and I wanted to meet other people at the party.

"I love your green eyes."

"I need to find my friends," I said.

Frank nodded and opened the sliding door for me.

I found Yessenia and her boyfriend in Frank's bedroom, along with my friend John and his friends, sitting on chairs around a small table. Yessenia looked up when I entered and said, "We're going to play quarters. Want to join us?"

A shot glass sat empty in the middle of the table, surrounded by unopened bottles of beer. Quarters: the classic drinking game. I sucked at it. I couldn't flip the damn quarter into the glass and always ending up having to drink more than everyone else.

"I'll watch," I said.

Frank reappeared in the doorway, holding bottles of rum and tequila. "Let's play." He looked at me and grinned. "C'mon, we'll go easy on you."

I was suckered into participating. Sure enough, I was soon drunk on a mixture of beer and hard liquor.

After a while, most of the guests thinned out and John's friends wanted to leave. John had a worried expression on his face and signaled me to follow him into the living room. He bent down, wrapped his arms around me in a tight hug, and whispered into my ear, "I don't want to leave you here, but my buddies won't stay. I don't trust that guy Frank and the way he's been looking at you tonight."

Giggling and slurring my speech, I said, "Thon't worry. My fends are here. I'm g'be fin-n-ne."

"He's been making you drink hard liquor while everyone else has been sticking to beer. Watch out."

"Awww, you're soooo sweet, John-ee." My head felt floppy like a rag doll.

John took one last look at me before leaving with his now-irritated friends. By the time I turned around, it seemed everyone else was gone. I went back into the bedroom. Yessenia and her boyfriend weren't at the table anymore.

"Where's Yes-sen-ia?"

Frank smiled, took my hand, pulled me out of his bedroom and closed the door behind him. "They wanted to be alone in my walk-in closet for a while." He winked.

I couldn't quite process that information. I slumped down on his couch.

"You look tired," he said. "I have a futon over there if you want to lie down until your friends are ready to go."

"No thanks. I'll...I'll be fine," The TV was on. I yawned and zoned out to whatever was on the screen. Frank walked away.

Time lapsed and I woke up when I felt someone sitting next to me. It was Frank. "I didn't know I's sleeping," I said. "I'm sooo sorry."

"You're fine," he assured me.

I rested my head back against the couch cushion and everything went black.

In a dream, I felt warm lips touch mine. For a moment my lips automatically pressed back, until my brain caught up with them. Strong cologne invaded my nose. I opened my eyes and saw Frank kneeling in front of me. He leaned in for another kiss.

I turned my head and pulled away.

He jumped back. "I'm sorry. You were kissing me back."

I glared at him—or at least I tried. Whether or not my facial muscles complied is another thing altogether.

He left the room. I closed my eyes and instantly fell back asleep.

Something pulled at my arms. Even though my vision was unsteady and the room was shaking, I saw Frank reach out his hands and pull me up to a wobbly standing position—I hardly felt a thing.

"C'mon," he said. "You look so tired. Come lie down. It's no trouble at all." He leaned me against the wall while he slid open the futon, converting it to a bed. Then he led me over, helped me lie down, put a pillow under my head, and covered me up with a blanket.

"See?" he said. "No problem. I'll go check on your friends."

I thought he was being so thoughtful, such a nice guy. When he left the room, my eyes closed, my brain shut down, and again I was out cold.

In a strange dream-like state, I sensed something wasn't right. I couldn't wake up. My body felt like a heavy weight was on top of it. My neck tingled. I tried to swallow, but my throat was dry. I felt a light tickle on my neck, then my cheek, then my chin, until something wet pressed against my lips.

Open my eyes. Why can't I open my eyes? Wake up. Eyes open, please.

Finally, the synapses connected and Frank's face came into focus. He was lying on top of me—his jeans against mine, his arms around my shoulders. He kissed my neck.

Please stop. I don't want you to do this.

I couldn't move.

Get off me.

I was paralyzed. Frank and the room spun in circles in front of me. I felt like I was on one of those centrifugal force rides at the county fair, which slam you up against the wall. My brain lost communication with my body and I fell back into a deep slumber. Blackness, blank mind—I was far away.

Some instinct woke me up like a battery backup after a power outage. My eyes flashed open. I saw Frank much more clearly than I could feel him. He didn't notice me being awake because he was too busy groping at my breasts.

No, this isn't happening to me. Wake up!

Frank's teeth latched onto the bottom of my shirt and pulled it up. He hands slid across my bra, cupping my breasts.

Stop it! Fucking stop it, Frank! Get off me, mother fucker! I screamed in my head, but not a sound escaped my lips.

I felt cold air on my midsection. My shirt had been pulled up to the bottom of my bra. He was licking my stomach.

No, you can't do this to me! Why can't I get up? Why can't I move? Why can't I speak?

With one hand still fondling my breasts, Frank slid his other hand south. His body pressed harder on top of me. He unbuttoned my jeans.

I'm not going to let this happen. C'mon brain, wake up. If I can't move, please let me at least scream.

I yelled in my head over and over again, hoping the words would materialize. *No! No! No! Okay, on the count of three, I'm going to scream.* I focused intently on my mouth, on making the sounds with my lips, on pushing the air up from my diaphragm.

No! No! "No!" I miraculously bolted up a few inches. Frank jumped off of me. Apparently, the last "no" had escaped my mouth. Then, as if by divine intervention, I was able to yell, "Get my friends! Now!"

Without hesitation, Frank went into his bedroom.

Having spent every last drop of concentration and control, I fell back down and passed out again.

"Miranda, wake up," I heard Yessenia's voice. She sounded so far away. "I heard you scream. What happened? Get up." She was kneeling down next to me and shaking my shoulder.

With her help, I sat up. "He was trying to rape me."

"Oh shit!" she said.

I was still pretty limp and she held me up.

"Joe!" she yelled. I blinked and her boyfriend was there. Yessenia lowered her voice. "Let's get the fuck out of here. Now."

I staggered out the front door with their help and slid onto Yessenia's back seat. She clicked my seatbelt. Thankfully, Yessenia was sober enough to drive.

I stared out the car window, unable to speak. *So much for safety in numbers. No one's going to watch out for me; I have to protect myself.*

I had been lucky. Never again would I get wasted unless in the safety of my own house with people I trusted. *As a matter of fact, why would I want to get drunk at all?*

I have a son. He needs me. I almost got raped and who knows what could have happened after that? How would I have been able to deal with that trauma?

At seventeen, after Henry raped me, I checked myself in to see a psychologist who diagnosed me with depression. I had stopped taking the medication two years earlier.

Later that night in bed, I tossed and turned. The stupid partying wasn't worth it. It was no longer fun, not after Frank.

I need to spend more time taking my job as Jacob's mother seriously and less time with Mr. Rum-and-Vodka.

I made a mental note to see another psychologist—if I could remember to when I woke up.

CHAPTER TWENTY-TWO
DECISIONS

WINTER 1999

SPRING SEMESTER WAS ABOUT to start. I was fortunate to have locked in a Monday and Wednesday school schedule. This meant that I needed to see Giovanni, the general manager of Century Lounge, to request a schedule change—no easy task since he was an arrogant, chauvinistic asshole.

But better to speak to Giovanni than with the disheveled, gray-haired owner of the nude club, Howard. He was an old lunatic—he was known to randomly come in, watch the stage for a few sets, and make nonsensical complaints about the girls to the managers. For example, one week he could be unhappy with a girl and request that she cake on more eye shadow, bright blush and red lipstick and she'd have to comply, at least until he left the club. The following week, he could call a girl over and lavish her with flirtatious compliments. Sometimes this was the same girl he complained about the week before.

We dancers came to the conclusion that Howard was senile. He often ordered walls to be constructed in random places of the club, constantly changing of the layout of the dance booths; the club was always construction zone. Howard changed the dance prices so often that even the dancers didn't know what to charge—we'd have to check the sign daily. On occasion, he would change the token or dance prices in the middle of the day, so our tokens were like stocks in the stock market, they increased or decreased in value; it was impossible to predict.

In his apparent lack of good judgment, Howard had hired Giovanni, a war vet with anger management issues and possible PTSD, as our general manager. Bob, our nice daytime manager—the one who had hired Yessenia and me—was an old war buddy of Giovanni's. I couldn't quite picture Bob as a soldier. Or as a strip club manager. He reminded me of an accountant. Bob was the only buffer between us dancers, Howard's crazy whims and Giovanni's firecracker temper.

The girls gave me last-minute advice on how to deal with my Giovanni meeting.

"If it comes down to it, cry," Tyger said. "Crying works for me every time. It helps if you can get him to feel sorry for you."

Tyger often cried and I felt sorry for her. I heard she'd hallucinate and scream at invisible apparitions. We tried to attribute it more to mental illness than her likely drug use. Regardless, I didn't think the pathetic act would work for me, but I supposed if it came down to it crying was worth a try.

Bob came into the dressing room to fetch me.

"Good luck," the dancers called out as I followed Bob to the hidden back room.

I felt like I was being led to the gallows. I had no idea if was Giovanni was going to scream at me in the midst of some battlefield flashback.

Bob didn't say much along the way.

I followed him through the near darkness. "Is it true that this used to be a bowling alley?" I asked, trying to ease my nerves.

"Sure was." He pointed to the darkness. "The lanes are still over there."

I had the impression that Bob wasn't any happier than I to be heading back to Giovanni's office.

"Wait here," he said when we reached a corner lit up by a single light bulb.

I bit my lip and watched him disappear behind a wooden door. I tugged at the bottom of my dress and dug my heel into the old carpet.

Bob reappeared, his hands trembling. "Did you bring your college schedule like I asked?"

"Yes." I unfolded the paper in my hand. I knew Giovanni liked to be in control and didn't like to change dancers' schedules unless he felt it was warranted, or if he was in a good mood. I sensed the latter wasn't happening that day.

"Good," Bob said. His voice was shaky. His apparent nervousness only made mine worse. "Go on in. I'll wait out here."

I managed to fake half a smile and entered the small room. Giovanni, with his full head of black hair, dark skin, and cold beady eyes, sat behind a large wooden desk littered with piles of papers. No windows, no artwork, no plants—only a desk, chairs, and filing cabinets. Giovanni raised his chin and motioned for me to shut the door and sit down, which I did. I opened my schedule. He leaned back in his chair and crossed his buff tattooed arms.

"Hi." I plastered on my friendliest smile, hoping to appear more confident than I was. My smile was met with his stone-faced expression, my greeting met with his grunt. I slid my schedule across the table. "I need to change my shifts because my new college semester is starting. That means I can't work on Mondays or Wednesdays."

I saw a large ring on his pinky finger when he picked up my schedule. His button-up dress shirt seemed out of place in this office. His arm muscles bulged against the sleeves. He didn't say anything for a moment—only stared at my schedule. He took a long deliberate breath before leaning forward. "How's your attendance here?"

"Good."

"Have you been showing up for your shifts, or have you called out a lot?" He narrowed his eyes.

"I've been here every day I've been scheduled." Luckily, since I'd only been working for about a month, this was true.

"Have you been on time?" He barked questions at me like a drill sergeant.

"Yes." *Or within an hour of my scheduled time.*

"Are you going to ask for any other days off?"

"No, I don't think so."

"How do I know you won't drop these classes?"

What the hell? If he doesn't change my schedule, I'll lose this job. Then I can't support Jacob. I don't think I'm going to need to act—I may start crying in a moment for real.

"I have a baby to support. I'm trying to get my college degree, so I can't drop my classes. I can work those days after my semester ends." I held in my tears and focused my eyes down to stare at some papers on his desk.

"I need girls to work Mondays," he said.

How was that my problem? "I can't work when I have classes."

"What about the evenings?"

"I can't because I don't have daycare at night." I managed to look him in the face again. "Please, Giovanni. Please, I need this."

He paused a long while, studying my face. I felt I was being judged for some crime. At last, he responded, "All right."

I waited for something more before I realized the conversation was over. "Thank you. I appreciate it."

He no longer acknowledged my presence. That was it. I stood up, exited the room and was escorted back to the dressing room by Bob.

After we were out of earshot, Bob asked, "How did it go?"

"Okay, I guess. He's not nice."

"Well, I think he has bipolar disorder or something." Bob led me back into the main club area. He glanced at my dress and smiled. "You look like you've lost weight."

I stared at the carpet. "Yeah, I lost a few pounds."

"Good for you! You look great." He wrapped his arms around me in a fatherly hug. "I'm so proud of you. I knew you could do it."

"Thanks." I blushed. "You're the nicest manager I've ever had."

"I'm glad I hired you and Destiny. You two are good girls with great attitudes, good heads on your shoulders—unlike some of the others here."

I didn't know if he was referring to freakish Emerald, unstable Tyger, drunken Blanca, or one of the other drugged-out dancers. At any rate, I appreciated the compliment and flashed him a warm smile.

*   *   *

Yessenia decided she didn't want to come to work when I wasn't working, so she asked Bob to change her schedule, too. That meant that she had to meet with Giovanni. I was worried for her since she didn't have a college schedule or a child to use as excuses—only the fact that we carpooled.

"How did it go?" I asked her on the way home.

"He's an ass," she said. "He had a gun on his desk."

"A gun? Are you kidding me?"

"He didn't have it out when you went to talk to him?"

"No." I was horrified.

"Yeah. He kept playing with the handgun, twirling it around, pretending to point it at me. He was trying to intimidate me."

"He's nuts. I mean, something is *seriously* mentally wrong with him. Weren't you freaked out?"

She shrugged.

"Did you get the schedule change?"

"Yes, but I don't know if he'll give it to me next time."

*　　*　　*

First Yessenia's 21st birthday came and went, then mine. Even though we were now legally of age to work in a topless club we decided to stick to the nude club. Yessenia had pointed out to me that "it's easier to deal with sober men than drunken ones," and I had agreed.

*　　*　　*

Valentine's Day was around the corner. How to celebrate? I decided a trip to Las Vegas was in order. But I didn't want to go alone. Dan was available, so we made plans to go with Yessenia and the firefighter she was dating at the time.

During the long drive there, I thought about whom I wanted to keep dating: Dan or Jason. After the Frank incident, dating men other than these two no longer appealed to me. Dan and Jason were kind but their patience with my wishy-washiness was waning. I knew it was time to choose one, but it was a tough choice.

I made a list.

Jason, pros: sweet, affectionate, smart, spiritual, honest, romantic, creative in bed, good with my son, gives massages to die for, treats me like a queen, seems genuinely interested in who I am, encourages me to continue my writing and compliments me on the stories I hadn't shared with anyone else since high school, and supports me in whatever I want in life.

Dan, pros: sweet, affectionate, shares part of my past and so he understands me, compliments me, willing to come over to my house whenever he can, has a son so he must be good with kids, has a stable job and income, is dependable, ambitious, intelligent, refined, and romantic.

Jason, cons: smokes cigarettes, smokes weed, no stable job or income.

Dan, cons: credit problems, lives with his parents.

Conclusion: none.

In Vegas, I lay on Dan's arm in bed in our hotel room. "I know I can't keep dating both you and Jason. I know it's not fair."

He wrapped his other arm around me and rolled me over to face him. Our noses were inches apart. "It's easy. I have a solution."

"Oh yeah? What's that?"

"Be my girlfriend and stop dating Jason and the other men. See? Problem solved."

"I'm sorry I'm putting you through this." I turned on my back and stared up at the mirrors on the ceiling. *Where was the pink champagne on ice? Ha-ha.* "Have you ever seen mirrors on the ceiling before?"

Dan pointed to the side. "They are mirrors on the walls, too."

"What time are our dinner reservations?" I smirked, running my fingers through his hair.

* * *

After returning to California, I still couldn't decide between Dan and Jason. I cared about them both. Why couldn't I create one person out of the two of them?

After much reflection, I stopped dating Jason and become exclusive with Dan. It wasn't because I had some epiphany. I simply figured it was better to chance making a wrong decision than to remain indecisive. Since these two men allowed me to continue hurting their feelings, it was up to me to stop them from being so permissive.

I had to think about what was best for Jacob, too. Dan had a stable job as a computer network administrator and a son the same age as Jacob. Meanwhile, Jason didn't seem to have any real ambition and certainly wouldn't be able to support a family. Jason acted like a doormat.

Like buying a car, changing careers, and applying to a university, I assumed choosing a mate should be a logical decision made with my mind and not with my conflicted heart. Dan seemed to be my safe bet. All the hours I spent on the phone with Jason, all the time spent cuddling with and talking to him, I ignored. I put all that behind me.

Everything was falling into place. Mostly.

Chapter Twenty-Three
Issues

February - March 1999

In addition to the gold heart pendent necklace and dozen long-stem red roses Dan gave me during our Valentine's weekend in Vegas, I also received gifts—albeit less meaningful ones—from my regulars at work: teddy bears, jewelry, flowers, and extra cash (which I took home).

Things I wished I wasn't taking home from work were swollen knees, crooked toes, and painful muscles.

Blanca placed a towel on her stool in the dressing room and sat down. Other than her black stilettos and lacy bobby socks, she was completely nude. Her tangled hair scattered across her brown shoulders. She cracked open a beer can and looked at Yessenia and me through the mirror while listening to us discuss our aches and pains.

She asked, "You two crawl on stage on your knees?"

"Yes," Yessenia said. "Why?"

"I sure as hell don't crawl on the dirty-ass stage," Blanca said. Blanca, the black-haired hard-bodied forty-year-old with perky implants and vaginal reconstructive surgery—whatever that was, I never wanted to ask—did not do "floor work."

I laughed. "Well, I don't have the muscle strength to do the pole work you do." And after the incident at the bikini club, I realized no job was worth paralysis. "I wish I knew how to crawl around on stage without messing up my knees."

"Use your shins." She tapped hers. "Don't put weight on your knees. That's what the other dancers do."

"That sounds hard," I said. I slipped stockings on to cover the bruising and swelling. "My knees hurt so badly that I have to ice them every night when I get home. And my feet are killing me. These stupid shoes squish my toes at the end. I'm getting deformed."

"Don't crawl until your knees heal. You don't want knee-replacement surgery." Blanca picked up her beer and took another swig. "Buy a foot spa and soak your feet in Epson salt every night. That's what I do." She gulped down half the can and belched.

"I don't want to crawl anymore," Yessenia said. "I only do that when I can't think of anything else to do on stage. The floor's disgusting."

Blanca finished her beer, crushed it, and tossed it into the trash can. "Hell yeah it is. Fuck the men. I don't get paid enough to crawl. They can kiss my ass." She took another beer from the cooler she had under the counter. "Buy some wraps in the drug store. Ones with long ice packs. Slide the ice in, wrap them around your knees, and Velcro shut."

I looked at Yessenia. "Sounds like we need to go shopping tonight."

Yessenia held her shoes. "I'm not wearing these until I get out on the floor."

I followed her lead. We limped down the hallway, six-inch platform stilettos in hand.

* * *

As long as there were at least ten dancers working the day shift, we each only had to go up on stage once per hour, leaving time to make money doing lap and table dances. Unfortunately, many dancers frequently called out sick, so one day we were terribly short-staffed— only six girls on the line-up. On top of that, one of those dancers, eighteen-year-old Kimmy (whose underdeveloped breasts made her look even younger), only did nude table dances—no lap dances (at her boyfriend's request). And, of course, the club was busy, which meant a small supply to meet a big demand.

"Serenity, you're up next," the DJ announced over the speakers at the start of another dancer's second song.

We much appreciated these reminders. Otherwise, there could be an empty stage.

"Do you have time for a dance?" a man asked me before I had a chance to go backstage to change.

I couldn't turn down easy money. "Of course." I led him to the lap dance booth, dropped in a token, and slinked around him, bathed in red lights.

The song came to an end and I heard the first notes of Aerosmith's "Rag Doll." My customer looked into my eyes longingly. "Can we do another dance?"

"I'm on stage next, so come watch me. We can do another dance afterward." I figured the other girl was probably done picking up her tips.

He opened his wallet and handed me a twenty. The dance prices kept changing. Today they were fifteen dollars. I thanked him for the tip and ran backstage. Running in six-inch stilettos was an art—albeit a dangerous one.

Marvin, the DJ who looked like a kind grandfather, repeated his introduction for me. Breathless, I shoved my purse through the red curtains onto the stage and made my entrance.

I danced my usual routine. Soon my second song, "Sweet Emotion," came to its three-minute cut-off point. I slipped into a robe and walked around the edge of the stage to pick up my tips.

"Thank you," I said to each man.

One gentleman leaned forward. "Can I get a dance when you get off stage?"

I looked over at my previous customer who had stood up with his drink and left the stage, awaiting my return. "Someone already asked me, but I can dance for you after him. Where can I find you?"

He agreed and pointed to a table.

Yes! Now I have some cash lined up.

Money was great that day, but exhaustion took over. It would figure that the club was packed with men wanting dances on the day that we had to go up on stage every thirty minutes. It was as if the customers were turned on by our sweaty bodies as we rushed from the dance area to the stage and back to the customers who requested dances.

My thighs burned from the squatting pain of doing slow-moving lap dances—trying to keep off of their laps.

I rushed over to the private lap dance area where yet another man was waiting for me. I stepped up the stairs and my heel caught on something. I reached for a table but didn't make it. My knees—my swollen painful knees—slammed down on the carpeted stairs. My shin hit the edge of a step. Pain shot through my body.

"Are you okay?" My customer extended a hand, which I readily accepted.

"Yes, thank you, I'm fine," I lied and forced a seductive smile. *I can pay more of my credit card balances or make another car payment if I can keep going.*

After doing two dances for him, I limped to the bar, ordered an ice pack, and headed to the dressing room to assess the damage.

Yessenia was in there changing. She stared at my leg. "What the fuck? That looks horrible."

I sat down and lifted my leg onto another stool. A purple bruise started to surround a big hard greenish lump.

"It hurts like hell." I whimpered. The ice stung, but I knew I had to reduce the swelling.

"Serenity, you're up next," DJ Marvin said over the loudspeaker.

"Shit." I wanted to cry. To distract myself from the pain, I counted my cash. In four hours, I had already made as much as I normally could in a full eight-hour shift.

"Want me to tell Marvin to skip your set?" Yessenia asked.

And stop making money? "No, it's okay. I'll put on a corset, garter belt, and stockings to hide this." I slipped my black stocking up my leg and flinched at the tenderness. "I'll be fine." *I hope.*

"Are you sure?"

I stood up. "Can you see it through the black stockings?"

"Not really." She shook her head. "You're fucking nuts."

I was ecstatic when our shift was over. At home and exhausted, I slept well, other than the throbbing pain which the ibuprofen couldn't erase.

*   *   *

The following weekend, still recovering from my bruised leg—fortunately the swelling had subsided—I took Jacob to the large park near our apartment to relax and enjoy the beautiful sunny California winter day.

I squeezed Jacob's hand. "Listen to me. Don't run around the lake. Be careful."

Jacob wiggled and squirmed until he freed himself of my grasp. "I know. I will."

I handed him a slice of bread. "This is the last piece I have. There's a duck over there."

A few feet ahead of me, Jacob ran to the water's edge. He held his hand over the water and bent over, inching closer and leaning further.

Before I could stop him, his footing slipped on the wet walkway and he slid into the green water.

I lunged for him, grabbed hold of his jean overalls and lifted him up out of the water. While he didn't fall all the way into the lake, he was dripping wet from the knees down and crying.

Time to go home.

*   *   *

On Tuesday, my alarm buzzed me awake at 7 AM, just in time to get ready for school. I stretched and rubbed my eyes. If Jacob wasn't already up, I needed to wake him so he'd have time to go potty, eat breakfast, and get dressed.

I shuffled across the room and peered around the room divider to find his toddler bed empty. My eyes widened and I ran to my bedroom door. It was locked. I flung open the blinds and saw him sitting on the carpet. He looked up at me and grinned. His hands and legs were covered in blue, red, and green ink. So was my carpet. Crayola markers, which I thought I had secured out of his reach, lay strewn across the floor.

"Jacob!" I yelled. "Why did you get into the markers?" I turned around to find the answer.

Jacob had precariously piled up his toys and clothes until he was able to reach the top of my dresser. "I want to draw."

"You can't do that! Help me clean up."

"No." He went to his bed, climbed on top, and started jumping on the mattress.

"Jacob, stop it!" I grabbed him and brought his flailing body back to the ground and used baby wipes to clean him while he screamed in my ear.

I spent the next thirty minutes on my bruised and swollen knees scrubbing the carpet. As usual, I was late to class. I wondered if God was somehow punishing me.

I paid attention when other parents I knew suggested that much of Jacob's constant lack of self-control, impulsivity, and defiance meant he should be tested for attention deficit hyperactivity disorder, ADHD. Even though I sensed something was amiss with him and I was frustrated, I didn't want to accept that my baby might be abnormal.

*   *   *

After I took a few days off to heal, I was back at work at the club. I settled down in one of the club's strange movie-theater-style seats. I leaned my elbows on the armrests and ignored the musky smell of old wood that permeated the air and mixed with cheap floral spray and customer body odor.

Business was slow. Lenny Kravitz sang "American Woman" while adorable petite blonde-haired Genie—with her thigh-high red vinyl boots, devil's horns headband, and nothing else—swung gracefully on the pole, wrapping, twisting, and contorting her tiny frame around it. With her short straight bangs, she looked like a twelve-year-old school girl—even though she was older than I. This thought disturbed me and I decided to sell dances instead of staring at her hairless pussy and feeling like a pedophile.

"Hi, I'm Serenity. What's your name?" I whispered into a man's ear. He told me his name, which I promptly forgot. "Would you like a dance?"

"What kind do you do and how much?"

"I can give you a lap dance or a nude table dance for fifteen dollars, whichever you want."

"All right. Let's do some lap dances." He stood up and followed me to the back of the club.

I wish it was always this easy. I wouldn't have to get frustrated over rejections.

After our dance, he tipped me, I hugged him, and we parted ways. I leaned against a brass railing next to Yessenia and watched the stage.

"Put your hands together and welcome Lisa to the stage," Marvin announced.

Lisa's typical song "Pour Some Sugar on Me" by Def Leopard blared out of the speakers.

A customer named Sarge—whom I assumed was a retired police sergeant—quickly made his way to the tip rail. He squeezed into the seat, his belly pressed against the counter even with his straight posture. After rubbing his hand across his gray buzz cut, he adjusted his square-framed glasses, and pulled a wad of cash from his pocket. He lined the rail in front of him with dollar bills until there was no brass visible. He folded more dollars in half lengthwise and set them up one next to another on the edge of the stage and put another layer on top of that one, like a stack of cards. This was Sarge's showy way of getting Lisa's attention.

Lisa, a hard-bodied blonde who modeled for several magazines—

I personally saw her nude on a motorcycle on the cover of one—had a loyal following. She rarely worked, but when she did, her fans were there waiting for her. Her stage routine was mesmerizing to watch—not because she was an amazing dancer, but because she didn't dance at all. She posed.

"Here she goes again," I said to Yessenia.

Her Barbie-doll body appeared on stage. She leaned against the wall and turned and posed, waited awhile, and turned and posed again in the frontal position. Lisa had the largest implants I'd ever seen... DDD would be an understatement. She could have lost a small animal in her cleavage. With her well-toned slender frame and tight bottom, she appeared unbalanced, as if her implants could topple her over at any moment.

After she ran out of wall space, Lisa pranced over to a pole, grabbed hold of it, and marched in circles around it—all the while holding her other arm up, bent at the elbow like one of Barbie's arms. Her bangs and straight blonde hair framed her doll-like face and her pink-glittered, plastered-on smile.

This Barbie was flexible and could drop down into the splits and hold one leg up to her ear like a telephone. Still, Barbie didn't dance. It didn't seem to matter.

"It shocks me that she stands there and makes money doing practically nothing," I said.

"Yep," Yessenia said. "She doesn't need to dance."

"She hardly talks either. She has it pretty easy." I didn't know anything about Lisa or why she couldn't make all her money from photo shoots. I figured modeling didn't pay well.

"I wouldn't say she has it easy," Yessenia said. "Do you ever see her eating or drinking?"

I thought for a moment. Lisa shared the princess dressing room with us, so I should've been able to answer this. "I don't know. I never see her eat. She always brings big bottles of water to drink."

"It's not water."

"What?"

"It's vodka."

"Straight?" I could believe it. Wouldn't someone die of alcohol poisoning if they drank that much on an empty stomach?

Yessenia nodded. "If she's downing those huge bottles of vodka each time she comes in, I'm sure she has her own issues. Everyone does. I wouldn't be jealous."

"I'm not jealous. I thought she had things pretty easy. Never mind." I was a little jealous. I worked my ass off for my money. Being a single mom was harder than I imagined, not to mention trying to maintain good grades. Then again, this was not going to be my life forever.

Lisa finished her set and barely-legal Kimmy was up next.

Kimmy was a mixed ethnicity girl with cascading black spiral-permed hair. I admired her. Although she was younger than I, wasn't in college, and lived with her boyfriend, she had agreed to informally adopt a friend's unwanted baby. Her boyfriend didn't want her to do lap dances. She stuck to her word and never did one. She never drank nor smoked. She was as clean-cut a dancer as one could be.

Kimmy danced across the stage with a perfect straight-toothed smile that accentuated her baby-faced cheeks. While she moved, I saw a small bump in her stomach area.

"Look," I whispered to Yessenia. "She's showing." Kimmy had told us she was pregnant and couldn't be happier. She swore me and Yessenia to secrecy.

"Yeah," Yessenia said. "I think that's a first."

"What?"

"Seeing a pregnant dancer on stage."

"How long is she going to keep dancing?"

"Until the managers notice her baby-belly and tell her to quit."

I wanted to be happy like Kimmy. I wish I had been as excited to have my baby as she was to have hers. I didn't understand. She didn't have another career lined up, or any college education to fall back on. How come she wasn't stressed out like I was? She was more at peace. What was her secret? I was struggling to keep up with my course-work, spend enough quality time with my now-difficult toddler, and maintain the façade of a bubbly confident stripper.

As it turned out, other girls had much bigger problems than I.

I went to the dressing room to take a break from the flirty cha-rade, try to regroup and put on my I'm-so-fucking-happy-to-be-here mask.

At a dressing station sat Nicole—a young scraggly blonde, not so bright, a Midwestern girl turned Hollywood whore. She was sucking air out of a strange red balloon—another one of her drugs. Not wanting to watch her self-destruct, I walked back out again.

After doing a couple of lap dances, Yessenia and I relaxed at the bar. I sipped my cranberry juice through the tiny red straw and stared at the nude dancer on stage.

"Watch Charlene." Yessenia motioned toward the waitress. Yessenia peeled back the wrapper on her bear claw pastry, took a bite, and leaned in closer to me. "See what she's doing?"

Charlene placed a plate into the microwave and stood by, waiting for it to finish.

"Microwaving her lunch?" I asked.

"Did you see any food on the plate?" Yessenia continued eating.

What kind of question was that? "No. But I wasn't paying attention." I stared at Yessenia. What was she getting at?

"Okay. Now watch."

I did. When the microwave oven beeped, Charlene took the plate out and headed through the back corridor that led to our dressing room.

"Okay," I said. "What was I watching for?"

"She's microwaving Nicole's drugs."

"What are you talking about?"

"Nicole's been doing Special K, animal tranquilizers."

"Why would you cook it? I don't get it."

"It's in liquid form," Yessenia said. "When it's cooked, it turns to a powder she can snort."

I couldn't imagine any benefit in doing those powerful drugs. "How do you know so much about this?"

"Because she told me," Yessenia said.

"Nobody tells *me* this stuff."

"Because they know you're more straight-edge." She smiled. "That's not a bad thing."

"What do you mean by that? What do they say?"

"Don't worry—they don't talk shit. They get high." She laughed at me. "I share cigarettes with the girls and they offer me hits."

I knew she was referring to the pot-smokers in the middle dressing room. The dancers offered me a smoke once, but I declined. Never did get offered again.

"I saw Nicole sucking a balloon." I wanted to feel like I was privy to some secrets.

"Yeah, that's Nitrous."

"Have you done it?"

"No. That shit kills your brain cells. Watch how stupid Nicole acts after doing it."

Near the end of our shift, after some of the night girls had arrived, Yessenia and I found ourselves alone in the dressing room, discussing whether or not we would stay later to do more dances to make up for a slow day.

Nicole stormed in, laughing maniacally. "Hey, you guys. I gotta tell you the funniest shit."

"You mean even funnier than you telling us some ultra-rich Beverly Hills douchebag paid you to come into his mansion, shit on a plate, and leave?" Yessenia asked.

"What?" I said, afraid to hear the answer.

"I got that bitch back," Nicole said.

Yessenia sat down, lit a cigarette, and puffed away.

"Who? What are you talking about?" I stared at Nicole's reflection in my mirror. She leaned in toward her mirror and adjusted her fake eyelashes. Like the other dancers in this dressing room, we often communicated through the mirrors.

Nicole burst into laughter. "I burned cigarette holes in the costumes she left hanging backstage."

Is she nuts? Who was she talking about? The dancer probably didn't do anything. I figured it was all in Nicole's head.

"Seriously?" I said. "Did she find out?"

"No. But it'll be funny when she does. Promise not to say anything, k?"

Yessenia shrugged. "You're crazy." She took another long drag before the plumes of smoke escaped her lips.

I feigned a smile. Thank God Nicole liked us. I'd hate to be her enemy. "Are you sure the clothes belonged to her?"

Nicole stopped for a moment. "Fuck. I hope so." She doubled over in more laughter.

Yessenia stared at me through the mirrors and I took the hint. We packed up our costumes, said our good-byes, and called it a night.

Once back in my car, I turned to Yessenia. "I think Nicole's going to end up dead in some alley somewhere."

"Probably. If not from drugs, then something else. But, not my problem."

That was true. Couldn't get too involved in anyone else's life, or risk endangering my own.

Chapter Twenty-Four
Sexual Identity

Spring 1999

Business slowed. The other dancers and I tried to find a way to increase our earnings. Candy—not-too-bright, skinny, flat-chested blonde, pale-skinned, fresh-off-the-bus-from-the-Midwest-and-now-I'm-on-drugs—came up with an idea: sell dances performed by two girls. She and I persuaded a few men to fork over the double-priced dances, until management caught on and put a stop to our fun. It didn't matter—we enjoyed dancing together and other men asked us for dances after seeing our erotic moves.

* * *

During one of my sets, I had a strange experience on stage. I was dancing to "Spin Spin Sugar" by Sneaker Pimps or "Sour Times" by Portishead, or some Hooverphonic song—I can't remember which it was—and I was exhilarated by the music. I felt each pulsating beat.

The men around my stage were spellbound by my slow slinky moves, and money kept going up on the tip rail. I slipped my hands across my body—caressed my arms, my breasts, my stomach and hips.

Men grabbed their drinks and came up to my stage. I swung around the pole perfectly and crawled—on my shins of course—sensually across the stage. Doing floor work, I opened my legs high in the air, twisting them about, and tickling the insides of my thighs with my manicured nails.

My eyes glossed over, fully enjoying the moment—the music, the attention, the money, the feeling of my own skin—the power. On my second song, I stripped off my thong panties and teased some more. With my arms, I squeezed my breasts together.

I skipped up and swung several rotations around the pole when something wet happened.

Confused and in a panic, I rushed backstage about twenty seconds before my song ended.

Yessenia and another dancer were back there, getting ready to go on. They gave me puzzled looks.

"I need a baby wipe!" I exclaimed. My legs were crossed as if I had to use the restroom.

Yessenia handed me one. "Why? What happened?"

"I'm so embarrassed. I can't believe it."

"What?"

"I'm all wet."

Her eyes widened in surprise as she watched me wipe myself off.

Neither one of us understood how such a thing could have happened.

I didn't want to face that I could have been turned on by what I was doing. Stripping was a job. I wasn't supposed to enjoy it. It wasn't supposed to turn me on. I'd heard about dancers having orgasms on stage, but I didn't have one—or at least I fled the stage before I could.

* * *

Another day, a male customer approached me and asked, "Can you dance for my girlfriend?"

Without hesitation, I smiled and said, "Sure. I'd love to. Where is she?"

He pointed to a young dark-haired girl near the stage who grinned and waved at me.

"I'll be over there in a few minutes." In a panic, I rushed backstage to ask the other dancers for advice.

"It's easy to dance for girls," Blanca, sober for once, explained. "But it's different. You can rub your knee in between her legs."

"You know women are sensual, so do more things like lightly blowing on her neck." Bodacious Sara—a Dolly Parton lookalike from Texas—sat naked on a towel-covered stool and brushed her thick blonde hair. "If you ask her, she'll probably let you know what she likes."

"Be careful," Blanca added. "Sometimes women think they can

get away with more than the guys. Watch her hands."

I went back out to do my first girl-on-girl dance. Her boyfriend wanted to watch.

"I'm nervous," she said. "I've never had a lap dance before."

I did as the other dancers suggested. I slithered around her, flipped my hair over her, and breathed warmly up along her neck. She squirmed and moaned. I straddled her and pressed my breasts gently against hers. She closed her eyes. I held her by the waist, squatted down in front of her, and slowly slid back up, in between her legs. She tilted her head back and her chest heaved.

Something happened to me when I heard her sigh and moan. I felt tingling warmth I had only felt with men before. Desire.

Much to my surprise, dancing for a woman came naturally, and I was more than happy when she asked me to continue for another song. I enjoyed watching her enjoy me. It felt completely different than dancing for men. That was business: calculated, choreographed moves. This was tantalizing pleasure: hers…and now mine.

I wanted to satisfy her but didn't cross the line, didn't let her hands wander, didn't let my fingers linger. Feeling this way about a customer, enjoying a lap dance, was new to me. I didn't understand at the time why dancing for a woman was more exciting for me than dancing for a man. It wasn't until years later I understood I wasn't as straight as I had assumed.

I leaned in, only inches from her, and licked my lips. I stared intently into her glossy brown eyes, which stared back at me. I breathed in her breath and she breathed in mine. Since we were in a more secluded booth, I allowed her to do what I wouldn't allow a man to do— place her hands on my hips. I faced away from her, bent over, and wiggled my butt gently against her chest. My lap dance shorts crept up my ass, but I didn't pull them back down. She giggled like a nervous schoolgirl. In one move, I grabbed her knees and leaned back against her, my head on her shoulder. I slid down her body in between her legs.

I flipped my hair over her jeans zipper and smothered my face in between her thighs. She moaned. I stood and danced in front of her, sliding my hands across my body.

The song faded out. Our time together was over.

"Thank you so much," her boyfriend said. He handed me cash. "I know she loved it."

"So did I." I didn't want to leave. I didn't understand why I was feeling the way I was. I was confused.

"That was so much fun!" she exclaimed. "Thank you."

"Yes, it was." I embraced her in a hug. "I hope you come back soon."

She never returned. But my eyes were opened that day to something I hadn't realized: I definitely had more than a platonic interest in some women. Gradually, a craving to experiment—should the opportunity present itself—blossomed.

Chapter Twenty-Five
Life Isn't Fair

Spring 1999

I REMEMBERED A LIVELY CONVERSATION I had, while still in high school, with my first boyfriend's mother. This was early on, before the relationship turned bad.

My boyfriend Henry and I were making French toast. His mother overheard me talking to her son about my future plans beyond college.

"Sure, Miranda," she said, "you're a smart girl, but things happen. Plans change. Life doesn't always work out the way you want."

"I don't agree. I can achieve anything I want in life." *Not like you who ended up dropping out of school, prostituting, having children with a married man and now living here in this poor community.* "If someone wants something bad enough and works hard enough to get it, then they will." I dipped a slice of bread in egg yolks and placed it in the frying pan. My boyfriend knew better than to argue with either one of us, so he quietly continued flipping the French toast.

"I feel sorry for you." She shook her head. "I used to think like that. But shit happens."

By "shit," I assumed she was referring to my boyfriend and his older brother. From what I had gathered, both were unintended pregnancies.

I scowled at her. Did she know who she was talking to? I wasn't some idiot. I had great grades, was intelligent, independent, and extremely ambitious. *You and I are not the same.* "You wait and see. I'm going to go to college, get my four-year degree, and be successful." I slapped another piece of toast in the frying pan, which sizzled in the

224

hot oil.

She pursed her lips together, looked at her son, and back at me. "Well, Miranda, I sure hope so. I hope everything will work out for you the way you *plan.*"

It sounded condescending. I knew her son—who didn't aspire to much—was not going to remain in my life beyond high school and I was going places. "Oh, I know it will. I'm not giving up, no matter what."

"That's great, but you need to know when to cut your losses." She slammed down some papers and left the room.

I grinned. *There won't be any losses. I can't help it if you're bitter about life.*

*   *   *

A few days after Easter, Yessenia and I arrived at work to discover that a tragedy had occurred the weekend before.

The morning was slow, and we took an early lunch in the middle dressing room. A bunch of us had Mexican food delivered. Yessenia and I sat down on the old worn-down pink carpet and munched on some chips.

Two of the women who had lockers there, the bony Hungarian immigrant Heidi and the sexy Russian immigrant Katarina, sat next to us.

"You will never guess what happened last Sunday." Heidi wiped her face and stuffed in another big bite of burrito. She was so thin it was hard for me to believe that she had two children.

Katarina's eyes widened. "Oh, yes. Unbelievable." Like Heidi and her husband, Katarina and her spouse had been in America for a couple of years, but Katarina's English was not good. "I could not believe."

Katarina had been an engineer in Russia, but her degree didn't transfer to America. Because of that and her limited English, she couldn't get an engineering job and resorted to stripping.

"What?" I scooped a bite of rice and beans into my mouth.

"A customer, after he left the strip club—you know how they have to exit through the sex shop? Well, he had a heart attack and died—right there in front of the dildos."

"Wow," I said. "Are you kidding?"

"No," Heidi said. "Even worse, they found Easter baskets in his trunk for his kids. It was terrible."

"Damn," Yessenia said. "That's crazy."

I shook my head. "How sad. How old was he?"

"Don't know, mid-forties."

"His poor kids." I thought of Jacob.

"He should have considered that before he came to a strip club on Easter." Yessenia took another bite of her burrito.

We didn't say another word about it. But, man, life could end at any moment.

Another bad omen hit the next evening. During dinner my mom announced, "I'm moving out of state. And I'm leaving next month."

My fork hit the plate. "Why?"

"Your grandma, who helped raise you, and your aunt have already said I could stay with them until I find an apartment."

"You'd move out there? What about money, a job?"

Mom shrugged. "I'll find a job up there somewhere."

Yessenia, Kirk, and Jacob continued to eat their spaghetti like nothing was amiss. I lost my appetite. Was I the only one who cared about planning a future?

Unlike her mention of it over Thanksgiving, this time Mom meant it. Kirk decided to move in with a friend. Yessenia and I went apartment hunting. When we visited a few complexes, we noticed the cheaper apartments were in a shady part of town.

Eventually we found a decent place with a good school district— Jacob would be starting kindergarten in two years and I didn't want him to have to move.

The problem was that we needed to show that we earned three times the rent to be approved for an apartment. Our strip club paystubs did not accurately reflect that.

"I don't want them to know we dance," I said. "I don't want dancing to spill over into my normal life."

"How else do you think we're going to get a place?" Yessenia said. "We have to tell them."

We entered the leasing office, and after a tour of the building with the leasing agent, we sat down across from her desk.

"So, what do you two think?" the agent said. "I have two side-by-side upstairs units coming available in a couple of weeks. It's a great location—you'll have a view of the pool. One is the one-bedroom model, and the other has two bedrooms and two bathrooms."

"How much is the rent?" I asked.

"The two-bedroom unit is $1050 with a twelve-month lease

agreement. Right now we have a special—half off the first month's rent. You do need to put down a $600 security deposit though."

That sounded like an awful lot of money, but Yessenia and I were quickly running out of options. We were ready to sign up. The agent ran our credit, but her face twisted when she examined our scant paystubs showing only 24 hours per week at minimum wage. The name of our club wasn't on the stubs; the club operated under a generic corporation title. That way men could safely use the ATM machines and pay with credit cards knowing that their companies or wives' prying eyes wouldn't see a strip club on any expense report or bank statement.

I had to say something, but I didn't want her to look down on me—I wanted people to judge me as the intelligent person I was, not by their preconceived notions of strippers.

"We make a lot more money than it says there because we dance," Yessenia said, sparing me the embarrassment of having to speak first.

The agent gave us a that-will-be-a-good-story-to-tell-my-friends-later-on look. "What do you mean?"

"We're exotic dancers," I said. "Paying the rent won't be a problem. Can we give you a larger deposit or something?"

"I can't do that." She laughed. "I need something in writing. You can provide a copy of your taxes and recent bank statements."

I groaned. "We work for cash, under the table." *What am I going to do? I'll have this problem at any apartment leasing office.* "Can't we use anything else?"

"I guess if you two can get a letter stating your income, I can approve the lease agreements." She cleared her throat, trying to maintain an air of professionalism while her tone of voice told me that we were the first dancers to ever come through her office. "It needs to be on company letterhead, I need a business card for your manager, and I'll have to call to verify it with your manager."

We agreed. The truth was we had no idea if we could convince our anxiety-ridden daytime manager Bob to do this for us. We sure as hell weren't going to ask unstable Giovanni or insane Howard.

Yessenia and I walked back to the car.

"What if we can't get a letter?" I said. "We don't have anywhere to go."

* * *

It took more than a heavy dose of flirting to convince Bob to help us out. I scanned the club's business card into my computer and used the image to create a fake company letterhead. The club didn't bother with traditional business communications.

I drafted the letters, typed Bob's name at the bottom and presented them to him for his signature. He hesitantly complied. Yessenia and I promised him that the apartment company would only call once, and that we would never ask him for another favor.

Fortunately, this satisfied our new apartment manager.

I created a list of furniture and household items I would need to purchase and focused on saving as much money as I could. Yet I was too afraid to put cash in the bank for fear of raising questions about my source of income.

Yessenia and I arranged a move-in date. I was about to move into my first apartment on my own with my son.

*   *   *

One day at work, Yessenia came rushing backstage to find me. I had just come off stage and was counting my tips, placing all the dollar bills in the same direction, folding them in half, and locking them into my purse.

She was hyperventilating.

"What happened?" I asked.

"Oh…my…God." She panted. "You'll never guess who's here."

"Who?" I asked. A few weeks prior, Yessenia thought she saw her cousin in the club, but we weren't sure if it was him. The man in question disappeared as soon as she pointed him out.

We had purposely found a job far away from home and near an airport, hoping to entertain random men flying in and out of the state as opposed to locals. We forget that locals would be picking up friends, family, and coworkers and that flights were often delayed. What better place for the locals to hang out than at a friendly neighborhood strip club?

"I think our neighbor is here."

The woman next door with the autistic girl? The fisherman upstairs? One of the people who lived in the 200-unit apartment complex across the street?

"Which neighbor?" I slipped my panties and dress back on.

She took a deep breath. "You know where your mom parks her car in the alley?"

I nodded.

"Well, across from our garage, you know how there is a row of other garages for the fourplexes next door?"

I nodded, still not seeing where she was going with this.

"You know the guy who has the Corvette? The one who's always hanging out in his garage?"

"No." I honestly was too busy running to and from school and work to pay attention to nameless neighbors. I primped my hair in the mirror.

"Well, the Corvette guy is here. I'm sure of it. Come here, I'll show you."

I followed her to the door that separated the backstage from the club. She cracked it open and pointed to a man slouched in one of the movie theater seats beyond the stage.

"That's the Corvette guy?" I said. "It's too dark. I can't see him."

"Well, I'm not going out there until he leaves."

Seeing how flustered she was, I asked, "Did he see me on stage?"

"Yes."

"I'm not going to worry about it. I have money to make." I reapplied a coat of lipstick. "Nobody knows we work here. It's so dark in here that we can easily be mistaken for someone else. Besides, if we deny it, how can anyone prove it?"

She raised her eyebrow. "You don't look like 'someone else.' You don't wear a wig or much makeup. You look like you."

The next day, Yessenia told me that she was calling out sick and Jacob was at the babysitter's. I had to go to work. I grabbed my duffle bag and was on my way to my mom's car in the alley when I saw him.

"Hello."

He was in his garage, leaning on his cocky yellow Corvette. I knew deep down that Yessenia hadn't been mistaken. Corvette Guy had seen me naked. *Lucky him.*

I gave a polite wave, tossed my sparkly blue metallic lockbox purse and duffle bag in the trunk and slammed it shut.

"How's it going?" He looked me up and down, nodding his approval. I was wearing sweat pants and a tight striped t-shirt, my hair tied up in a messy ponytail. I looked like an average college student.

"Fine."

"Damn right you're fine." His grin stretched from one ear to the other. "Going to work?"

My cheeks burned. I fumbled with my keys.

He started laughing.

I jumped into the car, turned on the ignition, and sped away as fast as I could.

In the rear view mirror, I saw he was still laughing.

Our moving day couldn't come soon enough.

*   *   *

I bought a new computer and printer on credit. When the bank approved me for a higher limit on my credit card, I bought furniture.

Rather than heading to the local assembly-required value stores, I searched through Pottery Barn catalogues. I wanted my place to have an upscale adult feel to it. I attempted to make my new home appear like any other urban middle class family's. My wooden chairs were delivered in boxes direct from Italy, my coffee table had antique etchings in the wood, and my sophisticated sleeper-sofa came with a washable slipcover. Quality furniture.

My son would come home to our apartment just as any other child in this excellent school district would. Never mind that his mother was stripping to maintain this façade of normalcy; no one would ever find out.

*   *   *

Not long after moving in, I picked up a flier from the university. My college professors strongly suggested we get involved in clubs associated with our major to make connections that could help us after graduation.

With my graduation date approaching, I joined a mentoring program. I was paired with a successful alumnus, Jay Johnson, a manager at a company that heavily recruited at our university. I had heard rumors that several students had lined up jobs through his company.

I was excited to learn about my post-graduate options from Jay and eagerly paid attention during every meeting.

Jay was a handsome dark-haired thirty-something who looked even more appealing in his three-piece suit. At our fourth meeting, he leaned across his desk toward me, ready to share something important. "Miranda, I want to level with you."

"Yes?"

"I can tell you're a smart young woman with a lot of potential."

I smiled. *He's going to suggest I apply for an internship at his company…where I could have a very bright future. Everything was going to work out.* I stared into his blue eyes. If it weren't for the gold band on his finger, my smile would have been more seductive.

"Now," he said. "This is only between you and me."

Great! Insider information!

"This company works people hard," he continued. "I mean I had to pay my dues. Everyone does in order to work their way up. It's part of the training process. But it is a lot of hours."

"I am prepared to do that," I said.

"When I say 'a lot of hours,' I mean that most of us are working well over 50 per week."

I didn't see where he was going with that.

"What I'm trying to say," he continued to continue, "and this is only my opinion, is that this job is not really for single moms."

Single moms. The words bounced around in my head like a pinball. "I don't understand," I said. "I can do it."

"Single moms never work out in this job. I mean, if your kid gets sick and you're the one running the office, what can you do? The hours are so long that you wouldn't get to spend enough time with your daughter."

"Son," I corrected him.

I stopped listening at that point. In fact, I couldn't wait to get the hell out of there. *I was hoping for a respectable job and now I had to hear this shit. Ironic that the strip club doesn't care that I'm a single mom. When I graduate, is this the workforce welcome I'm going to receive?*

I didn't want to believe it.

I couldn't.

If I did, there would have been no point in my hostessing, escorting, or dancing—it would all have been for naught.

In the past, every time someone had told me that I couldn't succeed at something, I was determined to prove them wrong. This, though, after exposing my body to get to a point of "success," hurt.

It was 1999, not 1959. Why was there still discrimination against single mothers? The strip club seemed to be more accommodating and fair than the professional world.

Even though my mentorship hadn't ended the way I intended, I figured it was a fluke and that nothing else would get in the way of my success.

I've since learned that not everything goes as planned, but I've also realized what I had already suspected to be true: many people give up on life. I made a promise to myself that even if all of my plans fell through, like with my mentor, that I wouldn't become one of the quitters.

*   *   *

Late one evening, Bonnie and Heather, two classmates from college, came over to my apartment so we could finish a project that was due in the morning. We gathered around the computer in my room, typing and deleting frantically.

I clicked the mouse to close a dialogue box. The mouse froze. The blue screen of death.

"Oh my God." I rolled my eyes. "Heather, did you use the school computer when you saved the file on this disc?"

Heather looked up from her notes. "Yeah, why? Isn't the file there?"

"It's corrupted. My computer won't even open it. It says there are too many viruses."

"Oh shit." Heather jumped up and leaned over the monitor.

"The school computers are always full of viruses," Bonnie whined, tossing her notebook on my bed. "This report's never going to get done."

I ignored Bonnie. "Did you email it to yourself?"

"No." Heather shook her head. "Oh wait, yeah, I think so. I'm so tired I can't think straight."

"I need some fucking sleep," Bonnie said.

"We're almost done." I stood up and stretched my arms.

"We just lost two hours of work," Heather said. "We're going to have to start over."

Bonnie flung herself back on my bed. "This is bullshit."

"Here," I said. "Heather, you can log on to your email and get our last uncorrupted version. Bonnie, let's look at our notes again."

Bonnie whimpered.

An hour later, we typed the final period and hit "print." We all cheered and watched the pages come out of the printer.

The fifth sheet of paper was streaked gray. The sixth was blank.

"Uh oh." I held up the blank sheet. "I ran out of ink."

Bonnie slumped to the ground. "We're going to fail."

Heather asked, "Do you have another cartridge?"

"No," I said. "What are we going to do?"

"There should be a twenty-four–hour copy place around here, right?" Heather asked. "Or at least one that's open to midnight. What time is it?"

I looked at the clock. "11:30. Damn, we better hurry."

Bonnie looked horrified. "No guys. I'm not doing this."

"What do you mean?" I asked.

"I'm done. Fuck it. I'm going home." Bonnie stood up.

"You can't leave us with this," Heather said. "We agreed to finish."

"I don't give a shit. I have other classes to worry about." Bonnie grabbed her purse.

"But you need to help us," I said.

"No, I need sleep. I don't even need this class for my major. Just leave my name off. I'll take the F." Bonnie stormed out.

Heather shrugged. She and I rushed over to the copy place, opened the file and printed the report.

Two minutes before the store closed, we were done. I helped bind everything together in a presentation folder.

Even though it didn't go quite as planned, Heather and I didn't quit.

*   *   *

My darling son, now an active preschooler, had a sneaky way of getting into everything—be it schoolwork, food, or my work bag. A cute ball of destruction, Jacob was missing Jiminy Cricket on his shoulder who would have advised him not to do half the bad things he did.

Every morning—fearing the worst—I would wipe the sleep from my eyes and tiptoe into the living room to survey the damage. Sometimes I'd find him on top of the kitchen counter, climbing up the cabinets. Other times, I'd discover that he had pushed a chair to the front door, unlocked all three locks, and had gotten outside. Child proofing meant nothing to him—it wasn't even a deterrent. Rather than try to twist the childproof door covers, he disassembled them.

On another such day, I yawned and stretched in my bed. It was too quiet. I peered over the edge of my bed to see Jacob entertaining himself with my makeup. There was a ring of mascara around his eye—he looked like a panda bear or a puppy with an eye patch. He had smeared my foundation into the carpet and all over the 6-CD cartridge that I had to use for my stage music—its hard blue plastic cover hardly noticeable underneath the beige crème. I didn't even know how he had managed to quietly drag my bag down off of my dresser.

Why me? Why does he make my life so difficult? I scooped Jacob up and dragged him to the bathroom for a scrub down.

"I can do it!" he wailed. "I can do it myself!" He stomped his feet on his stepstool.

"Fine." Satisfied that he was occupied with the water, I returned to the crime scene. On my hands and knees, I cleaned up the mess. Tears of frustration dribbled down my face.

I noticed that the water was no longer running, and wondered what he was currently destroying.

I peeked around the corner.

"Hi, mom," he said, a big grin on his face. "I'm going potty." He sat on the toilet backwards, the black ring still around his eye.

I shook my head. At least he wasn't smearing feces on the wall again.

Although I couldn't salvage the foundation, I was able to clean the disc changer cartridge in time for work.

* * *

After moving into my new apartment side-by-side with Yessenia, I became more serious with Dan. At my urging, he started to spend more time at my place. First it was only weekends. The weekend bag became larger. Soon his shampoo was in my shower and his clothes in my closet.

He didn't offer to help with the rent. He claimed he didn't have the money so I scowled when he bought an expensive Movado watch, aluminum rims, and new clothes. While it was true that he maintained a room at his dad's house and helped his dad with bills, he was eating and living at my apartment for most of the week. I already had a child to support; I didn't need two. On the other hand, I enjoyed Dan's company and his cooking, so I chose to keep things the way they were for the time being. Still, the underlying tension was building.

Months passed and my stress with dancing, parenting, and life increased. I came home and vented to Dan.

"Today totally sucked." I threw my duffle bag at the foot of my bed and kicked off my shoes. "Nobody tipped. Three guys actually sat on my stage and only left a dollar total. I was so pissed."

"Do you have to strip?" Dan asked. "I don't like it that my girlfriend strips nude for other men."

"Last time I checked, you haven't finished college either and aren't in any position to help me, so that's the way it has to be."

"There are plenty of other options for making money."

I laughed. "Are you freaking kidding me? How else can I make the kind of money I'm making? And work the number of hours I'm working? There's no way. Either I drop out or can't pay my rent."

"I hate hearing about men seeing you naked."

"Fine then. I'll stop talking to you about work. I'll be graduating in less than two years anyway. Then I'll get a respectable job, so you don't have to be embarrassed by me."

He shook his head and left the room.

*　　*　　*

During my next shift at the club, I was thrilled to find out that my annoyance, tweeker Emerald, had either quit or been fired. A new dancer going by the name of Butterfly had been hired in her place. I was used to seeing new girls come and go. Usually, I paid no attention until they had been there at least a week—many didn't last that long or they switched to the night shift.

I leaned against the upper level railing and watched the stage when Butterfly appeared. I blinked. She twirled around in her airy pink baby doll lingerie. I stared at her delicate nose, high cheekbones, and full lips. She was my mirror reflection. She was me and I was her. Except for her longer spiral curled hair, our faces and complexion were—well, we could have been twins.

"Wow, you're right," Yessenia said, "She does look like you. Except her breasts are smaller, and you're thinner."

I tilted my head and scrutinized her body and face, trying to see what I could pick apart to make myself feel better. She giggled and flirted with the men around her stage who were eating up every second of it.

When her second song came on, I scowled. I had never heard that techno beat before, but the chorus kept repeating "Sugar Daddy-O, Sugar Daddy-O!"

Mark and Hiroki flashed through my mind with each "Sugar Daddy-O." *Dear God, what did I do to deserve this torture?*

After her set, Butterfly, in her pink thigh-highs with satin ribbons on top, collected her tips. And each time she reached over to pick up her cash, she blew the man a kiss, and in a girly-little voice, she said, "Thank you, Daddy."

I turned to Yessenia and we made puking gestures.

A few minutes later, I asked a man for a dance.

"You're the one who was just on stage, right?" he asked.

My cheeks reddened. "No, that was Butterfly."

"Oh, I'll wait for her."

That was the last time I would be honest when asked if I was her. After that, I pretended to be whoever the hell the men thought I was, because I couldn't afford not to.

When my stage set ended, I put on a sheer robe and collected my tips.

A gray-beard leaned over and handed me a five dollar bill. "Can I get the next dance?"

"Sure." I smiled. "I'll be right out."

I threw on my dress, doused myself in more body spray and hurried out to the floor in time to watch Butterfly leading my customer to the lap dance booth. My jaw tensed. I turned around and walked backstage, slamming the door shut behind.

While Butterfly didn't stay at our club for more than a couple of weeks, I did get several dances from men who confused me with her and lost some as well, which irritated me to no end. Every time she danced, she used the "Sugar Daddy-O" song. At least it was a reminder that Yessenia and I no longer had any contact with our sugar daddy-o's.

I was overjoyed to see Butterfly go.

* * *

"It's slow today," I whined. "There's no money out there." I sat down in the dressing room.

Yessenia shrugged. "At least you made money yesterday."

"Not really. It was slow yesterday, too. You wouldn't know since you're always calling out sick."

Yessenia picked up a strand of hair and rolled it around her curling iron. "I'm burnt out on this fucking job."

Blanca stumbled over to her stool, drunk as usual. "It's because you two work too damn much. That's why you're burnt out. How many days a week do you work?"

"Four," I said.

"That's your fucking problem. This ain't a normal job. It takes a lot out of you, physically, mentally, and emotionally. You can't work four days a week. You need time to get the fuck away from here."

While Blanca had been full of useful advice in the past, I felt she was wrong this time. "But I need to work four days to pay my bills. Yessenia calls out sick all the time, so she's only here twice a week." I was jealous that Yessenia could work less than I; she didn't have a small child to support. It was hard enough to go to work with her and much harder to go alone.

"You call out sick, too," Yessenia said. "You only come in three times a week." She went back to curling her hair.

"Yeah," Blanca said. "And do you notice that you make more money on the weeks when you work less days?"

How was that logical? "No," I said. "If I don't work four days a week, I won't be able to make rent."

Blanca laughed. "You won't make shit if you burn out. You'll see." She glared at me through the mirror. "I don't come to this hellhole more than twice a week. Cut back, then you'll make good money when you're here. Or you'll end up jaded like most of the other dancers." She flipped her black hair over and sprayed perfume. "If you get tired of it, try a new club. I'm not saying quit here, but moonlight somewhere else."

I grumbled. "What does moonlight mean?"

"Work two places. But don't let Howard or Giovanni find out. They don't like that shit."

I decided that once again Blanca was right.

Rather than work closer to home, Yessenia and I auditioned at Bare Elegance, a high-end club nearby, so we could still get the airport traffic. The outside was sleek with blue and pink neon lighting. Inside, the clean carpet, plush armchairs, and shiny brass poles all looked new. In the restrooms, a woman handed out paper towels and miscellaneous toiletries for tips. A masseuse walked the club floor, selling shoulder massages. The air was cool and fresh. The speakers were clear, the bass tight. The caliber of the dancers was much higher.

I figured if I didn't get hired, at least I already had a job.

Greg, the pudgy general manager, looked like a power broker with his pinstriped suit—a suit!—gold watch and chain, and slicked-back blonde hair.

I volunteered to audition first. Surrounded by blonde bombshells, I swung around the pole for my audition. I crawled; flipped my hair; did the splits—now that I was flexible enough to do this—bent over; arched my back; and kicked my legs open. I let the music run through my veins. Customers came to my stage to reward my efforts.

The stage was a small circular platform with a tall pole in the middle. When, at the end of my song, a girl opened a side door for a cigarette break, I cringed at the bright sunlight that poured in. After working long enough in dim club lighting, I felt like a vampire melting.

I focused back on my show.

Fortunately, Yessenia and I were both hired, and allowed to work the more favorable weekend evening shifts. While it was busier than Century Lounge, there was also more stiff competition. The dancers were snobbier, and so were the men. The overstuffed armchairs on the floor were almost too comfortable for the men to bother leaving for lap dances.

There were three stages: the one I auditioned on, a smaller satellite stage near the bar, and the main stage. Behind the curtains to the main stage was the dressing room where I tried not to spend any length of time. I had absolutely nothing in common with these girls and their name brand clothing and personal trainers. I stayed on the floor, trying to hustle dances to make my money.

There were three separate dance areas: one rarely-used area for nude private table dances—similar to our other club, one semi-private area on the side of the club, and an upstairs private dance area. All lap dance booths—bathed in red lighting—offered the privacy of a sheer curtain. The men were bolder than what I was used to.

Following our other club's strict rules, I made the men keep their hands down to their sides. Yessenia and I soon learned that the rules here were lax—customers could place their hands on dancers' hips or thighs. I couldn't deal with having cold clammy hands violating me, which hurt my cash flow. After a couple of weeks, we left on good terms, retaining the option to return.

I didn't speak a word about my moonlighting to any of the other dancers at Century for fear of word getting back to Giovanni or the owner.

With a year left in school, it wasn't good I was already burnt out. Yessenia and I would have to find another way to supplement our income. I thought Bare Elegance would be the answer, but it wasn't. Last time I got burnt out by work—Club Flamingo and escorting—my earnings drastically declined and I ended up having to go out with men for money. I didn't want to resort to that again. Why did life have to be so difficult? Why couldn't dancing be like other jobs—go home at the end of my shift and leave work at work?

It wasn't fair.

CHAPTER TWENTY-SIX
VEGAS

I ZIPPED MY DUFFLE bag and slung it over one shoulder. "We'll only be gone for the weekend." I gave Dan a kiss. "Thanks for watching Jacob. I appreciate it."

Dan gave me a solemn stare. "Good luck." With eyes down-turned, he added, "I wish you weren't going to do this. But I know I can't stop you." He squeezed me one last time. "Jacob," he called out, "Come give your mom a hug goodbye."

Jacob charged into my legs. I picked him up and gave him a peck on the cheek. "I love you. Be good for Dan." Once released from my arms, he took off running back to his toys.

I went next door to get Yessenia. Neither of us liked to wake up this early. But with a five-hour drive ahead of us, we had to get on the road before the Friday morning rush hour. We had only until the end of the work day to find a club to sponsor us, get hired, and acquire a license from the Las Vegas Police Department.

Bleary-eyed from the nonstop desert landscape, I welcomed the sight of Sin City. We drove past the clubs we were considering and decided to audition at two classy topless ones: Cheetah's and Crazy Horse, Too.

"We can't wear sweats there," Yessenia said. "Where do you want to change?"

"Up there, at Denny's."

With an eyebrow raised, she said, "Are you sure?"

I pulled into the parking lot. We took our bags and moseyed into the diner. *Don't call attention to ourselves.* We maneuvered our way to the

239

restroom in the back of the restaurant and found a single stall, a sink, and paper towels crumbled on the floor.

Yessenia went into a stall and changed in the lightning-fast speed that dancers are accustomed to.

When she came out, she plugged in her curling iron to do her hair while I went into the stall and slipped into my trashy red dress—the same one I actually stripped in.

For fear of being too short to get hired, I put on my tallest platform heels—a nauseating four-inch platform shoe with nearly eight-inch spiked heels. The black straps hugged my foot and I leaned against the wall for support. I was as tall as Yessenia in her low heels.

"Are you going to wear that outfit in public?" she scoffed.

"Yeah, why? I need to make up for the fact that I'm not blonde and six feet tall like the other dancers here."

She shrugged and applied another coat of mascara.

The restroom door swung open and a grandma holding her granddaughter's hand entered. After their eyes jumped out of their sockets, the older woman glared at me and quickly escorted her innocent little one into the stall.

Bet you weren't expecting to see a couple of strippers in the restroom. You are *in Las Vegas, you know.* Actually, my first inclination was to be ashamed or embarrassed. Then I thought, why not own it? So I did, and laughed it off.

I smacked my lips together to spread the glossy coat evenly. "Ready?"

Yessenia and I picked up our bags and headed for the exit. With perfect posture and a sexy sway from the heels, I followed her through the restaurant. Along the way, everyone—old and young alike—craned their heads.

Yes, we are strippers, here in your family diner.

Patrons hushed and nudged each other upon seeing us. A dead silence ensued while we passed by, and a flurry of conversation followed in our wake.

Your husbands and fathers will be seeing more of us later tonight.

By the time we got back in my car, we were laughing so hard, we had to try not to smear our eyeliner.

Looking back, I wonder what the hell I was thinking. It wasn't necessary to dress like a hooker to get hired at a classy club—talk about an amateur mistake. I'd been dancing long enough that I should have known better. Because of me, a bunch of families in a Denny's would have some explaining to do to their children that night.

Off we headed to Crazy Horse, Too—our first stop. I had to have Yessenia drive, because pushing the pedals was impossible in the shoes I was wearing.

Yessenia parked the car at the front of the first club.

"Ready?" I asked.

She shrugged. "Not really."

We approached the security guard at the door.

"We'd like to audition," Yessenia said.

I was too nervous to do much else than follow her lead.

The club was gigantic and glamorous, with ten times the mirrors and lights of the Los Angeles clubs. We left the bright sunny day at the door and entered a world of mirrors, neon lights, plush chairs, and shiny stages. The manager, who could have doubled as a personal trainer, looked us up and down and walked toward us. His polo shirt was two sizes too small.

"We want to audition for the night shift," Yessenia announced.

"Sorry, sweets, each manager hires for his own shift. If you want to work the evening shift, come back around six or seven."

Since we weren't looking to work the day shift, we'd have to return later.

Once back in the car, I said, "That's not going to work for us, because of the police. We need permits to work in Vegas. The station closes at five. We have to get a club to hire us now, not at six or seven."

"Okay. Let's go to Cheetah's."

At the next club, we spoke with a dark-haired middle aged manager whose greasy combed-back hair was tied in a ponytail. He asked, "Have you two danced before?"

"Yes." Yessenia ramped up the charm. "We've danced at several clubs in Southern California. We're the money makers at our club." This was true—we were two of the more successful day-shift dancers, consistently racking up more dances on average than most others at our club—with exception of the dirty-talking Brittany, a nineteen year-old who indulged in tanning salons so often that she bought a tanning bed. This also aged her by ten years.

"Have you heard of Bare Elegance?" I mentioned the classiest of the clubs where we had recently worked. "We worked there. Other dancers suggested we work weekends out here in Vegas."

We had no problem getting the manager to sign the forms to

sponsor us. He told us to come back once we had our permits.

We drove downtown, parked, and walked around the corner to the police station, not at all expecting to see a line wrapped around the building as if this were the queue for a roller coaster ride at Disneyland.

"What the hell?" Yessenia said.

"I don't know." The middle-aged men and women in line were definitely not there for stripper licenses.

As it turned out, everyone who works in a casino in any capacity has to get fingerprinted and licensed. We not so patiently waited our turn.

"This fucking sucks." Yessenia twirled her hair

"I hope we earn enough money to make this worth it," I said.

It was like a slaughterhouse assembly line. Each police officer stood in place, performing the same job hour after hour. Our forms were checked against our California IDs and our pictures were taken.

My fingers were dipped in black ink and rolled across the paper, one at a time in each square. They sent us to the Lava soap station to scrub off the oil before being handed laminated ID cards. We were officially legal to strip in Vegas. Fortunately, no club name was typed on the card, so we were free to work wherever we pleased.

Since it was evening by the time we finished, we decided to check into our crappy hotel room on the strip. The red paisley carpet was faded, the queen beds lumpy, and the air stale and smoky. We chose this dump because it had the cheapest rooms available. We decided to try our luck with the night manager at Crazy Horse.

"What did he say?" I asked Yessenia when returned to the lobby after she spoke with the night manager.

"He said he'd hire me, but not you. He only wants tall girls. I told him we came together. So he said to come back to work the late night shift."

Should I be disappointed or relieved? Fuck those tall skinny bitches. I hate being short. "What time is the next shift?"

"Around 2 or 3 AM."

My jaw dropped. "Are you serious?"

"Yeah, fuck that. I'm not working that shift."

"But we're already here. We can at least try it out. Let's go back to the place that already hired us and try to work a shift there right now, and come back here afterward. That way we can see which one's better."

I realized how lucky I was to have such a great friend who didn't put herself ahead of me. That was the second time she had refused to accept a dancing job without me.

Back at Cheetah's, we auditioned and were hired on the spot. I couldn't even count how many dancers were in the dressing room, all in varying stages of getting ready or leaving. The girls were packed under the fluorescent lights, along the wall mirrors in between rows of lockers.

"There're too many girls working," I said. "How are we going to make money?"

Yessenia shrugged.

We busted our asses on stage and hustled the floor, but there were more dancers than men by almost 2 to 1. The men were content sipping their drinks and watching the stage. After offering dances and being rejected for the fifth time, I looked up to see Yessenia motioning me over to her. She was sitting next to a customer at a table near the wall. When I approached, she stood up and pulled me aside.

"Serenity," she said. "He recognized us from a club in California."

"Seriously? Oh my God, now we're being recognized across state lines?"

"I know. Crazy."

"Damn it. How am I supposed to hide this job when I graduate from college if this shit keeps happening?" I took a deep breath. "Are you making any money? How are we going to pay the hotel and gas? Let's go back to Crazy Horse."

"I'm tired. Let's go back to the hotel or I'll get a cab."

"Well, we can go back and take a nap, but let's get a wake-up call, so we can get up in time to try it out."

"Not promising I'm going."

After a few hours, the hotel room phone jarred me from my sleep. My back was sore because the bed sucked. It took every ounce of determination to get myself and Yessenia up and ready to leave.

"I'm too fucking tired." Yessenia parked the car at Crazy Horse.

"We can work for a couple of hours to get a feel for the place. If we don't like it, we don't have to come back tomorrow night."

We stepped inside and I realized how much fancier it was than Cheetah's—there were more mirrors, more neon, and plusher chairs.

The late night manager, a short pudgy Italian in a suit, was more laid back than the earlier managers. He took our dancing licenses.

"You have to keep our licenses?" I asked.

"As long as you work here," he said. "Make sure you check in with me to tip out before your shift ends."

"Don't we tip the bar and the DJ?" I asked.

"Tip out your twenty percent to me—we'll split it with the bar and other staff."

We nodded and exited his office.

"Let's go to the dressing room and change," I said. "Where is it?"

Yessenia pointed to a tall, blonde bikini-clad dancer who was heading through a door. We followed her into the largest, most elaborate dressing room I'd ever seen. It was as big as some entire clubs in California. We walked past rows upon rows of well-kept lockers. There were benches and mirrors and everything was clean and in good condition, not falling apart like the dressing rooms in Century Lounge back in Los Angeles.

An older woman, in maid-like attire, complete with apron, approached an Amazonian—tall, hard-bodied—brunette who was sitting in a robe at a chair-and-mirror station. Her makeup bags, clothes, curling irons, and brushes were strewn across the counter. A few pairs of platform heels lay around her feet.

"You want two egg whites and a piece of plain wheat toast?" the woman with short black curls asked the dancer.

"Yes," the dancer said. "Make sure egg whites only. You know how I like it. Only the egg whites. Thanks, momma." She blew a kiss, picked up a drink and sipped it before applying more makeup.

The older lady nodded and went back toward the kitchen.

I rolled my eyes and kept walking behind Yessenia. She pointed out different rooms. "Look, tanning beds…and showers over there."

"Dang. This is like stripper paradise."

But not entirely. As soon we left the dressing room and walked out to the club floor, I was shocked to find out that the lap dances were actually topless "lap" dances done in plain view—not in a separate dance area—on the customers' chairs. I discovered that the men expected to be able to put their hands on a dancer's waist, hips, or thighs—like at the high-end club, Bare Elegance.

"Fuck. I need a drink." Yessenia ditched me.

Like in the casinos in Vegas, people could smoke indoors. I pulled my hair in front of my nose and took a whiff. Mixed in with the smell of floral spray was cigarette stench—and not the good-smelling cloves like Jason used.

"Serenity, you're on stage next," the DJ called out.

I was too overwhelmed to even request any music. It was obvious I was in a whole new world unlike my clubs in California.

After the small glassy platform stage was empty, I grabbed the shiny brass poles and ascended the slippery steps. A handful of customers tossed down a few bills, nothing to get excited about. I zoned out and fell into one of my typical floor routines. It wasn't until my second song started that I realized floor work was pointless in a topless club. All the men could see were my panties, no real show.

I stood up, took off my top and swayed to every third beat. These men looked half-asleep and weren't putting any additional tips up, so I checked out the club as I danced. While tousling my hair and twirling around a pole, I scanned the perimeters. Most men scattered around the club seemed to be well past the fun buzz stage, nearing the hangover part. Dancers hovered around them, helping them empty their wallets.

I crawled in front of the tip rail. I leaned back and kicked and twisted my legs around, in the sexy stripper style. *How much was the hotel for two nights? Plus dinner, and breakfast tomorrow, and the gas?* Another couple of dollars went up. I considered cheating to get a few extra bucks, in the way that I'd seen other strippers do—"accidentally" move my panties aside a bit. Nah. Not worth the risk. I sat on my knees and bounced up and down. *Wait, divide that total by two. But I need to make more than break even, so how much do I need? A couple hundred?*

My song ended. I collected my tips, exited the stage, and circulated the room, offering lap dances.

"What's your number, baby?" asked a young good-looking guy who'd probably downed a pitcher of beer. "Come here. Come sit on my lap." He patted his khakis.

"Do you want a dance?"

"How much you want?"

"Twenty dollars."

"Come sit here. Talk to me."

I leaned over him and whispered in his ear. "Want me to dance for you?"

"Nah, I don't have any more money. But you can sit right here, baby. What are you doing later?"

I backed up. "I'm working." I turned and walked away. *I don't need men to waste my time. I'd had enough of that at Cheetah's and had nothing to show for it.*

Why was it that the more men drank, the less they were willing to pay up? I didn't know how the other dancers were doing it. Were they talking dirty like overly tan Brittany from Century Lounge? I didn't know how to sell dances to drunken men, yet. All the places I had worked were nude, which in California meant alcohol-free.

Through the smoky haze, I made out a short man struggling to pull his golf shirt down over his protruding belly. As I approached him, a pungent cloud of beer, cigarettes, and old Chinese food almost stopped me in my high-heeled tracks. He licked his lips and rubbed his thigh as I approached. My stomach turned. *A few dances, and I can pay the hotel.* I plastered on a smile, took a deep breath, and put my hips in motion.

A few hours later, I learned about the Emperor's Room, a VIP private room. For $125 ($100 to the dancer and $25 to the club) a customer could take a dancer back there for three songs, but he had to show the bouncer the money up front, which saved me from worrying about getting stiffed. From a dancer's perspective, this was much better than the $20-per-dance fee on the main floor of the club.

However, I learned men demanded more attention and touching in the VIP room. My intention would be to provide the illusion that I was doing more. I wanted to try it out.

"Why don't we stay and keep doing dances here?" a Hispanic man in his thirties handed me another twenty dollar bill for a second dance. "Why should I go to the VIP room?"

"Have you been in the VIP room before?" He shook his head so I added, "It's more private. Out here, everyone's staring at us." I winked.

He agreed. The next song, we waited for the bouncer to let us into the Emperor's Room. After my customer settled into a sofa seat, I leaned close and swayed my body in slow motion.

"Why don't you do what she's doing?" He pointed to the strippers in the darker corners of the private room.

"If we stay in here for another three songs, we can move into that corner and have more fun." I giggled.

He declined and I was relieved because I didn't want to follow through with my empty promises.

I found Yessenia sulking at the bar. "I'm falling asleep." She crossed her arms. "If you're staying, I'm taking a cab back."

"But we've only been here for about three hours," I said.

"No way I'm coming back. Unless they let us to work the earlier shift, I'm done."

"Did you make any money?"

She raised her eyebrows and glared at me.

I knew she wasn't a hustler. That wasn't her style. She was used to being approached by men and drunken men didn't do that often at 3 AM.

Irritated that my shorter stature had kept us from the better shift—as if I wouldn't make enough money for the club—I stormed into the manager's office.

"We're going now and would like our IDs back," I said.

Sitting behind the desk in his expensive suit with his gold watch and rings, the manager leaned forward. "Leaving already? Why?"

Yes, asshole who reminds me of the mafia-like manager from the bikini bar. "We don't like this shift."

"Well, you have to work to make money on any shift. Try to stay to the end."

Fuck you. "I am making money. That's not the issue." *Even though I could and should rip you off—in fact you probably expect me to—I'm going to tip you out close to fair and square to prove to you that you guys fucked up by not giving us both the earlier better shift.*

I reached into my purse, flipped through my $520 and pulled out $90. I held it out to him. "Twenty percent, right?"

He raised his eyebrows, nodded, took our IDs out of a drawer and handed them back. "I'm sorry you two are unhappy. You can come back later and talk to the day shift manager."

"No thanks." I turned, locked arms with Yessenia who was barely awake, and exited.

On Sunday, we slept in, checked out of the hotel late, ate at the worst buffet ever, and left Vegas.

"So wasn't worth it," Yessenia said.

"Yeah, but at least with our IDs, the option is open to us in the future." Not that I ever wanted to do that again. I couldn't wait to get back home, back to my baby Jacob and my boyfriend Dan. I needed a hug and some encouragement to make it through two more semesters of college and stripping.

CHAPTER TWENTY-SEVEN
BOUNDARIES

SUMMER – FALL 1999

I PUT JACOB TO bed and logged onto my computer to finish a college assignment that I had neglected. Dan was in the living room watching TV, again. Speaking of neglect, to avoid dealing with some relationship issues we'd been having, Dan had been distancing himself from me.

To go into my college email account, I clicked on my "favorites" button. Or, at least I had intended to. Instead, my mouse clicked on "history."

My jaw dropped and my cheeks went flush with anger. *This must be a mistake.* A list of porn addresses appeared on my screen. Frantically, I clicked on them. *How could this be? I never look at porn.*

I despised porn ever since I met several dancers who had been entangled in that industry. They confirmed what I had heard: unlike the lucky men, many girls in that industry were on serious drugs to perform the acts they were hired to do, and most did it because they urgently needed the cash. It was worse than stripping—porn actresses' bodies were internally violated.

For the most part, it seemed the porn industry wasn't filled with women with ravenous sex drives; it was a male industry that exploited desperate women for money. Some men offered to work for next-to-nothing to be able to fuck So-And-So anally. I couldn't in good conscience support that. On the other hand, I also knew a dancer who wanted more than anything to be in adult magazines with another girl (which she succeeded in doing).

Although many women and men outside of the adult entertain-

248

ment industry might lump strippers, dancers, geishas, escorts, porn actresses, and prostitutes into the same category, I now understand that every girl has her limits as to what she will and won't do. For me, and for most other exotic dancers, as the saying went, "you can look, but you can't touch."

If I were to allow myself to be groped for money, I would have crossed that line and lost respect for myself, which was why I couldn't work in Vegas.

However, I felt that every woman should be able to make her own decisions about how she used her body. It was only when a woman was coerced or forced to do something she wasn't comfortable doing, either because of the sex slave trade, drug addiction, or manipulation, that I drew the line. At that point, the woman was no longer the one making the decision, had nothing to gain, and was simply being used for another's benefit. From what I'd been told, many porn actresses fell into that category.

Stunned, I stared at the porn sites on my computer screen. Degrading images of cum dripping on women's faces and breasts flashed in front of me. I kept clicking on the links, as though I was punishing myself.

"Dan!" I screamed. "Come here now!"

Dan, who had been watching TV in the living room, entered the bedroom. "What?"

With tears in my eyes, I pointed to my monitor. "What the hell is this? Why the fuck are you looking at porn on my fucking computer?"

He paused for a moment. "Miranda, don't be so dramatic. Why is it your business what I look at? Looking at porn isn't nearly as bad as your stripping in Vegas."

"On my fucking computer? You know how I feel about porn!"

"Get a grip. We've made videos before. Want me to get them out?"

"That's different. That's us. This is you looking at other women."

He shrugged and rolled his eyes. "You dance for other men."

"I've danced for you, too. Remember, you're the one that wanted to see me strip?" A month earlier, since Dan had never been to a strip club, I invited him to my work so that he could feel more comfortable about what I did, but I didn't want him to see Yessenia nude, nor did she—talk about awkward.

When Dan showed up at the club, I didn't notice he was there until I walked out on stage and saw him sitting at the tip rail. I thought I could handle it. I was wrong. Whereas I—like any good actress—was comfortable on stage in front of strangers, having him there shattered the illusion. My "act" met my "reality." I felt naked in every possible way. I couldn't look Dan in the eye. And by the furtive glances he gave me, I knew that neither could he.

When the torture ended, I dressed and went out to the floor where I took Dan to the private booths. I gave him a nude table dance and a clothed lap dance.

Dan and I had been having problems because of my dancing and I had been hoping that by showing him what I did, he would feel better and might even be turned on. But rather than being a sexy turn-on that brought us closer together, the whole fiasco only distanced us further. His being there removed my veil of anonymity. Someone from the outside world had broken into my dancing world, which I had worked very hard to keep separate.

Dan shook with anger. "Going to your club was a fucking mistake. Now I can picture you dancing on other men's laps."

"If you paid me rent, I wouldn't need to dance so much." I couldn't forgive him for the porn. I felt betrayed, much like the way he—working in computer networking—might feel if I went to another man to help me with my computer. "If you wanted to see a sexy woman in lingerie, why didn't you ask me? That's so fucked up."

"No, what's fucked up is that you show strangers your pussy for money."

"You're so mean." I fought back the tears. "You're not being fair. I have to support Jacob and finish college. You knew I was stripping when we started dating. If you couldn't handle it, you shouldn't have started dating me."

"God dammit, Miranda, that was before I loved you so much."

"If you cared about me so much, you wouldn't be looking at porn on my computer."

"And you wouldn't flaunt your body to assholes for money."

"At least other men pay attention to me and give me money, unlike you. On both issues."

"Oh? So you enjoy parading nude in front of a bunch of fucking strangers?"

"Screw you."

The fight didn't end well.

* * *

After a horrible day of stripping, I couldn't wait to get home. I wanted to drink away my sorrows. A customer had stiffed me out of part of the money he owed me for two lap dances. It wasn't just that I lost twenty dollars—I could recover that by doing more dances—it was that a man had succeeded in getting a lap dance from me for free. I felt violated.

Dan was working late and I put Jacob to bed early. I opened a bottle of rum and alternated between crying and drinking.

Finally, the front door opened and Dan entered. He sighed when he saw me. "What are you doing, Miranda?"

"Nuffin. Not doing nuffin'." I slid down the wall, slumped to the floor, and took another gulp from the bottle.

"Why are you drinking?"

I couldn't tell whether he was confused or annoyed. I couldn't tell whether the room was standing still or spinning. I wiped my mouth on my sleeve, slurred out a response and took another swig.

Dan wrestled the bottle from my hands. He held it up for inspection. There was only about two shot glasses worth left.

"Gimme back it. Thas, thas mine. Gimme it." I reached out to grab it, but fell over instead. My face was streaked with mascara and tears.

"You've had enough."

In my drunken stupor, I let out a maniacal laugh. Dan looked at me like he didn't know who I was anymore. He didn't give me the sympathy I expected and needed.

Life was full of let-downs.

* * *

Not long after, Dan and I separated.

I didn't want to be alone.

I called Jason and invited him over. "I'm upset and I don't want to be by myself."

"Do you want me to come over because you want to be with me," Jason said, "or do you just want someone for the moment?"

"I just want you to come over. I'm having a hard time. Please?"

Silence.

"Jason?"

"Miranda, I can't. I want to, but I can't. I got hurt by you the last time we saw each other. You made your decision. You chose him over me. I'm sorry things didn't work out with your boyfriend."

"Fine. I gotta go."

I went online and chatted with other men. I met Rafael, an Italian accountant who had a daughter about the same age as Jacob. He was tall, average build, and cuddly with piercing brown eyes, a large pronounced nose, and slicked-back black hair.

I told him I was an exotic dancer. He told me he was divorced.

We agreed to meet offline at a kids' pizza place with our little ones. Soon, he was staying at my house every couple nights, then every night. After a month of dating, he had unofficially moved into my apartment. He didn't bring all his belongings over, but he was there all the time after work. I didn't plan for that, but we wanted to see each other every day.

Looking back, I can't believe I lost my mind to the point of making such poor judgment in allowing a practical stranger to prance his way into my life and into the apartment I shared with Jacob. Not one of my wisest moments, but then again, all my young and dumb actions were snowballing.

Rafael introduced me to his family. He brought me to his brother's birthday party where I met a myriad of self-proclaimed flamboyant gay men and had an altogether fascinating time.

On Thanksgiving, Rafael took Jacob and me to his older brother's expensively designed and decorated house in La Jolla, where I met his mom and, in a side conversation with his chiropractor brother, I found out the truth.

Later that night, when Jacob was asleep in his bed, I confronted Rafael. "You're still married! You told me you were single."

"I haven't been with her for a long time," he said. "So, we're separated. Same thing."

"Separated is not the same as divorced!" I yelled. "I don't date married men. Leave now."

"Aw, sweetie, come here. You need some loving."

"No, I don't need any loving from a married man. Get out of my house."

"Is it that time of the month?" He wrapped his arms around me and held tight.

I squirmed in his arms until I could pull out of his grasp. I stared at him in disbelief. "This is so over. You lied to me. Get your shit together and leave."

He laughed. "You're so cute when you get like that. C'mon, it's late. Let's get some sleep." He reached to caress my face. I pulled back. "You'll feel better in the morning." He turned over and, to my dismay, went to sleep.

Why don't people take me seriously when I'm angry? Is it because I'm short?

The next day while he was at work, I stacked his CDs, clothes, and shoes by the front door. When he arrived at my place, I held out my hand for the key. He complied.

* * *

Dan and I missed each other and got back together. We made promises to treat each other with more kindness.

When he returned to my apartment, he was more than a bit irritated over my dating Rafael during our separation.

After taking a look around, Dan said, "What the hell, Miranda? So you replaced me?"

"What do you mean?"

"My razors? My shampoo? You let that asshole use my things. My condoms! Really, Miranda? How could you?"

"I'm sorry. I didn't know you'd be coming back."

One of things we did to increase communication was we spoke through two Beanie Babies: a kitty and a puppy. I was the kitty; he was the puppy. They were displayed on a shelf on my desk in the bedroom. Whenever we were happy with each other, one of us would place the two stuffed animals side-by-side in a hug, or make them kiss. But when we weren't happy, one of the animals would be strangling the other.

Chapter Twenty-Eight
Worlds Converge

FALL 1999

At the beginning of the fall semester, I met with my guidance counselor and discovered that I was not on track to graduate in May of 2000 like I had assumed, but that I would likely finish half-way through the following school year. I could accept that—it was still meeting my goal to get my degree. That's all that mattered. I needed a real job, one that I didn't have to hide from people, one which Jacob would be proud to say his mommy did.

In one of my upper division classes, I was assigned a group project with ten too many members—each with our own work and school schedules to maneuver around. All of us chipped in a few dollars for supplies. One of our group members, a middle-eastern man about my age, forgot to bring cash. I offered to cover him until our next class. He thanked me.

When our next class started, he admitted that he had forgotten the money again. He apologized and asked, "Can I take you to lunch today instead?"

He seemed harmless enough, so I agreed.

The entire time he flirted with me. I tried to make it clear these were unwanted advances.

On the drive back to school, he said, "Would you be interested in joining me on a trip? I'm taking a vacation soon, and I'd love for you to come with me. I'd pay for everything."

"Don't you have a child?" I asked. "Aren't you married?"

He persisted in his offer with flattery. Completely disgusted, I couldn't get out of his car soon enough.

He never paid me the money he owed me.

I felt men were all the same as him. He was a client in training. He didn't even know I stripped, yet he was making the kind of offer I got in strip clubs. However, I wasn't at work and wasn't being paid to deal with his harassment, to be paid to be the girl on the side for a married man.

After going through the stressful break-up with Dan, the drama with Rafael, and the awkward reunion with Dan, I couldn't tolerate much more.

That was when I had a family crisis. My grandmother had been admitted to the Intensive Care Unit, ICU, and the doctors didn't anticipate her living beyond the week. At hearing this news, my mom, my son, and I caught the next plane out of state. I had the good sense to take my backpack and all my schoolwork with me. Being the conscientious student I was, I phoned all of my professors the next morning to report my absence and to make arrangements to turn in assignments and take tests upon my return to school, presumably the following week.

"Don't worry about the test or your paper," one teacher said, "You take care of your family and see me when you get back."

I thanked yet another one of my understanding professors and made my dreaded last phone call, to my arrogant communications teacher. He was a gray-haired-I-should've-retired-five-years-ago-because-I-fucking-hate-my-job kind of teacher. His boring lectures droned on and on. He had little tolerance for differing views and for anyone whom he considered to be disrespectful in any way—be it from tardiness, lack of note-taking, or excessive questions.

His gruff voice on the other end bellowed. "You'll be missing a test."

"I know," I said. "That's why I'm calling you."

"That test has been scheduled since the beginning of the semester. It's in your syllabus."

As if I couldn't read. "I know. I'm sorry, but I had to fly out last minute. Can I take it during your office hours as soon as I return?"

"No. There are no make-up tests."

"But if I get a zero, I won't pass the class."

"That's your decision to make."

He doesn't believe me. "I can give you the name of the hospital and my grandma's doctor's information so you can verify that this is an emergency."

"I don't need that. You know my policy."

That was it. After only spending two days with my mother visiting my ill grandma, I took an early flight home—in time to take his royal highness's test. By some divine intervention, my grandma recovered.

I saw an opportunity for passive-aggressive revenge. Our next communications class assignment was a how-to speech. I approached my arrogant teacher after class.

With a glowing angelic smile, I said, "I wanted to know if it would be all right with you if I did my speech on how to become an exotic dancer."

He grunted and raised one of his bushy white eyebrows. "So long as you are professional, I don't care what your topic is. Remember your peers will be grading this next speech in addition to me."

I knew it was a risk, but frankly, I didn't give a damn. I was going for shock value, for anything that I thought might annoy him in the slightest.

Remembering that one of the requirements was a visual aid, I smirked.

On a bright sunny day, I strolled to the front of the classroom with my folded display board and paper bag. "Good morning," I said cheerfully. I cleared my throat.

"Let me start out by asking how many of you know someone who has worked as or is currently working as an exotic dancer?"

To my surprise nearly a fourth of the class raised a hand. Not my professor. He and the remaining three-fourths of the room fell silent. All eyes were on me.

"Today I'm going to explain how to become an exotic dancer. I've danced in six clubs in two states, doing bikini, topless, and nude dancing."

Some students leaned back and some leaned forward, but all seemed to hold their breath in anticipation.

"First of all," I smiled, "you need to find out the local laws." I glanced at my professor. He sat on the edge of his desk with one hand over his mouth, stroking his gray whiskers. I then explained an overview of laws, restrictions, and guidelines pertaining to the industry.

Every student had an evaluation form in front of them, but nobody was writing anything down.

Toward the middle of my speech, I picked up the paper bag and pulled out a pair of six-inch black stilettos and lap dance shorts.

"Here are some things you need."

My professor's eyes nearly popped out. He loosened the knot in his tie.

Satisfied that I had made him a little uncomfortable, I worked the classroom like I worked the stage—lots of eye contact and self-confidence.

Before I wrapped up my speech, I opened a tri-fold board which displayed several photographs. Some of my coworkers, Blanca and Nicole in particular, were kind enough to allow me to take pictures of them.

I pointed to a photo in the middle. "And here's me in a cop uniform."

Audible gasps.

My professor looked thunderstruck.

At the end, the students gave me a nice round of applause. I put my stripper gear back in the bag and returned to my seat.

Later at home, I gloated while reviewing my feedback. With the exception of a couple of religious zealots, everyone gave me good scores. Some commented on how I "surprisingly handled such a difficult topic with professionalism."

Since my campus population numbered in the five digits, I figured I wouldn't see that professor or most of those classmates ever again. I was satisfied that everything went as I planned.

Looking back, I'm not sure what the presentation accomplished in terms of sticking it to the professor other than showing him that I could do whatever I pleased and he couldn't stop me.

I had gotten used to being center stage and being haughty and dramatic. Speeches, even peer graded, were too easy for me, no thrill at all.

I wanted more thrills and more attention.

* * *

Now that my boundaries had been completely blurred, I decided to do another project on dancing for a different class. Unlike Mr. Arrogant, this teacher was completely intrigued by my chosen topic.

The assignment? To research "job satisfaction."

This assignment would be easy. No research required. Hell, I already knew the answers. All I needed was another dancer to echo my sentiments, type it up, and turn it in.

My hypothesis was that money did not equal happiness.

Dancing was a job where I could tell a customer "fuck off" if I wanted to, where it was possible make my rent in a couple of shifts, where I had plenty of freedom—all of which, according to my textbook, equaled a high level of job satisfaction.

Yet most days I hated my job. My self-worth was tied to a constantly fluctuating dollar amount. When I had a bad money day I felt like shit.

Candy, my not-too-bright bleached blonde from the Midwest 20-year-old interviewee, mirrored my views.

"How do you feel when work goes poorly?" I asked, pencil in hand.

She flipped her hair. "I don't know. It sucks. Like do you mean money?"

"You can say whatever you want. I need to write something down about how it makes you feel, you know, when you can't make money. Why?"

She dropped her shoulders. "I guess I feel it's because I'm, like, ugly or have a bad personality or something, in some way."

"Aww, you know that's not true." I scribbled notes. "Okay, here's another question. Do you feel joy or pleasure at work or from doing your work? And how so?"

She snickered. "No, I hate my job. I hate the way business has been. When I don't make money, I get angry with customers. I just wanna go home."

"So you never get any pleasure? Nothing's ever good?"

"Well, I guess so, but only when I do good, when I get a lot of tips." She ran her fingers through her straight blonde hair.

"Well, can you just answer, do you have any fun at work?"

Candy grimaced. "Seriously?"

"Yeah."

"With the dancers or the guys?"

I shrugged.

"This isn't fun," Candy said.

"Why not?"

"It's boring. There's nothing to do except talk to the disgusting customers."

I took notes then looked back at my assigned questions. "What could make work more fun?"

She laughed. "I could work in Vegas. Or I could get high, 'cause I don't drink."

"Anything else that would make it better?"

"If they had less girls on the day shift, that would make me happier. Then I'd make more money and have less personalities to deal with, if you know what I mean."

"Tweeker Emerald?"

Candy laughed. "Freaking glad she isn't here anymore."

I scribbled on my paper, "This job [dancer] has a very high burnout and some symptoms of burnout were present in the respondent interviewed."

I looked at the questions about feedback and asked, "Do the customers ever tell you how they think you're doing?"

"What's that supposed to mean?"

"Like, do they compliment you?"

"Yes, all the time, every day. Some guys say, 'You do your job well,' 'You're very talented,' 'Have you gone to school for this?' Of course other guys compliment me by giving me extra tips."

When it came to the category of feedback from coworkers, she answered, "I don't usually get comments, but when I do I've been told 'You're dancing good on stage,' 'You're doing many dances today,' 'I don't like those shoes,' or 'What's that on your ass?'"

Of course I earned an "A" on my paper, like the majority of my grades since I was five. I expected it.

Who'd have known that exotic dancing could have complemented my college work so nicely? Stripping was making me money and in a weird way helping me get good grades. However, it still wouldn't be a great conversation opener when meeting moms to schedule playdates for Jacob.

Chapter Twenty-Nine
Reality

Spring - Summer 2000

"What's your real name?" asked a forty-something businessman in a suit who had dropped $100 on dances with me.

"Serenity," I said.

"Come on, that's not true."

"Yeah it is. My parents were hippies. They thought it sounded cool."

"Serenity's your real name?"

"Yes. I use it because nobody believes it's my name."

Most men bought my story. He did and bought another dance.

On slow days, when customers continued to badger me and I thought there was potential for more money, I said, "Okay, I'll tell you my real name but keep it a secret. My name's Beth. I hate it, it's so boring. Promise not to tell anyone."

They'd coo over me, insist it sounded cute. Then we'd continue the charade for another dance or two.

* * *

Yessenia and I each had a handful of regulars who believed they were in love with us.

If a man was naïve enough to fall in love with my stripper persona, I was smart enough to take his money until he figured it out. I never lied about how I felt, but remained aloof.

Eventually they'd catch on and I'd move on to the next customer, until Matthew, a young good-looking Jewish man with short tight curls, glasses, and a sweet disposition, showed up at my tip rail. He smiled at me and stared into my eyes during my entire set. That's how I knew he would be good for a few dances.

When I collected my tips, he leaned over and said, "You are absolutely lovely. May I have a dance with you?"

Of course I agreed.

Matthew showed up every week. I appreciated his manners and gentle attitude, so I would sit and chat with him during a song or two when I needed a break. He worked in marketing, selling Lakers and Clippers tickets, and would come to the club after work near the end of my shift. Whenever he showed up, I convinced Yessenia to stay later so I could collect an extra hundred or two from him. Like Zach and my other regulars, Matthew preferred spending time talking rather than having me undress for private table dances. I slinked my body around him while dancing for him while he would stare intently into my eyes, speechless.

One day, after we spent a couple of songs in the lap dance booth, Matthew bought me a cranberry juice and we sat down to chat.

"I have something for you." Matthew reached into a bag and pulled out three CDs. "I know you like rock, and you've danced to Pink Floyd before, so I thought you might like these."

I accepted the gift—three Pink Floyd CDs containing not a single song I liked. "Thank you. That's so sweet." I gave him a hug and his arms lingered around my waist. I could smell his cologne.

Yessenia approached us, crossed her arms, and narrowed her eyes. "Come on, Miranda. We need to go. Now."

The following week, Matthew acted nervous around me. He would open his mouth to speak then stop and smile at me instead. I liked his smile, his straight teeth and full lips, and his blue eyes; however, my interest in him stopped at appreciation and fondness.

After an hour of dancing and talking with Matthew, I saw Yessenia glaring at me from across the room. It was past time to go.

"Yessenia's waiting for me," I said. "I need to leave. Will I see you next week?"

Matthew took a deep breath and reached into his coat pocket. He pulled out a letter. "This is for you."

I unfolded it and glanced at the two pages of handwritten sentences. Skimming it, my eyes stopped at the word "love." There was a phone number at the bottom. I felt uncomfortable.

I stared into Matthew's eyes with dismay and shook my head, my mouth open in surprise.

He took a moment to register my reaction before sighing and rounding his shoulders forward, making no effort to hide his disappointment.

Yessenia tapped me on the shoulder. "Miranda, if you don't come now, I'm leaving without you."

"Okay, I'm coming." I stood up and slid the letter into my purse. "Thanks, Matthew. I'll look at this later. Have a good night." I avoided his stare and, without giving him our customary hug, I hurried away, following Yessenia to the dressing room.

While we packed our costumes and makeup, I read the love letter at least twice. I forced myself to throw it in the trash on our way out to the car. No sense in dwelling on it.

Didn't Matthew realize a strip club was nothing more than an adult Disneyland? I was a Cast Member. I played the part of whatever fantasy girl a customer wanted. It wasn't real. I wouldn't let it be.

Matthew never returned.

Maybe if I hadn't met him in a strip club, things might have been different. But I refused to date men—no matter how wonderful they seemed—that I met through work.

The fact that they hung out at strip clubs meant they were not the kind of guys I wanted to date. Strip clubs contained all that I thought was unholy about men—lying, married men; creeps who wanted to brag about "hooking up"; pathetic men who never tried to meet women in real life.

Or they couldn't meet women in real life. Lack of confidence. Lack of desirability. Lack of something. They wanted to or had to pay for women's attention—attention without emotion or strings attached.

I wanted a man to want to know me, to date me for *me,* not for me "the stripper." Besides, they'd already seen me naked before a first date. No mystery there.

*   *   *

After another unproductive—no money—set on stage, I retreated to the dressing room for a break.

Yessenia and the other dancers in there were laughing.

"What's so funny?" I asked.

Yessenia giggled. "The other manager put a dildo in your bag."

"What?" Horrified, I ruffled through my outfits. *Who knows which cunt it was in?*

"No, it's not there anymore. He smacked another girl with it and chased after her." She wiped tears from the corners of her eyes. "You had to be there."

Somehow the hilarity of the situation didn't materialize for me. I couldn't wait to get out of this job.

Yessenia and I changed into our street clothes—sweatpants and baggy t-shirts—and prepared to go home when Blanca stormed into the dressing room, giggling.

"Listen to what happened," she said. "A creep propositioned me for sex during a lap dance. I was all by myself in the secluded dance booths in the back of the club."

"What a jerk," Yessenia said. "What did you do?"

"Asked him if he wanted to get fucked."

My jaw dropped. "You what?"

"No, listen," she said. "So he says, yes he wants to get fucked. I asked him how much he was going to pay. He flashed several hundred dollars and told me he'd pay me the rest when I showed up at his hotel."

"No, way," I said, "Tell me you're not—"

"Hell no. I took his money and did a couple of dances and told him I'd go to the dressing room to change. When I was a few feet away from him, I stopped, turned around and yelled, 'you've been fucked,' and flipped him off."

"Are you going to get in trouble?" I asked.

"Who's going to tell?" she said. "It's my word against his. He's the idiot. But, I'm going to hide the money for now in case they want to check. Bet he learned his lesson."

I never asked where she hid the money.

Never a dull moment at work.

Cops started to crack down on the local strip joints. Rumors were that dancers had been arrested at clubs not far from ours. Any customer could be an undercover officer. Many of us dancers became suspicious.

Even though I didn't think I was doing anything illegal, I was afraid of getting in trouble. I mean, it's not like an exotic dancer has much credibility. *Me versus cop. Cop wins.*

Graduation was only a few months away. Getting arrested would ruin everything I'd worked so hard for.

Bob handed us a paper and said, "These are the new rules." He cleared his throat. "You can't touch your pubic area or your breasts."

"What?" one dancer whined. "That's not fair!"

The dancers stroked their skin and caressed their bodies, and asked for clarification on what exactly would be allowed and what moves were banned.

"I don't understand," another said. "Can I touch here?" She cupped her breasts and squeezed them together.

He stared at her for a moment. "Yes, that's okay, but don't touch your nipples."

"What do you mean by pubic area?" I said. "That's vague. It's not like I finger myself on stage." The other girls laughed. I bent over in front of him and reached a hand between my legs. "Can I still do this?"

He looked at my upside down face. "Don't touch your ass there either."

The dancers grumbled.

There went a few profitable dance moves.

Money had been getting harder to come by lately. I needed to hang on until December, which was a money-making month.

For the next several weeks, our stage shows and lap and table dances were a bit more tame than usual. I was even afraid to let my hair touch a customer during a dance, since I heard rumors that police could arrest you for making contact.

Even rent wasn't worth getting arrested for. How would I explain that one to my family? *Um, Dad, I need you to bail me out. I'll tell you why when you get here.* Haha.

It turned out I did have some explaining to do. Jacob's babysitter started asking questions. An upstanding Christian woman with three adopted children and a licensed in-home daycare, she said, "What exactly do you do for work, Miranda? I need better contact information for the emergency card."

She no longer believed that I was a waitress. My occasional overnight sitting arrangements and odd schedule were suspicious. I thought I had a foolproof story, but apparently not. Ultimately, I respected her and didn't want to lie anymore.

"If I tell you," I said, "please don't say anything to anyone."

"You have my word."

"I'm an exotic dancer." *Exotic dancer* sounded a bit more respectable than *stripper*. "Only until I graduate from college," I added, as if this were putting a stamp of approval on the whole deal.

She gasped and squealed. "You're kidding me. No way." She laughed and smirked. "I would have never guessed. You wild thing."

When the police activity died down, everything at my club went back to normal and the stage rules were no longer strictly enforced. *Thank God I didn't have to stress anymore about touching my ass.*

Yessenia had a customer who lavished money on her on a regular basis, so she soaked up his cash. When he next visited the club, she danced for him for a while then came up to me.

"Hey, Serenity," she said. "My customer is going to buy both us vibrators."

If I'd been drinking, I would've spit it out. "What are you talking about?"

"Since he thinks we're roommates, I said you'd be jealous if I got one and you didn't."

"Shut up. Seriously?"

"Yeah. Let's go into the sex shop and pick out which ones we want."

"I don't see why I need one. I can have a real dick whenever I want."

"But this one takes batteries."

She wouldn't take no for an answer.

Damn. Vibrators were expensive. Especially handheld multi-speed made-in-Sweden hot pink vibrators.

We bought two matching ones.

On a dull Monday morning, I parted the velvet curtains and was about to walk on stage when "The Tide is High" by Blondie blared through the speakers.

Oh, crap. Another damn free dance promotion. Thanks, DJ, for clearing my tip rail. I love nothing better in life than stripping my clothes off on stage for the fun of it. Money is so overrated.

To stir up business, the manager would have the DJ play that song and announce to the cheapskates that there would be a free dance with any dancer of their choice. This free thirty-second teaser dance almost always resulted in at least one or two more dances, putting more money in dancers' purses and the club's pocket.

However, since I was up next, I couldn't participate. I peeked through the curtains and watched my coworkers pull all of the men off my tip rail, leaving me with no reward for pulling off my panties and bra.

With a pout, I waited backstage for my song to start.

Gotta love Mondays.

That night, Yessenia and I sat down in my living room and drank. More and more we were relying on alcohol to relax us after work. If it was a bad shift, one glass of wine apiece turned into a bottle.

"I hate stripping." I gulped the rest of my wine. "I can't make money anymore." It was becoming increasingly difficult for me to clear three hundred a night.

"Think I like it?" she said. "I don't even go to work half the time."

"Yeah, I know. It sucks when you don't. I hate going in by myself."

"Do what you want. Stay home."

"I can't. I need the money, but when I'm in a bad mood guys can tell and I don't make money." I emptied the bottle into my glass. "At least I only have a few more months of this shit."

"Wonderful. *I'll* be doing this forever." Yessenia finished her last glass of wine.

"I didn't mean it like that. My rent went up over a hundred and fifty dollars."

"Duh. Mine did, too."

"But what if I can't pay rent? I have Jacob to worry about. What am I going to do?"

"Like you said, *you* won't have to do this after you graduate college."

I went to the kitchen and opened a second bottle of wine. "Want some more?" I refilled our glasses. "I'm burnt out. I'm not going to make it another two months."

Yessenia lay back on my couch. "I haven't paid my credit card."

"Why not?"

"I'm not a hustler like you. I'm not making shit."

For a while, we blamed our bad shifts on the economy, on slow business, or on the time of year, but in reality other dancers were doing much better.

She sipped her wine. "We need to look at other clubs again."

"I'm not going back to Vegas."

"There's a nude club opening up near our old apartment."

"I can't work that close to home." I felt the risk was too great for me to be recognized at school or by a future employer.

"That's up to you. I'm going to check it out. They're offering a major discount on house fees. I figure I can work there until they raise the fees."

That was a tactic new strip clubs used in order to attract dancers: no tip-outs until they had enough girls. Money was always a great motivator.

"Isn't there anything further away from here?" I forced down the last of the dry wine.

"Yeah, we can check out several places."

And so we did. We auditioned and worked a few shifts at several other clubs—none of which we liked, whether it was because of location, income, dancer attitudes, club fees, customers, or management.

As soon as I was ready to audition at the beautifully decorated newly-built club closest to my home, local city residents decided to take legal action and force it out of business. That newly erected building was razed.

Fortunately, they had a sister club only blocks away from an amusement park. Yessenia and I went to check it out.

"Why do we need to go to the police station?" I asked.

The manager shrugged. "In this city, you need to register as a sex worker."

"What are you talking about?" I said. "Sex worker?"

"You need to apply for a permit," the manager said.

So I went from dating a cop to dressing up as a cop on stage to getting fingerprinted by a cop. Talk about going downhill.

Wow. Registering as a sex worker at a local police department. Sweet. This would look great on a background check. I pictured my future boss saying, "On your application, you didn't say you did sex performances. You don't fit our company image. I think we're going to have to let you go."

If I were to ever have political aspirations, I could only imagine the news report: *Local candidate's seedy stripping past revealed!*

With trepidation, I went to the police station. The officers' smirks shined through their serious demeanor, so Yessenia and I played the part of bimbo strippers by giggling and acting stupid. *Might as well amuse everyone during the awkward procedure.* A uniformed officer handed us our laminated "sex worker" licenses and we headed to the nude club nearby.

Money at the new club was dreadfully slow. They did far too many "2-for-1" dances where we had to parade around on stage in bikinis and do two bikini lap dances for a measly ten bucks. Worse yet, the club pressured us to sell drinks. Yessenia and I were always coming up short, and had to fork over more of our hard-earned cash to the club to compensate for our poor drink sales.

"There's more money by the airport," Yessenia said. "Let's go back to Century."

"It's not that easy," I said. "I need to get an internship now. I can't get a real job after December without relevant work experience, so I can't dance on the dayshift anymore. Would you work the night shift with me?"

"No, I can't compete with those hustlers."

"What if we try the topless club around the corner from Century Lounge?" I was referring to the Wild Goose, a topless burlesque club, a longtime establishment that we'd heard provided cheap drinks, decent food, and good entertainment.

She snickered. "And deal with drunken men? No thanks."

"But they don't make dancers work on a schedule because you're not an employee. We can come and go as we please; you don't have to go in when you don't want to. Plus, their stage and house fees are cheap since they make their money on the liquor."

"I'd get shit-faced," she said. "That would be the only way I'd be able to deal."

"We can try it out, work a few hours on Friday and Saturday nights. I don't want to work there by myself. It's easier when we're together."

"I'll think about it."

* * *

Back at Century Lounge, I listened to Blanca describe her side job as a dominatrix at an underground club in Los Angeles. She talked about racks, and whips, and satisfying her lust for getting back at the male race because of her lame husband.

"What did your husband do?" I said.

Blanca puffed on a cigarette. "I came home from work one night and caught him."

"Cheating on you?"

"No. See, I had noticed but couldn't explain how come my lingerie kept getting stretched out."

"He was wearing your lingerie?"

"That's not all," Blanca said. "His testicles had a chain tied to them. He was dragging the chain down a runway he made from some sheets. He had lamps set up along his runway."

"And you were okay with this?"

"Hell no. Screw him."

"So you left him?"

"No, I'm not leaving until my baby is grown up."

"Baby? How old is your son?"

"Seventeen." Blanca, at over forty years old, had a better-toned body than most twenty-year-olds. With her caked-on makeup and strange habit of hanging her hair over her face, no man would ever guess her age. "It's not good for kids to have divorced parents." She opened a beer.

And this situation is somehow healthier for a child? I dropped the issue.

*   *   *

I attended a job fair at my university.

I approached an investment company booth. A couple of men in suits and ties were speaking with other students. When it was my turn, I handed my resume to the thirty-something-year-old with short curly red hair.

"Your major isn't finance," he said. "Why do you think you're qualified to work for us?"

"I've been investing since I was sixteen," I said, "which is when I bought my first CD. Investments are a hobby of mine. I regularly read blogs like the Motley Fool."

He smiled. "You know about Motley Fool?"

That conversation led to an interview, which led to a part-time paid internship at the firm where I would be working under a female broker who grossed over $5 million a year. I had to wear dark-colored skirt suits with jackets, pantyhose, and low heels—something I was definitely not accustomed to. To say I looked conservative would be an understatement.

My final semester was tough: college on Tuesdays and Thursdays, internship on Mondays, Wednesdays, and Fridays, and topless dancing every Friday, Saturday, and other nights I could.

Good-bye social life.

Not a morning person, I detested the 7 AM start time at the firm and compensated with coffee. Five other interns and I sat around a cherry wood conference table in front of computer screens and telephones, making sales calls, filing paperwork, and sending out marketing mailers at the direction of four supervisors, the brokers working under the big boss.

I folded papers into a tri-fold, sliding my fingers to make a perfect edge, and placed them into envelopes so the header would be the first thing the recipient would see. *Stuffing envelopes. Now that's a skill I can be proud of.*

The other two female interns discussed their night life.

"This party last night was so crazy," one slender black-haired woman said.

"Dude, I can't drink." The other, a petite Vietnamese woman, giggled. "My face gets all red."

The male interns laughed and chimed in, discussing their own parties and inviting us women to join them for one on the next Friday night.

I continued folding paper and stuffing envelopes and didn't say anything.

"Don't you ever go out and party?" one of the girls asked me.

I kept my head down. "Nah, I don't have time with school and my son." *Let the other college girls have the limelight; I got my fill of it at my night job—the one that paid my bills.*

*   *   *

Staring at a computer monitor on an expensive wood desk in a little glass-walled office at the financial company, I typed "lmtcb," meaning "left message to call back," and put a check mark next to a name in the aerospace company's phone directory. My boss offered bonuses—all cash—to anyone who could get a hold of these proprietary phone books. I moved my finger down to the next number and dialed the phone.

An older man answered.

I identified myself and my employer. "She does free retirement workshops for the employees at your company every month."

"How did you get my number?"

"At her workshops, people who are interested in our services give us referrals."

"Who referred me?"

"I'm not sure," I lied. "I only get the list of names and numbers on the referral list."

"Well, I'm not interested. Don't call me again." He hung up.

I crossed his name off the phone book, moved my finger down to the next name and dialed the number. After five more rejections and one confirmation for our next workshop, I took a break. In the large conference room, the other interns were joking around while shredding old financial documents.

"Damn, that stripper was hot," one male said.

"She was all over you," another said.

Laughter, even from the two females.

"When are we going again?"

I averted my eyes and shifted uncomfortably in my seat.

The guys glanced in my direction and lowered their voices.

It wasn't long before everyone at the office started to watch what they said around me. They assumed I was a prudish conservative, which was fine with me. It felt nice for a change.

"You coming tonight?" one of my male supervisors asked two other supervisors.

"To see some hot dancers? Hell yeah." They laughed.

"Shush," the first one motioned toward me and raised his eyebrows. "We wouldn't want to offend anyone." The others followed him into a closed office to further their conversation.

I stared after them. Somehow I didn't make the connection until that moment that my coworkers in those fancy company offices were the same men who put dollar bills on my tip rail and asked if they could touch me in lap dance booths.

Inside or outside of the strip clubs, many men were the same.

I had put these professional guys on a pedestal thinking I would only have to deal with creeps at the clubs until I could earn my degree and earn the right to work around respectable men.

The veil had been lifted.

CHAPTER THIRTY
COVER BLOWN

YESSENIA AGREED TO TRY out Wild Goose, the burlesque club around the corner from Century Lounge. The rowdy topless place was more of a neighborhood dive bar, close to LAX. With its airport-ready location and cheap drinks, it was always packed. There was ample room for a large stage with two brass poles and a long dressing room hidden behind the curtains, as well as an L-shaped bar, lots of tables and chairs, padded booths around the perimeter, and several pool tables in the far back.

The girls on the night shift were a wide variety of pretty, in all different body shapes, ethnicities, and hair styles. Some of the dancers had tattoos. One even had an electronic monitoring ankle bracelet because of her one-too-many drunken driving charges. For the most part, the dancers were good looking and good-natured.

The kitchen served fries and juicy burgers all night. Dancers could get free food, only having to tip the cook. Yessenia and I would eat dinner there sometimes. If we ate at a table, guys bought us drinks. I was surprised to find a dancer from Century Lounge behind the bar at Wild Goose. Maybe she was trying to figure out if being a bartender was easier than stripping nude.

While dancers commonly adopted new stage names when they switched clubs (and sometimes on a whim while working at the same club, occasionally even mid-shift), I still used the stage name Serenity. Yessenia was still Destiny. Our names together had a nice ring to them.

Not only would customers buy us drinks, but they would try to get us to catch up to their level of drunkenness by pushing us to down shots.

I actually preferred shots to mixed drinks because I could drink them faster, which made it easier to move on to other customers rather than stay to sip one mixed drink, allowing one man to suck up my money-making time. It was impolite to accept a drink from a customer then walk away with it.

"Want another shot of Midori and Bailey's?" a man asked me and Yessenia.

"Got anything better?" I leaned my head on my hand with my elbow on the table.

"Let's have those buttery nipples," Yessenia said.

"Oh yeah," I said. "I love buttery nipples."

The customers laughed and ordered some.

We giggled and waited for our shots of butterscotch Schnapps and Bailey's.

"Serenity and Destiny to the stage," the DJ said over the microphone.

We finished our drinks, thanked the men, and walked across the club to the DJ booth.

"It's busy tonight," the DJ said. "The manager wants me to put two girls up at a time. Do you two want to go up together?"

"Yes," Yessenia and I said in unison.

"What music do you want?"

"I don't know," I said. "What do you think?"

"Surprise us," Yessenia said.

We rushed backstage and changed into miniskirts and buttoned-up dress shirts, clipped up our hair, and refinished our makeup.

If our skirts weren't so short and our heels weren't so tall, we'd pass for a couple of businesswomen or secretaries, exactly the look we were going for. *If businessmen can be creeps at the office, I'll bring the office into the strip club.*

"Let's welcome delicious Destiny and sexy Serenity," the DJ announced.

Duran Duran's "Girls on Film" blasted from the speakers.

"Good choice." I grinned. "After you."

Yessenia led the way through the curtains and onto the stage.

I twirled a strand of hair around my finger and playfully pranced across the stage. Whenever a man made eye contact, I averted my gaze and bit my lower lip. With one hand on the pole, I swung around, stood up and put a hand up to my mouth as if to say, "Oh, dear me, did I do that?"

Crumbled dollar bills littered the stage. Men wadded money up into balls and tossed them up—effortlessly tipping us without having to approach the tip rail.

Destiny and I switched sides. Mirroring one another, we acted like two shy girls from the office who felt the sudden urge to reveal ourselves, one button at a time. Men showered us with money and cat calls.

We opened our blouses to reveal our lacy bras. The men whistled and howled. The energy was electrifying.

Facing away from the men, I unclasped my bra, took it off, held it out for them to see, and dropped it. They shouted for me to turn around.

Arching my back, I reached up my arms and leaned against a brass pole, wiggling my bottom back and forth at the men. With two hands covering my breasts, I twirled around. The guys groaned and begged me to remove my fingers.

When the second song started, I giggled and thrust my hands into the air letting the men see me topless. Yessenia and I slipped off our miniskirts. We of course still had on thongs.

More money went on stage.

Our song ended. I blew the guys a kiss.

Backstage, Yessenia and I split our tips.

"That was good," she said.

"Not just good, it was awesome." It was one of the best sets I'd ever performed—both in energy and money. We were both really into the act. The costumes made us better actresses and we fed off each other's demure but confident attitudes.

When I would go onstage alone, I often danced to Metallica. With a tight faux leather mini-dress and strappy platform leather stilettos, I allowed the beat from "Enter Sandman," "Sad but True," and "The Unforgiven" to rush through my veins.

One night, a few customers, tired from too much booze, sat at one end of my stage. They were half-asleep. I thought I'd have a little fun.

I stomped my heel down in front of them. Their eyes opened wide.

"Wake up and watch," I said. "No one sleeps on my stage."

They laughed and put more money on the rail.

I spun around the pole, crawled up to them (they were definitely awake now), and swung my legs open to flash my thong.

Yessenia and I became accustomed to the free drinks at the club—now we could get drunk at home and at work. I escalated from one drink to two shots to three or four to be able to finish out my shift. Eventually I turned to as many as seven shots in one night, which caused me to fall in my platform heels more than once. Yessenia wasn't far behind me.

She would also smoke pot or make out with a hot Brazilian dancer—who had her own bodyguards—in a women's restroom stall.

Yessenia had already started to experiment with other women on the side. I was a little irritated that she hadn't given me details sooner. I wanted to know what it was like to be with a woman.

With Yessenia smoking and me drinking, I thought of Blanca's warning about dancers eventually succumbing to a vice. But I didn't really care. I was graduating in a couple months. I missed out on the college parties, so I decided to party at work. No big deal.

*   *   *

At college, I had made few friends besides Wesley. Wesley and I continued to shoot pool, maintaining our purely platonic relationship. In between classes, we hung out at the student union and studied together.

I didn't think anything of our friendship until the night when everything between us changed.

At Wild Goose, after my set ended the DJ announced into the microphone, "Okay fellas, show your appreciation for sexy Serenity!"

I smiled, covered back up, and picked up the crumpled dollar bills scattered across the stage floor.

Backstage, I unraveled my tips, put them away, and shimmied back into my sheer dress and lap dance shorts. A customer was waiting for me.

I took the stranger's hand and led him to one of the walls adjacent to the stage where a row of armless chairs were used for dances. While this club only allowed table dances—no-contact air dances—we were also permitted to perform at individual tables and booths, unlike the nude clubs in the area.

With the club being so crowded, it was easier to take my customers to the chairs along the walls used for dances. That way, I wouldn't have to deal with being heckled by a customer's drunken friends at their table or booth. It was too hard to flirt for more dances when I had to entertain a group rather than one.

My customer sat down on the red padded seat and leaned back against the wooden wall. I kicked my blue metallic lockbox purse underneath his chair, and danced. I slinked around for his entertainment, squatted, put my hands on the back of a chair in front of me for support, and shook my butt, inches from the man's chest. I peered behind me, raised an eyebrow and smirked in his direction.

He wore a dazed-I've-had-too-many-beers-to-count-but-I'm-in-heaven grin. I twirled around and tousled my hair before diving in toward him—close enough for him to feel my hot breath on his neck.

He stayed for another couple of dances before he had emptied his wallet and had to return to his friends who high-fived him.

I put my money in my purse and reapplied a coat of lipstick.

"Hey, are you available for a dance?" A college-aged guy approached me.

I smiled. I loved nights when the dances came effortlessly. "Yes, would you like one?"

"Oh, not for me. I mean, yes I'd love it." He licked his lips. "But, my friend *really* wants you. He can't keep his eyes off of you. I'll pay for a couple of dances for him." He handed me a twenty—the dances were only ten dollars each.

I pocketed the money and followed him, snaking through the tables and chairs, across the room. I carefully placed one stiletto in front of the other, trying not to trip on someone's feet. When we stopped, I raised my head to find his friend.

It couldn't be. This is not possible. Please tell me I'm buzzed from the two shots of Bailey's and I'm mistaken.

"Miranda? Oh my God…Miranda." Wesley stood there in front of me, stumbling from a few drinks. He ran his fingers through his brown curly hair. "No fucking way. It's really you. Miranda?"

Did he see me topless on stage?

Besides my mortification, I became concerned when Wesley kept calling out my name—nobody there knew my real identity. "Wesley." I held a finger up to his lips. "Shhh. Please, don't say my name in here."

His friend punched him in the arm, turned to me, and said, "Wesley couldn't stop talking about you since we walked in here. He's totally into you. When you were on stage….damn! He's right, you're fucking hot."

Wesley's eyes widened as if he'd discovered he'd won the lottery. "I...I can't believe this." He banged the back of his head against the wall and squirmed in place. "Miranda." He reached out for a hug.

I shrank at the touch of his warm hands on my cold skin.

His two buddies reveled in the moment and tried to get the two of us to go do dances. The second friend took more money from his wallet. "I'll buy him a dance, too."

This wasn't supposed to ever happen.

I shook my head, opened my purse, pulled the original twenty-dollar bill out and thrust it into Wesley's friend's face. "Here. Take this. I can't do this." I took one last look into Wesley's puppy dog eyes. "I'm sorry, Wesley."

I hurried back to the dressing room to hide. The door shut behind me. I slumped down onto one of the chairs in front of the mirror. Shaking, I stared at my reflection—at my thick black mascara, at the glitter around my eyes, at my sparkling pink lipstick.

Wesley was my friend. My friend. A male friend who never tried to get more from me than just friendship.

I remembered when Wesley and I first started hanging out. I had been amused at his apparent lack of romantic interest in me. That was a novelty: a man who wasn't trying to get more from me. Men had always been trying to get more from me—men at the clubs and in real life. I felt cheated out of being able to have male friends.

And I wanted male friends because men didn't seem to judge me as harshly as women did.

Wesley never judged me.

But then he never knew the truth.

I had sprinkled stripping into my real life when I spoke about it in class, but Wesley wasn't in that class. I didn't care about that teacher or about that class. I would never see any of them again. But I did care about Wesley. And I did want to see him again.

Plus making a presentation in class was my decision. This was not.

Wesley was my real life from the world I was trying so hard to become a part of, the world I felt like a stranger to. Stripping was my fake life, my acting life, the world where I wasn't myself, where I couldn't be myself.

That night my worlds had collided.

Maybe I had screwed up too much to be accepted in the real world.

I lay down my head and cried.

*   *   *

From that day forward, Wesley avoided me at school. He looked away from me in class. He didn't hang out with me. When I finally invited him to shoot pool, he made up an excuse and turned me down. I got the point.

I had rejected him in the club. He had rejected me in real life.

*   *   *

Besides Wesley, why did I hate dancing? It paid my bills, the cash was immediate, guys were always happy to see me, I was constantly flattered with compliments, gifts, and tips.

But most of us didn't like stripping. Sure the odd exhibitionist or the girls who loved the power and money liked stripping. So did the girls who were so far gone on drugs or the glitzy lifestyle with all the accompanying gifts—breast implants diamonds, cars and houses.

For me, stripping was a daily compromise. I was putting mind over heart, distorting a moment that should be special between two people who care about each other—who choose to see each other naked—into a crass business transaction. I was removing my clothes by will of mind and becoming a sexual object for strangers. I needed their acceptance of my body—their appreciation in the form of money—and when I got it I deluded myself into thinking that we were somehow even.

But the sad fact was, whether I made only a couple of dollars or hundreds for standing nude in front of customers, they couldn't pay me enough to make up for the embarrassment of stripping off my clothes, of wearing nothing but painful, impossibly high-heeled shoes, of smiling at men who often repulsed me, of acting thrilled at the opportunity to dance on their jeaned laps and play the game of keeping their hands off of me or to strip nude in a private booth only inches from their faces—oh, how lucky for me!

I did it all because I needed their money, but every single stage set, every single time I unclasped my bra and pulled down my panties, I felt—if even for a single moment before I hid it deep inside—my vulnerability. My nakedness was—fortunately!—not reciprocated, but it was on display like a cheap magazine for eyes who didn't appreciate who I really was, for men who didn't care about me.

Stripping nude was not glamorous. It was a job.

And for me, it was a necessity.

Chapter Thirty-One
Graduating to the Real World

December 2000 – December 2002

I PULLED UP MY pantyhose and glanced at the clock. It was almost time to leave for my internship at the office and I still hadn't eaten breakfast. I slipped into my heels, tucked my white blouse into my knee-length skirt and put on my blazer. I grabbed my purse, rushed down the hallway and looked into the dining room to see Jacob spooning another bite of Cheerios into his already stuffed mouth.

"Ready to go, sweetie?"

His droopy eyes looked up at me. I figured mine didn't look much better. I snapped a banana off the bunch on the counter, picked up Jacob, and tossed his mostly empty cereal bowl into the sink.

"Mommy, my blanket," he said, "and pooh bear."

How dare I forget? Balancing my purse and Jacob with one arm, I grabbed the blue blanket and well-worn teddy bear and hurried out the door.

The drive to the sitter's house was short. I didn't have much time before I was supposed to be at work. Although my job only paid minimum wage, I wanted to make a good impression on the boss in the hopes she might offer me a paid position after I received my bachelor's degree in a couple of weeks.

I needed it to work out. I needed money which a low-wage job wouldn't provide. I needed to stop dancing because incidents like what just happened with Wesley weren't good for me emotionally.

I put the car in park but kept the motor running while I took Jacob out of his car seat. "Are you going to be a good boy for mommy?" I asked as we walked in the babysitter's front door. I had to be at work before she normally opened for business. Because she knew me and liked Jacob, she unlocked the door for us so we could come in while she was upstairs still getting ready for the day.

Jacob rested his head on my shoulder and grabbed my neck tighter. "Don't go, Mommy. Don't leave."

"Oh, sweetie. Mommy has to go to work." I squatted down and sat him on the couch. He refused to let go of me.

"Mommy, I want to go back to sleep."

"I know, sweetie. I'm tired, too. I'll be back to pick you up as soon as I can. I love you." I gave him a kiss on the cheek before I pried his hands off of my neck.

My now four-year-old son lay down on the sitter's couch to watch cartoons. I covered him with his blanket and tucked his bear under his arm.

"Bye, sweetie. I love you." I kissed his hand.

He ignored me.

"Mommy loves you."

No response.

I had to go. Now an expert at running in heels, I jogged out to my car. As I drove away, I couldn't shake the emptiness in my stomach. I bit my lower lip to try to stave off depression.

Always moving—life was nonstop—I never allowed myself time to sit and reflect. I was afraid of the thoughts I restricted to the back of my mind.

Jacob had been in daycare around the clock since he was three months old.

I'm missing out on his childhood.

A stranger is raising my child. She gets to see all of his firsts.

Meanwhile, I'm stressed trying to make money. I'm stripping off my clothes for strange men, playing the part of the seductress. Then for the rest of the day I have to change my personality when I'm out in the "real world" lest people not take me seriously.

I felt like I had developed a dual personality. A third part of me had to play mom when at twenty-two I still felt like a child myself.

Yet supporting Jacob was the reason I started to dance. I think somewhere along the way, I had lost sight of that. What good was it all if I couldn't enjoy watching him growing up?

I made that decision to have Jacob.

What other choice did I have? I got pregnant too young and this was the consequence.

If I had been without child, life would've been simpler. I could've lived in the dorms to go to college. My expenses would've been lower. No daycare. No stripping.

But Jacob had grown on me. I kind of liked him. Playing peek-a-boo when he was a baby just to hear his giggle. Chasing him so I could tickle him while he laughed. Kissing his boo-boos when he had tears in his eyes. Feeling his bear hugs around my waist. Answering the constant why's he asked. Seeing the world through his green eyes.

I drove without the radio on and let myself think.

At least I took Jacob to the park to ride his bike every other weekend. We played games and watched movies together. I read him bedtime stories on nights I wasn't working at the club.

I knew those things weren't enough, but graduation wasn't far away. I wouldn't leave Jacob in daycare as often once I had a real paying job. Then I'd quit dancing and have more time and energy for him in the evenings.

That degree couldn't come soon enough.

*   *   *

Finally I finished my last midterm. When my grades came in the mail, I tore open the envelope to find A, A, A, and A—I'd achieved a 4.0 during my final semester at the university. With a grin, I picked up my Bachelor's Degree and had it framed.

Once that paper was hanging on my wall, it was official.

I had won.

Goodbye dancing, goodbye escorting, goodbye hostess clubs…forever.

I earned my degree, paid off my car, and walked away without student loans to repay. All thanks to Yessenia and a willingness to look beyond my immediate discomfort to achieve success in the long run.

Excited, I filled out job applications and sent my resume to a dozen companies.

After some interviews, two job offers came in, one from the company where I had been interning and one from another prominent company. Both offered me a nice salary with benefits, paid sick days and vacation, and paid holidays. And I wouldn't have to take off my clothes (apparently most jobs didn't require you to do that).

I couldn't decide between the two offers.

During the last week of my internship, I expressed to my supervisor the difficulty I was having in making the final decision.

He pulled me aside. "Miranda, you'd do great here. I have no doubt in my mind. But, considering your circumstances, you know, with your kid, you might want to think twice about this job."

"What do you mean?"

"Look, I can match the other company's offer. But this job would require so many hours during the first couple of years. You need to decide what's best for you and your son."

I wondered why companies didn't allow all of their employees to work less, so they could have an outside life and a family. Employees would be happier, companies would have a lower attrition rate and workers would be more productive.

Heeding my manager's advice, I declined their offer and went with the other company instead.

I put away my dancing shoes and put on my business attire.

After I filled out my new employment paperwork, I drove over to Century Lounge, the nude club, to pick up my year-end tax forms. Although Wild Goose listed dancers as independent contractors, Century Lounge had us listed as W-2 employees. Secretly, I wanted to show off my new costume—a business suit—to prove that it was possible to exit the money trap, and that I had done it. I grinned and hugged the girls and my old manager Bob who all said they were happy for me.

On my first day at the new company, I sat down and looked around at the small office. My four new coworkers were busy tapping away at their computers, negotiating over the phone, and assisting customers who came into the office.

I leaned back in my chair, opened up my training binder and read the opening page: *Welcome to the management training program. You're starting out on an exciting path, which will be outlined in the following sections.*

That's when it fully hit me. I had my own desk, my own computer, my own phone, a salary and a nameplate. I ran my hands along the smooth wooden desk. I wouldn't ever have to strip again. This was it. I had succeeded. Everything would be all right now.

And so goes those famous last words: *What could possibly go wrong?*

* * *

Now that I had a legitimate job, I could put money into the bank. Without needing the evening daycare or the gas to drive to Los Angeles and back to strip, my living expenses had dropped significantly.

By May of 2001, I gave notice to my apartment complex and purchased a condominium. I put every last dollar I had saved into the 3% down payment. Jacob loved his new room. Dan agreed to move in, and this time, he would pay me rent. Everything seemed perfect.

I stood on the wooden floors of my new place and stared up at the vaulted ceilings. This was actually mine. I owned it.

A week after moving in, I received a letter from my homeowners association.

"Dan, look at this." I held up the paper.

He read it. "Are you kidding? How can they do that to you?"

The Homeowners Association (HOA) dues were increasing by more than $100 per month and I needed to pay a bill for supplemental property taxes and a utility surcharge.

"How come no one warned me while I was in escrow?" I slumped down onto my couch "I don't have the money." I looked at Dan.

He shook his head. "Sorry. You know I'm broke. I have to cover my attorney fees and the back child support." Dan had a mess to sort out with his ex.

Was my high school boyfriend's mom right when she warned me that life wouldn't turn out as planned and that I'd only be disappointed?

The following Friday night, I slung my familiar old duffle bag over my shoulder, kissed Dan, and tiptoed downstairs—this time it was critical to be incognito. I didn't want my new neighbors to suspect a thing as I slipped away. I drove to Yessenia's apartment to pick her up—at least we were together again—and to Wild Goose without allowing myself time to reflect on the decision to return to dancing.

I felt like a failure. But I tried to stay positive.

As soon as I pay the supplemental bill and save up a few hundred dollars, I'll be done with dancing. Seriously done.

* * *

On a slow shift at Wild Goose, I sat down next to a customer to have a drink.

After we watched a few stage sets, he pulled out a $100 bill and slid it across the table to me. "I've seen you here for a while and I know you're having a bad night tonight."

Money had been slow, so I accepted it. "Would you like to do some dances here or over by the wall?"

"Honey, I don't do dances."

Even though men sometimes paid for conversation and my time because they knew I could be making money doing dances, I sensed that this man had an ulterior motive.

Time to play stupid.

I put the money away. "Thank you so much. You're so sweet." I reached over and gave him a hug, then picked up my drink and sipped some more Midori Sour.

"My wife's out of town."

"Is everything okay? Is she going to be gone long?"

"I'll be all by myself for a few days."

"Sometimes it's nice to have a break and relax."

"I don't think you get what I'm trying to ask."

The DJ's voice bellowed over the loudspeaker, "Serenity, you're up next. Come see me to pick out your music."

"Oh, that's me. I need to go on stage. Hopefully, I'll see you around later." I finished my drink. "Let me know if you want to do some table dances."

I've learned that self-preservation is a strong motive for doing some of the things we do. I needed money at the time, and I felt like punishing this man for his unfaithfulness. The fact that it happened to work in my favor was an added bonus.

Integrity was a quality with which I needed to reconnect.

* * *

Months passed by. At my day job, because of my experience selling dances, I was a natural at sales. I consistently found my name printed at the top of the district monthly performance reports. I outperformed my coworkers with higher per sale amounts and higher overall sales. I was getting fantastic reviews every three months and received small pay increases with each review. After a few pay raises I was able to quit dancing. Again.

See? I was right. I didn't have to strip for very long. That wasn't so bad. Nobody I know since Wesley has seen me at the club.

I can pay my mortgage, HOA dues, bills, and have enough for food. I don't need extra money for entertainment. As long as I can support Jacob, I'm happy.

Now I'm done dancing for good! Finally.

At the end of the year, my district manager took me to lunch, as was customary, for another quarterly review.

I took a bite of my salad and listened to him go on about my stellar sales results and new goals. The conversation turned.

"Let's talk about your future with the company," he said. "You know you were hired for the management training program, which means you intend to run your own branch in the near future, right?"

I loved hearing those words. I wiped my mouth and nodded.

"Miranda, your numbers are where they need to be. The next step is to become an assistant manager at a different branch, so you can shadow another manager. I'm ready to promote you, but you do know it's going to require more time than you're putting in now."

"I understand." I took a sip of my iced tea. Inside, I was jumping with excitement.

"Honestly, Miranda, not too many single moms do this. I know how you have to come in late at a certain time after taking your son to school."

"I could get someone else to take him."

"Well, I know that you also need to leave work by a certain time to pick him up from daycare. We agreed to those terms and conditions when you were hired."

I focused on moving the lettuce soaked in dressing across my plate. "Yes, I know."

"That's going to be a problem."

I drowned out the rest of the conversation, nodding when appropriate, like I'd done so many times at the strip clubs when talking to customers in hopes of getting dances.

The gist of the conversation was that he expressed his concerns about me being a single mom and therefore I wasn't going to get promoted yet.

What was I going to do?

A month later, one of my sales appointments took an unexpected turn. I slipped the papers in front of the tattooed man and his bleached blonde girlfriend whose skin was starting to show signs of overexposure to the tanning salons.

"Go ahead and sign here." I pointed to the bottom line.

While he read the terms of the agreement, his companion brought one of her long manicured pink fingernails up to her sparkly lips and said, "Don't I know you from somewhere?"

I nearly choked on my saliva. "No, I don't believe we've ever met." I flipped to the next piece of paper. "Please read and sign."

She ignored her boyfriend and stared intently at my face. "I'm not sure where I know you from, but I'm positive I've seen you somewhere before." She shifted her sequined purse onto her other bare shoulder.

I looked away. "You must be mistaken. I've never met you before." Which was true, but deep down inside, I figured this woman was a stripper and she had seen me at a strip club.

I turned to the man. "There's one last form here."

Once he set down the pen, I said, "Great. I'll go finish this up."

I could hear her whispering to her companion. I made his copies as fast as I could and rushed the two of them out of the office before my manager could overhear anything. That may have been the first time that someone I didn't know recognized me outside of the strip club environment. I couldn't have been more embarrassed.

By the beginning of the following year, I become frustrated with my office job. Every time I exceeded the performance goals they set for me, they raised them until they were nearly impossible to meet. Finally I realized I had capped out on the salary scale. They were trying to restrict my raises; otherwise, they'd have to promote me to manager.

Irene, the customer service rep who handled most of the clerical duties for the office, was a corpulent light-skinned Hispanic woman, with an infectious giggle and a pretty face. She and I became friends. We often ate lunch and gossiped together in the break room.

I also became friends with my manager, Marcie, a young freckled plain Jane with long brown hair. Irene, Marcie, and I went out together on occasion. Marcie even offered to babysit Jacob so I could attend my brother's Halloween party.

At the office though, I didn't play the business game by the company's rules. I incited unrest among the ranks simply by openly discussing salary, goals, and raises. I didn't accept what I was told as fact; I thought for myself and realized we were being trained to mislead customers.

"I don't want to hear it," Irene said. "I've been with this company for over fifteen years. I'm planning to retire from here. I can't jeopardize that." She put her hands over her ears.

"What are you talking about?" another coworker asked.

"Look at the figures." I pointed to a paper full of calculations. "It doesn't add up. We're basically lying to our customers."

It turns out I was right. Marcie had me speak to her boss, the district manager, and that was where the issue died.

Afterward, I couldn't in good conscience sell the company's products without being completely honest with my customers. My sales numbers plummeted.

Marcie revoked a day off that she had previously approved. At the end of a work day, she and I were in the parking lot getting ready to go home when she broke the news.

"But you already approved it," I argued. It was for my birthday and she knew it.

"Our branch's numbers are low."

"That's not my fault. I'm the one who's been closing all the big deals."

The district manager had made a point to acknowledge this during every one of our recent morning meetings in the hope of motivating everyone else. I thought it was a stupid tactic that only turned the employees against each other. After all, we were supposed to be a team.

"Have you closed a big deal this month?" Marcie asked.

"No, but—"

"If you can close a big deal by next week, then you can keep your day off."

Marcie knew damn well that that was impossible. I slammed my car door shut.

That night I had a breakdown. Dan witnessed it.

"I've made myself work in the sex industry for four years to get to this point, so I could get a nice office job, and now I'm being fucked with?" I couldn't breathe.

"Well," he said, "you have your degree."

"I've gone out with older men for money and did all that shit to get my degree!" My heart raced.

"But with your degree, you can get another job."

"I went against my beliefs and stripped nude for thousands of strangers to get this damn job!" My pulse quickened.

"You did what you needed to, to survive."

"I missed out on four years of my little boy's life to be treated this way!" My stomach churned.

"You don't need to work for someone who's a jerk."

"I tried so hard to earn respect only to be disrespected, this time not by asshole customers, but by assholes in suits!" I cried.

"Hey, are you okay?" Dan held me. "Try to breathe."

By the time Dan took me to the doctor's office for what turned out to be a panic attack, I was hyperventilating.

Dan filled out the paperwork. The nurse took my vitals. The doctor did an exam and said, "This is all a result of stress, nothing else."

"Stress can do this to me?" I said. "What are my options? Can I go on disability?"

"You can, but after a short leave, you'd be back on the same job, with the same boss."

I didn't know what to do, but I knew I couldn't work for Marcie or that company anymore. I felt used. They promised me a promotion. When I earned it, they withheld it to get more out of me.

A little over a year after my graduation, I walked into the office and handed in my resignation. Marcie and my district manager were shocked.

Irene understood.

* * *

I had quit back in February. Months passed and I couldn't find another job. Not to mention that the whole situation has depressed me so that I wasn't very effective in my job search. The summer was approaching and my credit card balances were getting higher.

Dan wouldn't pick up the slack while I was unemployed, which caused resentment to build inside of me.

"Why can't you help out more?" I asked, raising my voice. "You know I had to quit. And you know how much I hate dancing. I can't make money right now. What are you doing with your money? Why can't you pay more for the groceries?"

"Don't blame me for your situation," Dan said. "I'm paying you rent." He turned away from me and continued to play his computer game.

"Barely. It wouldn't kill you to pay more than half, even for a little while."

He put his headphones on and engaged in conversation with his online teammates.

I tapped him on the shoulder.

He pulled off his headphones and turned to me. "What do you want?"

"I want you to stop ignoring me."

"Then stop yelling."

"It has nothing to do with me yelling. You've been ignoring me for months now. You didn't used to be like this. You used to care about me."

He put the headphones back on and swiveled around to face his computer screen. He kept playing the game, talking to his teammates through the microphone, laughing now and then at their conversation.

It wasn't just the food or the money that was bothering me. It was what those actions meant to me. By not paying more, he sent the message that he didn't care any more about me than he would a roommate and that hurt. I realized he'd been distancing himself from me since I had quit my office job and returned to dancing.

"Dan!" I screamed.

He pretended I wasn't there.

I hit the power button on his computer, shutting it off.

He threw off his headphones and jumped up. "What's your problem?"

"You." I narrowed my eyes. "I've been ignored by you long enough. You don't care about me. I can't take this anymore. I want you out. Now. We're done. Over. Get your shit and get out. Now."

He took his wallet and car keys and stormed out of the apartment.

I called his cell phone. "If you don't come back and get your things, I'm going to toss them off the balcony."

He hung up. Thirty minutes later, he called me back. "I've called the police. They are on their way to escort me inside to get my stuff."

"Are you fucking kidding me?"

"You kicked me out and said you were going to throw my things out." I heard him mocking me with his tone of voice.

I didn't get a chance to respond before he hung up again.

He couldn't possibly have thought I was going to follow through on my threat. He knew me better than that. Basically, he was pissed that I was breaking up with him. By calling the cops, he was flipping me off.

Fine. Then I'll play that game.

Trying to control my breathing, I grabbed several black trash bags and marched into my bedroom. I threw all of his clothes and belongings inside bags and piled the bags on my couch. I unplugged his computer and monitor and stacked them next to the couch. I flung open drawers and cabinets, taking out any dishes, pots, or pans of his and tossing them into other bags.

The sound of footsteps echoed up the stairwell. I ran to my room and came back out again with a grin as I balanced Dan's pillow and teddy bear on top of the bags.

There was a knock on my front door. I took a deep breath, put on a serious expression and opened the door to let Dan and two uniformed officers inside. I was thankful Jacob was sleeping through this.

"May I have my key back?" I said, sweet as sugar, and held out my hand. "Your stuff is all packed up and ready to go."

While he carried his bags outside, I shrugged my shoulders at the officers and made small talk. I wanted them to believe I was calm and reasonable and that none of this was my fault.

I had never had anyone call the cops on me before. Such a betrayal hurt worse than the break up.

Dan grabbed the last couple of bags. Before going outside, he turned to me, pointed at his forty-gallon tank, narrowed his eyes, and said, "And don't hurt my fish."

I rolled my eyes at the officers. "Don't worry, I won't." I waved goodbye.

On the outside, I appeared calm. On the inside, I was fuming.

* * *

Financial ruin. No job, no boyfriend, a mortgage to pay, and a child to support. I had to once again rely on stripping.

My bills were higher than when I was living at my old apartment. Because of this, I had to dance more often than Yessenia and often found myself driving to work alone.

I was more burnt out on dancing than ever before. Money was so bad for me at Wild Goose that sometimes DJ Stephen wouldn't take my tip-out. To cheer me up, he sometimes took me out for pie and ice cream after work and would refuse to let me pay.

I couldn't make money dancing, not because there were fewer customers, but because my mood had noticeably darkened. I was cynical, miserable, and desperate, and even the drunken guys could see the anger under the façade of my smile.

Did I have to do more to make money? I had avoided the dark corners and the wall under the DJ booth because security couldn't watch the dancers as closely there for rule-breaking. The dancers knew it and the regular customers knew it.

I didn't care anymore. So what if a guy placed his hand on my thigh while I danced for him? It wasn't like I was letting him touch more than that. I actually found I got more dances that way. And I needed the cash.

CHAPTER THIRTY-TWO
SUGAR DADDY RETURNS

LATE 2002

I'D BEEN LIVING OFF my credit cards and hadn't slept well in weeks.

Faced with the choice of either moving far away and pulling Jacob out of first grade or retreating to what I saw as an evil corporate America, I gave the professional life a second try.

Irene had transferred to a different division of the same company. When a position opened up, she recommended me. After being hired, I cut back to only a couple of nights a month at the club to supplement my income. I was relieved to have a steady paycheck again.

While I was at the office typing up documents, a familiar number showed up on my cell phone's caller ID. I couldn't remember to whom it belonged, so I answered with apprehension.

"Mia? It's Mark."

I froze. It had been nearly four years since I'd been called Mia.

"Mia? Are you there?"

I turned around to see if my coworkers were within earshot. "Hi, Mark. I can't talk right now. I'm at work."

"So you graduated and you're not dancing anymore? Good for you."

"I still dance sometimes."

"I'd like to see you again."

Mark was from my hostessing and escorting past, a life I didn't particularly want to return to. Then I remembered the hundreds he used to give me. I thought of my credit card bill and said, "Only if you meet me at the club." I honestly didn't know how I'd feel about Mark seeing me topless.

He was silent for a moment. "All right, Mia. Where and when?"

It was settled. Mark was back in my life, for better or for worse. Later I told Yessenia.

"You're crazy," Yessenia said. "I wouldn't let anyone from our dark past back into my life." She danced as little as possible at Century and wanted an exit strategy, not a reentrance one.

"But now that Dan's moved out, I need extra money."

"I need money, too, but there's no way in hell I'd call up my old sugar daddy Gary. You're insane. Are you going to bring him around Jacob again? Now that he's older, isn't Jacob going to ask questions?"

"It's temporary."

"Yeah, sure. Whatever you say. It's your life—you can do what you want. You don't need my approval. But I am so done with that part of my past."

"How is stripping any better?"

"Fuck you," she said.

The tables had turned. Yessenia—the one who thought stripping was such a brilliant idea—now loathed it and harbored more emotional scars from it than I. During our four-and-a-half years in the industry, she had internalized what I had not: while I saw the job as a means to an end, for her the work had become too personal to bear. The men's stories became her nightmares.

* * *

Mark showed up at Wild Goose the following weekend and sat just beyond my stage. When I recognized the familiar Filipino man, I couldn't zone out and go through the motions. I felt self-conscious. He was watching me.

After I collected my tips, I went out on the floor and found him leaning back in his chair, dark arms crossed, bushy black eyebrows raised. His eyes hid beneath his gold framed glasses, his polo shirt tucked into his black slacks.

"Oh, Mia," he said. "Why do you do this? This is not right."

I sat down. "Because I need the money."

Mark slipped $200 across the table. "Stop this. I don't like it at all."

I took his money. "Quitting isn't easy. I can't pay my rent." I stared at the diamond-studded gold band on his left hand. "Aren't you married?" I had never confronted him about this in the past.

"Yes."

"Why don't you go home and spend time with your wife?"

"We don't love each other. We sleep in separate rooms."

"Why not get divorced?"

"It's not that simple. In my culture, divorce is not acceptable. She's the mother of my children. I'm obligated to continue to take care of her financially. And between my business and the race track, I'm hardly ever home."

"Don't you have a daughter my age?"

"Yes. She doesn't live at home, but I still help her out if she needs it." He reached across the table and took my hands into his. "Mia, I've missed you. Let's see each other again." He glanced around the room. "But not here."

I hated his touch, but couldn't hate him.

I appreciated that Mark cared so much about me that he was willing to pay me not to dance. Why couldn't Dan have cared this much? Mark had been nothing but kind to me ever since we met. Having him around again felt strangely familiar, like he was an old friend.

I felt sorry for him. It was sad that he had to pay me to claim any of my attention, but I could not return the emotions he felt for me.

*   *   *

I accepted Mark's offer for a paid date, but I felt more like his equal this time around.

He picked me up for lunch from my office.

"Miranda, who's that?" Irene peeked out through the blinds in the storefront window. "I saw you get into that car a couple of weeks ago. Are you dating someone new?"

"No, it's an old friend of mine. I'm going to lunch now. I'll be back in an hour." I grabbed my purse and headed out.

"Uh-huh. Friend, huh?"

I slipped into Mark's car before he could attempt to get out and open my door as usual.

We ate lunch and on the ride back, Mark said, "I brought a present for Jacob."

"What?"

"I have an extra television I'm not using, and I thought he might like to use it in his bedroom." He pulled in front of my office and parked behind my car. "It's in the trunk. I'll get it for you."

With no time to object, I unlocked my car. Mark placed the TV on my back seat.

"Thank you," I said.

"You're welcome, Mia." Mark reached into his wallet and handed me a couple of large bills. "This is for you." He smiled and leaned in for a hug, but pulled back, staring at my vehicle like a man checking out an obese woman in a short skirt. "Mia."

"Yes?"

"What have you done to your car?"

"What do you mean?"

"It's filthy. Look at your aluminum rims. They're black. Your car is layered with dirt. Have you ever waxed it?"

"No."

"Let me come over to your place. I'll clean your wheels and wax your car. You're going to ruin the paint if you don't take care of it. What about next weekend? I'll barbeque some dinner for you and Jacob."

I saw Irene peering through the tinted glass. "Okay, that sounds great. I'll call you."

He beamed and gave me a long hug before departing.

I hung my head and pulled open the office door. Without saying a word, I sat down at my desk and logged onto my computer.

It was no use. Irene started laughing. "Miranda, who the hell was that?"

"A friend."

"Okay, so you're friends with some old Asian guy?"

"He's Filipino."

She giggled. "Come on now. Do I look stupid? What are you up to? Are you sleeping with him?"

I swiveled my chair to face her. "No, but if you must know…"

We had been good friends for a while. I told her everything.

*　*　*

"Thanks for dinner, and for cleaning my car," I said to Mark after I had put Jacob to sleep.

"You're welcome." Mark swept my hair back behind my ears. "Do you own any diamond earrings?"

"No."

"Would you like some? I think one carat round studs would look beautiful on you."

First came the diamond earrings. Then, when my living room television broke, he bought me a new TV, a DVD player, a PlayStation game console for Jacob, and a subwoofer for my existing surround sound system. Plus he kept giving me a steady stream of cash. Because of Mark, I didn't need to dance as much.

My life had come full circle. I was back where I started—no more independent than before my degree and just as willing to fall into the same pattern.

I had wanted some paintings for my walls at home, so I asked Mark to buy them for me. He purchased the fine art prints and had them custom matted and framed. He patiently hung the Monet and Van Gogh artwork on my walls. When he had hammered in the last nail and lifted the final Van Gogh painting—*Starry Night over the Rhone*—up over my fireplace mantel, my doorbell rang.

Mark and I exchanged a look of surprise. I shrugged and opened the door to see my brother and his friend standing on my doorstep.

I must have looked horrified because Kirk said, "Surprise. Didn't you remember we were coming over tonight?"

I narrowed my eyes at him and held a finger to my lips. "Shush. Be good."

Without any other choice or way to explain Mark, I let them in. For the first time in my life, I found myself introducing Mark to someone with no connection to the hostess club, to my brother.

Mark stepped down. "Nice to meet you two." He brushed his hands on his slacks and turned to me. "Well, I think I better be going now." He embraced me in a hug, which I only halfway returned. "I'll phone you later."

It was all I could do to keep Kirk and his friend quiet until Mark descended my staircase and disappeared out of earshot.

Wild laughter and teasing ensued.

"So, Miranda," Kirk said. "Since you're hooked up, ask him to buy me a TV. I need a new one, too."

It needed to end. It wasn't right.

* * *

After several months of our budding work-related alcoholism and debauchery, Yessenia broke down. "I can't do it. I'm not going in to work."

She had been pulling this a lot lately. Coaxing sometimes did the trick.

"C'mon, it's getting late," I said. "We need to go."

Yessenia stood there in her doorway in sweat pants and a wrinkled t-shirt. She had a vacant look in her eyes. "You don't understand what this job's done to me. I can't do it. I'm over that place. I'm not going back."

With Jacob in bed, Dan watching TV, and it getting later, I dropped my work bag on Yessenia's doorstep. "What do you mean you're not going? How will you pay your bills?"

She shrugged. "I don't care anymore. You go without me. There's no way in hell I'm stepping inside that topless club again. I'm getting sick from all the drinking."

"Don't drink."

"If I don't drink, I'm going to have an emotional breakdown at work."

"Focus on making money," I said. "We don't have to stay until two, we can leave at midnight."

"I'm not making money. Unlike you, I can't deal with drunken men."

"What are you going to do?"

"Maybe I'll go back to dancing nude at Century where the guys can't drink."

The thought of dancing without her crushed me.

She can't quit. Not yet.

"Dancing nude again?" I asked. The thought seemed terrifying to me. It would be like starting all over again. I had gotten used to topless only.

"Come back there with me," she said.

I shook my head and sat down on her doorstep. "I can't. I can't work day shifts anymore, remember? Only Friday and Saturday nights. I have my internship and college during the day." I didn't want to drive to Wild Goose without her. Yessenia was my safety blanket and I wasn't ready to let her go.

Yessenia and I were unusual in the world of exotic dancers because we were always together. Nearly all dancers came to work by themselves. They hadn't been best friends since high school or next-door neighbors like us.

In fact, Yessenia and I were inseparable. DJs knew they had to put us on stage one after another, or one of us might refuse to go on stage. We drew strength from being together and until that moment when I was about to lose her, I hadn't realized how much her presence meant to me, how I had been able to strip because I had had my "sister" beside me every step of the way.

"Please come with me to work," I said. "We don't have to drink tonight. We can try to make a couple hundred and go home."

"You're more of a hustler than me." Yessenia stood there, her tangled hair hanging down on her shoulders. "I'm not going."

"Why not?" I put my head into my hands. I wanted to cry. Until that moment, I hadn't realized that my reality for these past several years had not been her reality. I had wrongly assumed that she was like me, never stopping to consider how my graduating college was going to affect her because to me stripping was a temporary job, while for her it was a depressing reality from which she had no way out.

Tears came to Yessenia's eyes and she didn't answer.

"Just tonight?" I asked.

She shook her head.

Maybe I can stay home tonight too, I thought. Then I remembered Jacob. *I have to pay the mortgage. And the daycare. And buy food. I need money.*

I stood up and grabbed my bag.

"I'm sorry," I said and gave her hug. "I have to go." Our paths were separating. I had been so caught up in my day-to-day living that I hadn't seen it coming. With my bag slung over my shoulder, I stared at the ground as I descended her apartment steps. I was separating from my stripper cohort.

I threw my bag in the trunk and sat in my driver's seat for a few minutes. I phoned Yessenia to give it one more try but she didn't answer.

She's really not coming.

It was getting late.

I need to make money. Think of the money.

I turned the ignition and headed onto the freeway, without Yessenia.

We never danced together again.

Instead, when her rent was due and she had no other choice, Yessenia went back to Century Lounge, hoping that the drinking men had been her problem.

I went back to Wild Goose, hoping that I didn't have a problem. But her absence made my dancing topless more real. It was just me and the strippers and the strip club patrons—no Yessenia who was my world of the past, my shield from my current naked reality.

I was lonely without her.

And without another driver I couldn't drink as much, which made it all the harder to cope.

With my regular work hours, Yessenia and I didn't find as much time to talk or hang out. I hoped she could find a way out of dancing soon.

And me, too. Stripping without Yessenia was miserable. I couldn't escape the scene inside the club for a few minutes to chat with her. I couldn't escape reality.

CHAPTER THIRTY-THREE
BREAKING POINT

JANUARY 2003

AFTER THE BREAK-UP WITH Dan, I had been dating many other men, but I wasn't feeling any chemistry with them. I continued to question my sexuality. If I couldn't be satisfied with a man, could I be satisfied with a woman?

I figured it normal for me to appreciate the female body more so than the male form because I had worked around naked women for years. I wondered if my feelings toward women were anything more than admiration. I didn't consider myself a lesbian. I had only seriously thought of being with a man until I saw Karina on stage at Wild Goose.

Karina was new to the club. Her long legs and gorgeous, commanding stage presence left me breathless.

I boldly approached her. With luxurious lashes, smooth skin and full lips, she was drop-dead beautiful and I was in luck—she was a lesbian.

"Yes, I'm interested." Karina gave me a flirtatious smile. "Are you looking for a long-term relationship?" She crossed her toned legs and swiveled back and forth on the barstool.

I couldn't lie. "I got out of one not too long ago and I don't know if I'm ready for another serious relationship yet. Maybe we could date for now?"

Karina's clear blue eyes stared deeply into mine. "I've been hurt before. I would need to know that you were committed to making something work."

Admiring her cascading dark blonde hair, I sighed. "I wish I could, but I'm not ready."

She pouted. "Let me know if that changes."

I couldn't focus on the rest of my shift, finding myself stealing glances in her direction all night, feeling a little jealous at the attention she lavished on the customers, even knowing she didn't like men at all.

*　*　*

The attraction I had toward Karina was new to me. I figured maybe it was a fluke until I met Carla through an online dating site.

Carla was Greek and had an open relationship with her boyfriend. Something about her intrigued me. I was drawn to her pretty face, her luxurious brown hair, her perfect complexion, her beautiful eyes, and her sweet laugh.

She and I couldn't wait to meet in person. Jacob spent the night at a friend's house, so I had the apartment to myself. I couldn't decide what to wear. I put on a short summer dress, then changed into a miniskirt, then resorted to jeans. I didn't want to look too eager. I dimmed the lights and sprayed perfume. I paced, waiting for her to arrive. Maybe she wasn't coming. I realized I was more nervous about meeting her than I had been for any date with any man.

She arrived and she looked hotter than the pics she had sent me. Carla and I laughed and talked about our lives and experiences. We both loved cats and starry nights. We both loved Italian and Greek food. It was cold in my living room so we headed into my bedroom and sat down on my bed. I turned on some music.

Citrus-scented shampoo emanated from her soft hair. I touched her honey-colored locks, which felt like silk against my fingertips.

I brushed her cheek.

She tucked my hair behind my ear.

We reached in and our lips pressed together. Slow and sweet. That was the first time I had kissed a woman. I was completely sober. It was electrifying.

Her soft lips, cheeks, and neck were inviting.

I completely understood why men adored women.

Hours after we met, we were undressed and discovering every inch of each other's bodies. The feeling of sitting atop Carla, straddling her waist and staring down at her voluptuous breasts was surreal, only matched by the view of her curves when she sat up, leaning over me as I lay down with an unquenchable desire to touch her.

Carla and I cuddled and kissed until the middle of the night. After phoning her boyfriend when she got to my place to say she was okay, she had been ignoring calls from him for hours. Instead we had sex.

"Are you sure you haven't done this before?" Carla asked, looking down at me in between her legs amid her moans of pleasure.

I giggled. "It just feels natural." And it did. It felt much more natural to me to go down on her than to go down on a guy.

When she figured it was time for her to leave (before the sun came up), we kept kissing each other goodbye, promising to get together again soon.

After she left, I lay in bed smiling. Being with her had felt so right.

Carla and I kept in contact by phone and computer. We made plans for another rendezvous, but Carla's boyfriend wanted a threesome. I wanted no part of that—I had enough men at my disposal already—so he wouldn't let her see me again.

I mourned her absence and filled the emptiness with as many men as I could—all of whom were weak replacements for Carla.

I scoured the Internet for other local ladies, bisexuals or lipstick lesbians. It was so much easier to meet men than women. A lot of the women seemed too serious or too flaky—like they were "bi-curious" but not willing to try it out.

I finally met another woman offline, a bodacious blonde with double Ds, overly-tanned skin, and a slightly aged face. We took a dip in my condo's Jacuzzi, but that's as far as it went. Nothing happened, nor did I want it to. I wasn't attracted to her. No chemistry at all.

I was so confused.

* * *

Yessenia and I planned to throw a party on a Saturday night for my twenty-fifth birthday. We invited Kirk and his friend, some high school acquaintances we hadn't seen in years, some current party friends, and my neighbors (to preclude any noise complaints).

Jacob stayed at the sitter's house for several nights.

On Thursday, the night before my actual birthday, Yessenia, Kirk, and his friend came over unannounced. Kirk unveiled a bong and bag of weed. "Miranda, it's your birthday. This is the good stuff, the buds. You go first."

"I can't," I said. "I don't know how to. I wouldn't know what to do."

Yessenia laughed. "Come on, birthday girl. I'll go first."

After we each took a couple of hits, I sat down on the couch and sulked. "I don't feel anything. It didn't work." I held my hand out in front of me. "Look, it's like, it's like, lllliiike." I babbled incoherently, amazed at the texture of my skin.

The phone rang. Caller ID announced my mom.

Kirk and Yessenia looked at me in horror as I answered the call. "Hi, mom." I giggled. "Huh? Oh, sorry. I'm really tired. Can I call you back?" Or at least that's what I thought I said to her before hanging up. I don't remember anything else about that night.

The next morning, I woke up thinking of weed, which reminded me of Jason who smoked a lot of weed. I hadn't seen him in a while. I phoned him and after a long conversation, he came over to spend the night.

Jason and I were sexually compatible and that was how we spent our evening. I did not mention the party I had planned because I could not have two men I was sleeping with at the same time be there and meet each other, could I? Jason didn't know I had invited Sam, the adorable dark-haired Cuban Jew I had recently started dating, to spend Saturday night with me.

Saturday morning after overhearing my phone conversation with Yessenia, Jason realized it was my birthday. He insisted on going out and getting us breakfast. When he came back, he surprised me with a gift: two candles and candle holders to compliment both sides of my fireplace.

His gestures made me feel guilty, but I tried to hide it; however, Jason knew me too well.

"What's on your mind, Miranda?" he asked.

"Nothing." I looked at the clock. Yessenia would be there soon.

"Are you doing anything tonight for your birthday?" he kissed my neck.

Like I had always done with Jason, I ended up telling him too much. "Yes. Yessenia and a few friends are coming over."

He raised his eyebrows. "Oh, you're having a party? Would you like me to stick around for the day?"

I looked away. "I don't think that's a good idea. Yessenia and I are going to be busy getting my place ready."

"Miranda, you know I can help."

"It's not that."

"Then what is it? You can tell me the truth."

"I don't want to hurt you."

"Is there another guy?"

I closed my eyes and nodded.

"That's beautiful, Miranda. You always call me and invite me over when it's convenient for you. Then you drop me for the next guy." He shook his head. "You're really not the same girl. You used to care about me." He sighed. "I'll miss you." He hugged me then left.

That was the last time I saw him.

A few hours later, Yessenia arrived to help me decorate my house with streamers, balloons, black lights, a lava lamp, and curtain beads for the hallway. We replaced my ceiling fan light bulbs with red lights. We installed a green light on my balcony for what would be the "smokers' lounge" and turned up the bass on my new subwoofer—thank you, Sugar Daddy.

While rearranging my furniture, the doorbell rang. I opened it to find a delivery man holding a bouquet of two dozen long-stemmed red roses from an anonymous sender.

"Oh my God." Yessenia rolled her eyes. "Are those from Mark?"

"Probably." I felt Mark had delivered guilt in a vase. "Let's put them on the table in the corner."

Pizza was delivered. Irene, my friend from work, arrived and much to her delight my neighbor showed up with a twelve-pack of beer. He had already been drinking and was quite entertaining with his slurred jokes.

The guests kept coming. My friend Jonathan, a nightclub promoter whose parents owned a Chinese restaurant, came with a cute blonde he was dating. He gave me a gift certificate to his family's restaurant.

Kirk played bartender and the drinks flowed freely. The bass pounded. I danced atop my coffee table amidst sticky spilled beer. Strobe lights flashed.

Sam, my adorable date for the night, arrived and I welcomed him with a kiss. No sooner had I sat on the couch to snuggle with Sam then one of my best friends from childhood, Eric, showed up with his wife.

"Eric! It's so good to see you." I jumped up to give him a hug hello then resumed my make-out session with Sam.

Another knock on the door. Another childhood friend, Kay, had come with her husband after enduring a two-hour drive to my house.

Surrounded by friends, I danced against Sam and accepted the drinks Kirk kept mixing, downing them like water.

Kay, I'm so glad you're here (Is that your bag of weed on my bedroom floor?). It's like good ol' times with me, Eric, Yessenia, and Kay. Lights off, black lights and red party lights on. Techno music and bass fill the air. "Hey neighbor, have another drink," Irene says. Drinks are plentiful. What did you say? Who cares? Does anybody want to dance with me? C'mon it's my birthday! Fine, I'll dance by myself. Here this chair is great for dancing on. It's your birthday, do what you want to. Why is the floor all sticky? Who spilled beer? Who cares? The imitation wooden floors are easy to clean up later. Doorbell, who's there?

Yay! Carla and her boyfriend (who cares about him?) are here! I am pleasantly surprised. Carla made it. I thought I would never get to have another lesbian experience with her again. Maybe I will tonight. How lucky am I?

Sam, I'll be right back. He settles onto the couch. I kiss his lips then casually disappear into my room with Carla and her boyfriend. I'm in the mood to play some piano music for her. Drunken piano music. As I straddle the piano bench, Carla moves close behind me. Her beau is on my bed, watching. I start to play. Impulsively, I turn my head around to face hers. I reach out and meet her lips with mine. She does not fight it but returns the kiss with passion. We embrace.

I lock my door and she undresses me. We become one and stroke each other's bodies. Her boyfriend at some point is no longer an observer but instead an active participant.

Bass fills the air. Music pounds in my head. Alcohol swirls in my veins. My vision blurs into a relaxing dizzy motion.

Whose hand is that? Who is licking me? Who am I kissing? Who cares? It feels great. He and I take turns on Carla then they took turns on me. Constant motions and an even flow fill my senses.

Who's knocking on my bedroom door? Hold that thought, sweetie, I will be right back. Slipping my dress back over my head, I open the door and step into the hallway. Kay says her good-byes. Yes, that is your weed? Here's your stuff back. Thanks for coming. Good-bye.

Jumping back into bed I toss my dress onto the floor. The sweet sensual touch of a woman's caress, the gentle feel of a woman's breasts against mine, licking her is like being licked by her. Moistened fingers and soft moans accompany the passion and lust.

Is someone knocking on my door again? Be right back, Carla. You two can keep yourselves occupied I am sure. Eric and his wife, you two are leaving already? I hope you had a good time…What was I doing? Aw, nothing really.

My devilish smile can't be hidden. Have a good night.

No sooner do I attempt to lock the door and get more comfortable than I hear yet another knock on my door. Oh, hey you two didn't leave yet? Do you need something, Eric? What do you mean you are insulted I am not inviting you into my room to join in on the "real party"? Are you serious or are you kidding? If you are serious, we should discuss this another time when I sober up. Have a good night. Oh Sam is getting antsy? Okay, thanks.

I saunter back out to the living room to make my rounds. People seem to be coming down or getting restless. Not many people are left. Hi, Sam. No, please don't go. I want you to stay the night. Has it really been an hour? I am so sorry, I didn't realize. Yes I am only playing with her, not him. Okay, I will be back in a few minutes. I kiss him then turn back to my room.

My fleeting moment has passed. Carla and her boyfriend want to leave. Sorry for the interruptions. We should continue this another time! Let me walk you to the door.

Party is over. Irene crashes on my living room couch. The music is off. The room is cleaned up. The beer spill is gone. Thanks Yessenia and Kirk and Kirk's friend.

Party…What party?

Too bad Carla's gone. My friends are gone. What a letdown. Now what? Sam waves me over. Oh yeah. He's on the menu for tonight.

Sam and I retreat to my bedroom. Let's finish this night off right.

Now I am twenty-five.

Tomorrow this will all be over.

* * *

Sunlight burned through my eyelids. I moaned and rolled over. The bed was empty. Where was Sam? He always liked to snuggle in the morning.

Prying my eyes open to look at the clock, I saw it was afternoon. Sam was gone.

My head throbbed. My stomach churned. The room spun. I pulled my hair into a ponytail and ran to the bathroom to throw up. I had only thrown up from alcohol a handful of times. This, by far, was one of the worst. Each lurch tightened my stomach and made my throat feel raw. I crumpled onto my cold bathroom tiles, unable to move, and fell asleep.

When I awoke, the sun was setting. I called and arranged for Jacob to stay one more night at the sitter's, crawled back into bed, and pulled the comforter over my head—the same comforter that had covered four of my sex partners over the last two days. It smelled clean but felt dirty.

There was a terrible heaviness in my heart. Without understanding why, warm tears streamed down my face and I fell back asleep.

I opened my eyes. It was dark. The house was quiet. Crickets chirped outside my window. I checked my cell phone and home phone. Not a single call had come through. Not from Sam. Not from Jason. Not from Yessenia.

My head pounded and my stomach ached, but I had nothing left to throw up. I took a couple of aspirin and lay back in bed and stared at the ceiling until my vision blurred and the tears came again.

I felt the same way I did after stripping, after dancing on men's laps all day. I felt gross and unhappy.

What the fuck is wrong with me?

My wild birthday was over. All I had to show for it was two candle holders, a hangover and an empty bed. Tears came faster, until I sobbed and shook. I wanted a hug, someone's embrace, but I was alone, completely alone and I had done this to myself. The void hit me.

The sex had been great. The attention had been fantastic. But in the end, none of my lovers really loved me. How was this different from stripping? Different scene, different players, but same ending: going home alone and feeling empty.

Whom did I love?

Jacob.

I had gotten rid of my little boy for the weekend. He would've liked to have spent my birthday with me.

Did I even know how to love another person or how to love me?

Emptiness was creeping up on me. I didn't want to deal with it.

How to escape? A bottle of wine? Another man? A woman?

No. No. No.

I lay there, questions flooding my mind. What was the point of all this?

Everything I had dreamt about since I was a little girl felt beyond my grasp: a successful career, a satisfying marriage, a fulfilling family. "Happily-ever-after" was a fraudulent idea peddled by Disney, pushed on little girls like a drug dealer pushes crack on an addict, and I had bought it.

The cockiness I had been brandishing all weekend was gone.

I had no direction.

Should I strip until I'm forty and drunk—like Blanca at Century?

I craved change, but didn't know how or where to start. *My self-*

esteem and happiness shouldn't be determined by the cash in my pocket or the lovers in my life.

When I had no more tears to cry, I took a deep breath and sat up. I stretched my arms and walked over to the open sliding glass window. Through the tree branches, stars sparkled in the sky. Moonlight illuminated the leaves outside. A cool breeze blew across my skin. My curtains billowed in the wind. I lay back down.

Every pore, every hair, every inch of my skin tingled. Hyperaware of the light and darkness, the warmth and cold, the rustling and stillness, I couldn't sleep. I lay awake in bed for hours. My mind went blank. No memories replayed. In that moment when I couldn't think of anything at all, I took in several long, cleansing breaths and closed my eyes.

CHAPTER THIRTY-FOUR
A NEW DAWN

JANUARY 2003 – PRESENT

WHEN DAWN'S FIRST LIGHT appeared, I opened my eyes, not realizing I had fallen asleep. An infectious energy rapidly grew within me.

I set out to change that which I could, beginning with Mark. He knew too much about me and my personal information. I needed to find a safe way to release him.

I told Mark I was a lesbian and that I was dating a woman. I stretched the truth, knowing there was no longer anything between me and Carla. The story felt like a safe way to cut ties with him.

He coughed. "Mia.... Are you...are you joking with me?"

"No. I had to tell you. I didn't want to keep this from you. I don't think we should see each other anymore because I want to be with her."

Mark looked at me with the same horrified stare that he gave me after seeing me topless on stage at Wild Goose.

When he descended my stairs for the last time, I sat on my couch and looked at the framed paintings on my wall, gifts from him.

I phoned Yessenia. She expressed relief, as did I.

* * *

I considered moving out of state. I didn't want to leave, since my family was in California, but I had accepted my harsh financial reality. I refused to dance anymore. I refused to be unhappy any longer.

Before listing my condo for sale, I turned to my brother for advice.

Kirk, his friend, and I sat in my living room, watching late-night TV and discussing my situation in an attempt to find a solution.

"Don't get stuck doing something you hate," Kirk said.

"I am doing something I hate," I said.

"Life's too short to be miserable. Change careers."

"Besides dancing and office work, what else can I do?"

At that moment, a television commercial grabbed our attention. A phone number floated across the screen and the announcer asked, "Are you unhappy with your job and looking to change direction in your life? Do you want to do something more meaningful? If you have a bachelor's degree and are a midcareer professional, consider working with the community with our program. Help underserved inner-city youth."

I couldn't believe it. Surreal. *Was this the voice of God?*

Kirk pointed to the TV. "Write down the number." He handed me a pen. "You've always liked helping others."

He was right. *But to go from stripping—where I take as much as I possibly can—to being a giver to the community?* Was that the answer? And if it was, could I do it?

* * *

After passing a grueling interview process and challenging tests, I was offered a position. It was exhausting learning a new career, but I came home from work every day feeling good about myself and my contribution to society. I felt fulfilled.

I spent more time with Jacob. I read to him in the evenings and played board games with him on the weekends—sometimes by the fireplace with hot cocoa.

Jacob didn't have to spend nights at a sitter's house anymore.

After my last party, I realized my drinking had gotten out of hand. Fortunately, I was able to quit drinking when I quit dancing. It turned out that dealing with exotic dancing had a lot to do with my out-of-control behavior. I limited myself to one or two drinks. No more binge drinking. I was one of the lucky ones who could control that.

I had also learned that I was open to men or women. It didn't matter to me. I could fall in love with a person, regardless of their sex. I was ready to date one person, to be open to falling in love, and I wasn't going to desperately seek out attention in the meantime. I treated the people I dated with more respect.

But most importantly, I never stripped again.

Epilogue
Yessenia

YESSENIA AND I KEPT in touch. She stopped dancing when she married a man she had dated for a couple of years. After she stopped stripping, she found herself unable to work anywhere for nearly a year and a half because of severe depression, panic attacks, and agoraphobia. She became afraid to go outside, afraid that everyone who saw her knew she was shameful, like Hester Prynne in *The Scarlet Letter*.

Yessenia engaged in intensive counseling. Because she found her passion in helping animals, she volunteered at animal shelters and pet adoption agencies until she built up the courage to get a job at a local pet store.

"Animals, unlike people," she said, "aren't mean and cruel. I feel good helping them."

I was relieved she was in a better place, but after eight years of marriage, her life as she knew it crumbled. She became embroiled in a dispute with an abusive employer and her husband physically and emotionally abandoned her.

I feared her spirit would break.

Instead, Yessenia discovered an inner strength, the likes of which I'd never seen in her before. She transcended her situation and rose above the abuse of her father, the pollution of dancing, and the failure of her marriage.

"Miranda," she said. "I don't need anyone to be happy. Don't worry about me. I can't explain this, but I feel different inside, in a spiritual sense. I feel at peace. I feel whole."

And she was right. With positive energy radiating from her, she drew more positive people to her.

Yessenia met a wonderful man and they bonded in a way she could only describe as being with a mirror image of herself. He was a different body, but of the same heart and mind. She had never thought it possible to be so understood by another, so accepted for who she was, and so completely at peace with herself.

I couldn't be happier for her.

*   *   *

MIRANDA

YEARS LATER, ON MY way to catch a plane to visit family, I purposely passed through downtown Los Angeles. I was approaching Flamingo's, the hostess club that started it all for me back in 1998. For memory's sake, I turned down that familiar street. It had been over ten years since I first stepped foot in that club.

I prepared myself to see the weather-worn building that housed many horrors, but became confused when I couldn't find it. I drove around again and again before I realized that it was gone. The red couches, the TV room, the time clock. It had all been razed to make way for the Staples Center, home of the Los Angeles Lakers.

The hostess club was gone, buried in my past forever.

In a satisfying shock, I continued to drive toward the airport. As I headed down Century Boulevard, I knew the familiar NUDE NUDES sign would be up ahead, after the next underpass. I braced myself for the flood of memories—dancing, stripping, drinking.

I drove under the bridge, but Century Lounge wasn't there—the stages, the sex shop, and the building were all gone, replaced by an airport parking lot. I couldn't believe it.

I turned the corner to find that Wild Goose, too, had disappeared.

A mixture of emotions hit me.

Nothing of my secret past remains.

I boarded my plane, buckled in Jacob, and settled into my seat. I stared out the window at the high-rise buildings of downtown Los Angeles. They shrank smaller as we rose higher.

All three clubs that had dramatically impacted my life were destroyed.

I was not.

ACKNOWLEDGEMENTS

First of all, I'd like to thank Erin Brown, my editor. Wow, you are amazing. Thank you for your guidance. To Yessenia: Thanks for sticking with me through this project. I value our friendship and memories. To writers Ingrid Ricks, Christine Macdonald, and Hyla Molander: Thank you for inspiring me to finish this. To my fellow writers who helped to edit this book: I respect you all and sincerely appreciate your help. To my brother: Your dry sense of humor rubbed off a bit. Thanks a hell of a lot. To my sister: Thank you for never judging. Your words of encouragement have meant more than you know. To my parents and son: This wasn't your fault. To my friends—you know who you are: Thank you for putting up with me, for providing occasional shoulders for me to lean on, and for giving me such invaluable input and guidance during the editing process. I'm lucky to have true friends like all of you. To all of the dancers (the nice ones) with whom I have worked throughout the years: Thank you for your kindness and generosity. Dear God: I'm no longer going to ask for strength. Wisdom would be nice, but peace, harmony, and happiness will suffice. To the Southern California Writers Conference (too many names to mention): Thanks for the great workshops led by great leaders that helped me to suck less as a writer. To my first literary agent: your early belief in my writing helped to ignite my creative passion. To all the assholes in my past: Thanks for the inspiration.

CPSIA information can be obtained
at www.ICGtesting.com
Printed in the USA
BVOW03*1556041217
501911BV00012B/320/P